PENGUIN BOOKS

KILLING BONO

'A fantastic book, which manages the difficult trick of being simultane-ously very funny and very sad. But then, clearly any would-be rock star who winds up as a rock critic for the *Daily Telegraph* must be a very sad individual. I brought the book to Africa, where several tribal ruffians fell upon it, tore it up and used it for their toilet paper and their fires. Which is no more than it deserved' Bob Geldof

'Candid, sometimes hilarious . . . delivering, in passing, some wonderful portraits of Sinead O'Connor, Bob Dylan and others . . . McCormick's a first rate raconteur' *Rolling Stone*

'Multi-tasks as an affectionate coming-of-age memoir, an intimate rock biography and a Nick Hornbyish meditation on growing up' *Blender*

'This book will make you laugh and wince but proves that McCormick is talented' *Ireland on Sunday*

'A great cautionary tale for all those who aspire to celebrity' *Daily Mail*

'This book has oodles of potential for falling flat on its face, but Neil McCormick has the bravado, the ego and the bloody-minded obstinacy to pull it off' *Sunday Times*

'This hilarious read about living in someone else's shadow will have you in hysterics' *OK Magazine*

'Honest and hilarious' *Daily Telegraph*

'Funny, painful and ironic, it's a heartbreaking ride of rock'n'roll wannabes' *Daily Record*

'Like Wile E. Coyote – equal parts inspiring, pathetic and hilarious – McCormick details his own repeated near-fame experiences and his eventual resignation to life as a rock critic. It might not get him an audience with the Pope but his memoir does let his talent shine out from under his pal's long shadow' *Tracks*

'By turns idealistic, disillusioned and unflinchingly honest, this memoir-cum-biography masquerades under chagrin, but its scope is much wider than that of a trusted-valet-tells-all ... It's an easy read but not a light-weight one' *Hot Press*

'I'd recommend this book to anyone – Bonophile or Bonophobe – who appreciates sharp writing. And if you've had any dealings with the music business, you'll love it all the more – though you may occasionally find yourself wincing in sympathetic pain ... traces two very different paths through the music world with equal measures of clear-eyed acceptance and lacerating wit ... a marvellous book' *New York Observer*

'What it means to be a nobody in the music business. A weirdly obsessive, strangely funny, and above all painfully real look at the life of the not-so-rich and never-quite-famous' *East Bay Express*

'A funny, jaundiced celebration of rock'n' roll fantasy and reality ... McCormick's is an authentic, gripping rock'n'roll voice, veering between self-importance and self-loathing on an unsteady journey toward self-knowledge' *Publisher's Weekly*

'With remarkable anecdotes about U2's earliest days, it is essential reading for any U2 fan and a fascinating account of making it (or not) in the music business. Moreover, it shines out as one of the most candid memoirs one could hope to read – an incisive meditation on the lure of fame' U2log.com

'You don't need to be a U2 fan to enjoy this book. McCormick's themes of friendship, ambition, jealousy, acceptance and growing up are explored using characters we know and admire which makes it all the more inviting' Interference.com

'Let's cut to the chase: this poignant, honest, conversational book is a must read for anyone, and especially U2 fans. It's a book that you won't be able to put down' www.atU2.com

'Neil McCormick gave rock'n'roll the best years of his life. This excruciatingly honest and painfully funny memoir is the result. A book for every dreamer who ever pouted in the bathroom mirror and saw a superstar grinning back. A love story of innocence and innocence lost'
Joseph O'Connor

'The best sort of book about rock, being both personal and intimate and written in a lovely way, illuminating a dozen big subjects by side-light'
Andrew O'Hagan

'The best book I have ever read about trying to make it in the music business' Sir Elton John

'I was Neil McCormick's fan in school. He was much cooler than me, a much better writer and I thought he'd make a much better rock star. I was wrong on one count. He's written a great book. It pulled me back . . . with a bit of a shudder. I can think of a few people who will wince when they read it and I am certainly one of them. You might imagine it would be very hard for me to like a book like this, it's excruciating to me at times, but it's very funny and it's very moving. I recognize myself in Neil's prose, which is very unusual. His own candour is extraordinary'
Bono

ABOUT THE AUTHOR

Neil McCormick is the rock critic of the *Daily Telegraph*. He has written for many publications, including *GQ*, *Hot Press*, *Observer*, *Sunday Times* and *Irish Independent* and regularly appears as a music pundit on the BBC. He was raised in Ireland and lives in London.

Killing Bono

NEIL McCORMICK

PENGUIN BOOKS

PENGUIN BOOKS

Published by the Penguin Group
Penguin Books Ltd, 80 Strand, London WC2R 0RL, England
Penguin Group (USA) Inc., 375 Hudson Street, New York, New York 10014, USA
Penguin Group (Canada), 90 Eglinton Avenue East, Suite 700, Toronto,
Ontario, Canada M4P 2Y3 (a division of Pearson Penguin Canada Inc.)
Penguin Ireland, 25 St Stephen's Green, Dublin 2, Ireland
(a division of Penguin Books Ltd)
Penguin Group (Australia), 250 Camberwell Road,
Camberwell, Victoria 3124, Australia (a division of Pearson Australia Group Pty Ltd)
Penguin Books India Pvt Ltd, 11 Community Centre,
Panchsheel Park, New Delhi – 110 017, India
Penguin Group (NZ), 67 Apollo Drive, Rosedale, Auckland 0632, New Zealand
(a division of Pearson New Zealand Ltd)
Penguin Books (South Africa) (Pty) Ltd, 24 Sturdee Avenue,
Rosebank 2196, South Africa

Penguin Books Ltd, Registered Offices: 80 Strand, London WC2R 0RL, England

www.penguin.com

First published as *I Was Bono's Doppelgänger* by Michael Joseph 2004
First published in Penguin Books 2005
This revised film tie-in edition published 2011

Grateful acknowledgement is made for permission to reproduce extracts from the following:
The Real Inspector Hound by Tom Stoppard. Copyright © Tom Stoppard, 1968. Faber and
Faber Ltd and Grove Atlantic.
'Blowin' in the Wind' by Bob Dylan. Copyright © 1962 by Warner Bros, Inc. Copyright
renewal 1999 by Special Rider Music. All rights reserved. International copyright secured.
Reprinted by permission.

Printed in England by Clays Ltd, St Ives plc

ISBN: 978-0-241-95380-8

www.greenpenguin.co.uk

To Gloria. Who saved me from myself.

Foreword by Bono

I was Neil McCormick's fan in school. He was much cooler than me, a much better writer and I thought he'd make a much better rock star. I was wrong on one count. He's written a great book. It pulled me back . . . with a bit of a shudder. I can think of a few people who will wince when they read it and I am certainly one of them. You might imagine it would be very hard for me to like a book like this – it's excruciating to me at times – but it's very funny and it's very moving. I recognize myself in Neil's prose, which is very unusual. His own candour is extraordinary. There is a deadpan quality to the description of his life that is very appealing, but his passion is never far from the surface. It is one of Neil's gifts to be able to write about really heavy things and make them feel weightless. There are a few narratives going on here, we bump into weighty subjects, but they sort of bounce past you like a big beach ball. And the truly astonishing thing is that the songs that he's written, that are quoted in the book, they ring like bells, and you can't even hear the melodies. The aspirations of his luckless protagonist are all fanciful until you read those lyrics. Then you realize this isn't just a guy who thinks he could have been a rock star. He fully inhabits the great line out of Marlon Brando's mouth in *On the Waterfront* . . . 'I could have been a contender.'

Bono

'Sometimes I dream of revolution, a bloody coup d'état by the second rank. Troupes of actors slaughtered by their understudies, magicians sawn in half by indefatigably smiling glamour girls . . . I dream of champions chopped down by rabbit-punching sparring partners while eternal bridesmaids turn and rape the bridegrooms over the sausage rolls . . . And march an army of assistants and deputies, the seconds-in-command, the runners-up, the right-hand men, storming the palace gates wherein the second son has already mounted the throne having committed regicide with a croquet mallet. Stand-ins of the world stand up!'

Tom Stoppard, *The Real Inspector Hound*

Chance is a kind of religion
Where you're damned for plain hard luck.
I never did see that movie
I never did read that book.
Love, come on down
Let my numbers come around.

Don't know if I can hold on
Don't know if I'm that strong.
Don't know if I can wait that long
Till the colours come flashing
And the lights go on.

Then will there be no time for sorrow
Then will there be no time for shame
Though I can't say why
I know I've got to believe

We'll go driving in that pool
It's who you know that gets you through
The gates of the playboy mansion.

U2, 'The Playboy Mansion'

Prologue

I always knew I would be famous.

By the time I left school, at seventeen, my life was planned down to the finest detail. I would form a rock band, make a series of epoch-shifting albums, play technologically mind-blowing concerts in the biggest stadiums on the planet until I was universally acknowledged as the greatest superstar of my era. And I would indulge in all manner of diversions along the way: make films, write books, break hearts, befriend my idols . . . Oh – and promote world peace, feed the poor and save the planet while I was at it.

You might think I was just another arrogant teenage airhead with fantasies of omnipotence. Indeed, there were plenty around me at the time who did their best to persuade me that this was the case. But I wasn't about to be put off by lesser mortals jealous of my talent. Because I knew, deep, deep in the very core of my being, that this wasn't just another empty dream. This was my destiny . . .

So there I was, thirty-five years old, sitting in a shabby, unheated little excuse for an office above a bookie's in Piccadilly, watching the rain drizzle down my single, grimy window, wondering where it had all gone wrong. I'd wanted to be a rock star and had wound up becoming a rock critic. To compound my torment, I was suffering from a bad case of writer's block with my newspaper deadline looming and the fucking telephone hadn't stopped ringing all morning with a succession of PRs pestering me about their shitty rock bands, all of whom I secretly resented for, I suppose, just being more famous than me. But at least talking on the phone gave me an excuse for not writing my column.

'It better be good,' I snapped into the receiver.

'This is the voice of your conscience,' announced my caller in a gravelly, wasted Dublin accent that reeked of smoke, late nights and fine wines.

'Bono,' I said, in recognition.

'You can run but you can't hide,' he laughed.

'The way I feel right now, I don't think I could even run,' I sighed.

It was, indeed, Bono: rock legend, international superstar, roving ambassador for world peace and (though it is unlikely to feature prominently on his CV) a schoolfriend of mine from Mount Temple Comprehensive.

'Where are you?' I inquired, listening to the echo of global distance bouncing down the phone line.

'Miami,' he said. 'Playground of America. Ever been to Miami? The gangsters look like fashion designers. Or maybe the fashion designers look like gangsters. Sometimes it's hard to tell . . .'

There was a time when we had both been singers in school-boy bands, playing every toilet in Dublin, convinced against all the odds that we were the chosen ones, bound for glory. We moved in different circles these days. I wrote for a newspaper. He was the news. But every now and then, when something brought me to mind, Bono would call up out of the blue to fill me in on his latest adventures in the stratosphere of superstardom.

'I was out at a club last night,' he said, slipping into raconteur mode, his voice an intimate whisper. 'It was very Scarface but, like I said, maybe it was just a fashion thing. Lots of men with moustaches, models draped over their shoulders, you know? Every man and woman in the place was puffing on enormous cigars. Clouds of smoke everywhere. Smoke-rings rising up to the ceiling. There's something about a beautiful woman and a cigar; it's a very powerful combination, don't you think?'

'Until you kiss them and find out they taste like an ashtray,' I grunted.

'You're such a romantic,' said Bono. 'So I'm led into this room at the back which is just filled with hundreds of little drawers, floor to ceiling. And each little drawer has a little plaque with a name on it: Schwarzenegger, Stallone . . . Madonna! You know, all the famous cigar smokers! It's like a walk-in humidor. All these personal stashes of illegally imported Cuban cigars maintained at perfect temperature and humidity for whenever they want to drop in and have a puff. I was looking for the President's name, 'cause I'm sure he has his own drawer in there somewhere. It's pure Miami. This whole city's like the shop window for the American dream. But then – and you'll love this, Neil – I see a box with the name "Sinatra"! Francis Albert! They keep one for him. How cool is that?'

As I listened, occasionally making encouraging noises, I watched a pigeon splashing about in a puddle that was building up on the ledge outside my rotting window-frame. Miami seemed a long way away. Bono sounded woozy and happy after his night on the tiles but I had a strange feeling welling up in my chest, a disturbing swirl of conflicting emotions. I was pleased that Bono had called me. Flattered, even. I liked and admired the man as much as anyone I had ever known. So why did his voice have the power to send a sharp stab of insecurity running right through my heart?

'I thought of you, 'cause I know you've always been a big fan of Frank,' said Bono. 'I can't quite believe this myself, but I have done a duet with the Chairman!'

That was it. Something popped in my head. 'Stop!' I spluttered. 'Enough! I should be doing a duet with Frank Sinatra! What's Sinatra to you? Just another famous scalp! I love Frank Sinatra. Leave him alone! Next you'll be telling me you've been asked to play James Bond.'

There was a moment's uneasy silence, then Bono laughed. 'Actually, the Edge and I have written the new *Bond* theme for Tina Turner.'

'Oh, fuck off!' I snapped. 'The problem with knowing you is that you've done everything I ever wanted to do. I feel like you've lived my life.'

Laughter echoed back down the line. 'I'm your doppelgänger,' Bono said. 'If you want your life back, you'll have to kill me.'

Now *there* was an idea . . .

When I put down the phone I started to brood. Was Bono really my evil twin? Or was I his? Now that I thought about it, our careers had diverged early on and just kept on getting wider and wider apart. As he rose to the highest realms of fame and fortune, I had plummeted to the depths of anonymity, a rock'n'roll casualty, leaving only the briefest of traces in the margins of pop history, and that for being the first person to leave U2.

Oh, yes. I didn't mention that, did I? But we'll get to it.

Perhaps I was the yang to Bono's yin. The dark counterbalance to his life of success and good fortune, absorbing all the bad luck and mischance that never seemed to go his way.

I pulled down a decaying, much-thumbed, hardback antique *Oxford English Dictionary* from my overcrowded bookshelves. **Doppelgänger** *(ad. Ger. Double-ganger): The apparition of a living person; a double, a wraith.* That's me all right, I thought. Just a phantom reflection of everything I ever wanted to be. And everything I ever wanted to be was personified by a bloke I had gone to school with. How cruel was that?

'Bono Must Die!' I typed into my computer. I blew it up, 72-point bold, and printed it out. It looked good. I knew a few people who would wear that T-shirt.

'I, Bono,' I typed. Perhaps I could sell my story to *The National Enquirer*. Bono Stole My Life.

Not that I hadn't achieved things in my own right. Deep inside, I knew that to be true. But, in the blinding glare of superstardom, the small triumphs of ordinary existence don't always register. Instead you can easily become a footnote in somebody else's story.

So let me get something straight from the start. Contrary to what you may have read elsewhere, I do not have the dubious distinction of being to U2 what Pete Best was to the Beatles: the man who missed the gravy train. I know, it is right there in black and white in the group's authorized biography, *The Unforgettable Fire*. In Chapter Four, biographer Eamon Dunphy informs his readers of the first fateful gathering of the band that would become U2, to which Bono, apparently, 'turned up with another Mount

Temple pupil, Neil McCormick, who, like everyone else present, fancied being lead guitarist'. However, after a few grim renditions of rock standards, including 'Brown Sugar' and 'Satisfaction', 'Neil decided to bale out'.

That rather trivial little tale seems to follow me around wherever I go, as the source of many other biographical presumptions. I still wince whenever I see myself described in print as an 'original member of U2', or, worse, 'ex-U2', as if the defining moment of my entire life was petulantly stomping out of a rehearsal room back in my schooldays. So please read the following carefully: I wasn't there and, even if I had been, any ambitions to become lead axeman in the nascent combo would surely have been hampered by the fact that I had only ever mastered three chords on my daddy's Spanish guitar – and I wasn't even sure which chords they were.

But if something is printed often enough it becomes the truth, or at least the official version of events. I think the members of U2 actually believe it themselves at this stage. Certainly, that was the impression I got when I finally made it to Miami, as a guest of the band for the launch of their 2001 world tour. At a backstage party, the band's manager, Paul McGuinness, kept introducing me as a member of the original line-up. The fact that a former alumni of his band was now music critic for conservative British broadsheet the *Daily Telegraph* seemed to amuse him immensely.

The pouting and gorgeous Andrea Corr was there, somehow looking even more desirable than usual with a pint of Guinness in one hand and a lit cigarette in the other. 'Did you really walk out on U2?' she asked, sounding suitably impressed.

'I told Bono the band wasn't big enough for the both of us,' I replied. 'If they'd have stuck with me, they could have really gone places.' (Come on. What was I supposed to say to the most beautiful woman in Ireland? That it was just a misprint?)

'How does it feel seeing them on stage?' Andrea asked. 'Do you think, "That could have been me up there"?'

Now *that* was cutting a little too close to the bone.

I looked around the room, crowded with familiar faces. The

sleek, über-rock figure of Lenny Kravitz lingered in a corner, dressed in fake fur entirely inappropriate for the climate, his expression hidden behind omnipresent, impenetrable reflective shades. He was silently accompanied by someone who appeared to occupy the role of mobile-phone roadie. Lenny would hold out a hand and a gleaming, metallic phone would miraculously appear in it. When his conversation was over, he would hold out the phone and the roadie would slip it back into his pocket.

Elvis Costello, an entity from a different end of the rock spectrum, portly, bespectacled and dressed like he had just been for a rummage in a charity shop, mopped his sweaty brow, engrossed in musical conversation with chrome-domed producer Brian Eno.

There were old friends of the band, such as the extravagantly talented singer-songwriter and one-man art installation Gavin Friday (who had an arm wrapped around one of the beautiful Corr sisters) and eternally poised press officer Regine Moylett. There was the red-blazered Irish aristocrat Lord Henry Mountcharles, perhaps slightly the worse for wear, directing his conversation into the unconvincingly inflated cleavage of one of Miami's beach-babe set. The small but perfectly formed figure of supermodel Helena Christensen flitted by in a flimsy summer dress while Christy Turlington posed resplendently on the other side of the room. There were members of U2's crew and management, familiar faces from Dublin, many of them looking red and puffy following a few days on the tear in the Miami sunshine. There were wives, girlfriends, children. And there was a smattering of tanned and immaculately attired local worthies who had succeeded in blagging coveted Access All Areas passes.

Upstairs in an enormous ballroom a party was in full swing, with superstar DJ Paul Oakenfeld spinning discs and scantily clad waitresses serving free drinks for several hundred regular, common-or-garden VIPs. But this was where the real insiders could be found, crammed into a narrow corridor behind the stage, basking in the presence of the band.

Bono, the Edge, Adam Clayton and Larry Mullen, the four members of U2, were scattered about the room, sweaty and exhausted after a two-hour *tour de force* performance, graciously accepting fulsome praise from this ragged assembly of celebrities, family, friends, colleagues, freeloaders, liggers and assorted hangers-on.

I watched it all and wondered where exactly I fitted in. This was the very life I had imagined for myself all those years ago, but here I was only by an accident of acquaintance. I caught Bono's eye. He was, as usual, the centre of a huddle of activity: rock stars and supermodels hanging on his every word. He winked at me and grinned.

I remembered a conversation we had, late one night, many, many years ago. We were talking about U2's first-ever performance, playing cover versions on some rickety school tables held together by sticky tape in the Mount Temple gymnasium.

'That gig changed my life,' I admitted to him.

'It changed mine too!' he excitedly replied.

The difference was, it changed his for the better.

I

I did have a life before U2.

In common, I suppose, with many children of the late-twentieth century, my earliest memories are of television. Specifically, in my case, a five-minute afternoon show for mother and child called *Bill and Ben, The Flowerpot Men*. I won't bore you with a detailed description of plot and premise. Everything you really need to know is encapsulated by that particularly prosaic title. One day, feeling the time had arrived to discuss my career plans, I solemnly informed my mother that when I grew up I was going to star in *Bill and Ben*.

My mother affectionately explained that my idols were actually puppets. But I was way ahead of her. 'I know,' I petulantly insisted. 'I'm going to be a puppet too.'

She just didn't get it. You see, what I really wanted was to be inside that magic tube, looking out, with all of my little friends watching my every move, laughing and applauding. I was only an innocent child but I had already been bitten by the Bug, that most sinister and pernicious creation of the mass-media-saturated modern era. You must know what Bug I'm talking about. It breeds in celluloid and vinyl, crawls across cinema screens, rides the airwaves and mingles with the beams of light emanating from cathode tubes, infecting vulnerable egos with delusions of grandeur. And it had me in its grip.

I wanted the camera to confirm my existence. I wanted to be somebody. I wanted to be a contender. I wanted to be . . .

. . . a Flowerpot Man.

Over the years my career plans changed, but the fundamental motivation remained the same. To paraphrase David Bowie, a much later influence of my psyche but no less damaging: fame was the name of the game.

My family moved from Scotland to Ireland in 1971. The Beatles had broken up, a new brand of so-called glam rock was in the ascendant with T-Rex, Slade and Sweet and the pop charts seemed to be crammed with singalong gobbledegook with titles like 'Chirpy Chirpy Cheep Cheep' and 'Bridget the Midget' but the truth is that none of this was of much significance to me. At the age of ten, I regarded the music business with a healthy disdain, an attitude which, had I managed to maintain it for another twenty years or so, would have spared me a great deal of personal pain.

While my older sister, Stella, watched *Top of the Pops* with something akin to religious veneration, I saw myself as having much loftier tastes. I liked Frank Sinatra, a mature artist who could act as well as sing and never wore eyeliner. My younger brother, Ivan, was a willing ally in the hugely entertaining sport of tormenting my sister about whatever teenage idol currently occupied centre stage in her fantasies. But I began to harbour deep suspicions about Ivan's allegiances when he started wearing tartan trousers with turn-ups in the style of the Bay City Rollers.

The last of the McCormick siblings was our little sister, Louise, seven years my junior, who was too young to have an opinion on the great Sinatra/pop schism (or, at least, too low down the family pecking order to have an opinion that counted). Louise listened to whatever anyone else played and seemed to like it, even tolerating the Aran-sweater-wearing, kilted folkies from the Scottish highlands whose tunes my father favoured and the collections of classical highlights my mother would occasionally try to foist on us in the name of education.

Apart from musical differences, a symptom of a sometimes unpleasantly intense sibling rivalry, ours was, by and large, a happy family. I report this with no pleasure whatsoever, for reasons that I hope will become clear. Both my parents came from staunchly working-class, British-coal-mining backgrounds but my father had (through a process of apprenticeship, night studies and endless exams) hauled us up to the comfortable plateau of middle-classness (to which my mother, in particular, had taken like one to the semi-detached born). Having started on the factory floor at fifteen years old, Dad had become a qualified engineer before being fast-tracked for senior management in car manufacturer Chrysler. We relocated to Ireland for his latest promotion, moving from a bungalow in a dreary Scottish town to a five-bedroom, two-storey house in Howth, a beautiful fishing village on a peninsula at the northern tip of Dublin. It was quite an idyllic place to grow up – fields and forests bordered by the sea, with a city within easy reach.

I have to say that my parents treated us children exceptionally well, apparently wishing upon their offspring the education, opportunities, financial security and, crucially, freedom of expression and artistic fulfilment that had never been an option in their own childhoods. I have often complained about this to them.

'Do you think we should have made you suffer more?' my mother tuts whenever I essay my theory that family hardship is an essential ingredient in the otherwise almost intangible metaphysics of fame, acting as a kind of psychic spur on the drive for stardom, especially in the music business. Think about it: how many well-balanced rock stars can you name? From the shared grief over the premature deaths of their mothers that united John Lennon and Paul McCartney to the divorce that rocked the childhood world of Kurt Cobain and the paternal abandonment that fired up the Gallagher brothers, the family backgrounds of rock idols are littered with misery. In particular, there is something about an absence of parental love that drives some individuals to entirely give themselves over to audiences, seeking out the approval of mass applause not just for glory but also as a balm for their tortured souls.

Perhaps, like my mother, you think I am being melodramatic; but while I was comfortable in the bosom of my family, positively revelling in the sense of freedom and almost unlimited possibility I felt in those early years in my newly adopted

3

country, over in another part of Dublin a boy I had yet to meet was having his world turned upside down.

Paul Hewson – the boy who would become Bono – was fourteen when his mother died, suddenly and unexpectedly, in September 1974. He grew up, with his older brother, Norman, and father, Bob, in a household of men numbed by grief, unable to share their feelings. It is something we have talked about over the years. 'You don't become a rock star unless you've got a lot missing somewhere – that's becoming increasingly obvious to me,' Bono once admitted during another rambling call down a transatlantic phone line in the middle of a US stadium tour. 'If you were of sound mind you wouldn't need 70,000 people a night telling you they loved you to feel normal. It's sad, really. It's the God-shaped hole. Everyone's got one but some are blacker and wider than others. When you've been abandoned, when someone's been taken away from you, when you feel like a motherless child, the hole opens up. I don't think you ever fill it. You can try to fill it up with time, by living a full life, but when things are silent you can still hear the hissing.'

For Bono, the opening up of the God-shaped hole was the defining moment in his life, pushing him in two directions simultaneously: towards the emotional sanctuary of rock'n'roll and towards the salvation promised by a profound faith in his maker. If I had anything resembling a God-shaped hole, I think it would have been God (Him, Her or Itself) that was missing.

I was raised as a churchgoing Catholic boy, and my gradual estrangement from the comforts of faith was a long and torturously painful process (as much, I suspect, for those around me as it was for myself). At seven years old, I served a brief tenure as an altar boy in the local church. For me, the altar was a stage, the worshippers merely a captive audience, but my scene-stealing posturing during service did not go down well with the priest, who quietly took me aside after a particularly melodramatic dispensation of the Holy Host and suggested that I might not be cut out for the job. (As it turned out, neither was he: some months later he eloped with a member of the congregation.)

My faith was to be seriously tested by our move to Ireland – still a rigidly Catholic country, with little separation between Church and State. At the tender age of ten, I fell into the grip of the Christian Brothers, an order of repressed sadists who operated a policy of beating the fear of God into you. Violence was deemed a healthy way for boys to occupy their time. Certainly, the pupils in St Fintan's Primary School did little else but fight, usually under the approving supervision of their teachers. At breaktimes the playground was a seething mass of young bodies gripped in a variety of wrestling positions. I think I spent most of that first year in a headlock.

With spirits low, my parents made the decision to remove all their children from the clutches of the various religious orders (Stella was being educated by nuns up the road) and install us in a private school of excessively liberal inclinations. In its own way, this proved every bit as ill judged. Sutton Park was full of rich kids whom no one could discipline for fear that their parents would withdraw their fees. Needless to say, I loved it.

There was no religious education in my new school. Acts of worship were reserved for music appreciation classes, to which pupils were encouraged to bring in their own records. Our teacher would play us a piece of Mahler, which we would listen to in bored silence, and then it would be the turn of someone in class to get up and stick on an Alice Cooper or Mott the Hoople record, every aspect of which would be furiously debated while the teacher rolled his eyes in despair.

When it came to my turn to bring in a record, I did not exactly have a lot of choice. I only owned one single, Terry Jacks' number-one hit 'Seasons in the Sun'. It remains a source of embarrassment to me that the first record I ever bought should be something so trite. I wish I could claim, like most rock critics, that I was into the Velvet Underground before I even learned to read. But there you have it. In 1974, this maudlin ballad of a dying man bidding farewell to those he has loved appealed to the tragic self-dramatist in me. All together now: 'We had joy, we had fun, we had seasons in the sun . . .'

To my horror, my selection did not go down at all well among the young bohemians in Sutton Park, some of whom groaned loudly while others sang along with the chorus in silly voices. My teacher praised the song's melody and economy of story-telling, which only made my peers' mockery worse. I felt my cheeks burning with humiliation when he decided to spin the B-side, a sentimental country song about an old lady who couldn't feed her dog because there were no bones left in the cupboard. I was suddenly confronted with the sheer banality of my musical tastes. Terry Jacks did not even wear make-up, for goodness' sake. I was thirteen now, and there were no excuses for being so uncool. When I got home, I contemplated the seven inches of black vinyl with a sense of intense shame. Stella, who had always hated the song, finally put me out of my misery. She took the single from my hands and with a nail file proceeded to gouge an enormous scratch across the record's surface before coolly replacing it in its paper bag and handing it back to me. 'There,' she said, with assured finality. I didn't even protest. I simply returned the scratched record to the rack, never to be played again.

The next single I bought was Ralph McTell's 'Streets of London'. Would I never learn?

The McCormicks liked to think of themselves as a musical family, although our instrumental skills left something to be desired. My grandfather would proudly proclaim that he had never had a lesson in his life as he regaled us with near-unrecognizable organ renditions of 'Amazing Grace' and popular classical pieces replete with false starts and bum notes. He was the first in a mercifully short line of self-taught musicians. My father learned to play guitar by following a series on television, frequently blaming his inability to play a complete piece from beginning to end on the fact that he had missed episodes two and five. My mother, mean-while, shrugged aside the minor handicap of being tone deaf to apply herself to mastering the out-of-tune piano that occupied our dining room. Our regular family sing-songs were not for the faint-hearted.

Ivan was the first to apply himself to learning to play an instrument properly, attending guitar lessons from an early age. While at Sutton Park he formed his first group, Electronic Wizard. They made their debut at a lunchtime concert in the school, kicking off with an original composition, the opening couplet of which I still vividly remember: 'Electronic Wizard is our name / Playing electric music is our game'. This bold assertion was somewhat undermined by the fact that the quartet's line-up consisted of three acoustic guitars and a snare drum. I swiftly concluded that Ivan's musical ambitions represented no significant threat to my plan to become the first famous McCormick.

I wanted to be an actor and, while waiting to be discovered by Hollywood, I landed the lead role in the school's annual end-of-year theatrical production. In 1975, at only fourteen years old, I was to make my debut as Hamlet. I prepared by walking around reading poetry, muttering to no one in particular and generally affecting intense self-absorption, although I doubt anybody but me noticed a great change in my behaviour. I even started spending time in the cemetery that bordered the rear of the school, which was where, two weeks before the end of term, disaster struck. Posing dramatically on a cemetery wall, I lost my balance and plummeted to the gravestones below, breaking my ankle quite badly. My drama teacher visited me in hospital, where I was lying in traction. I gamely tried to persuade him that I could play the part on crutches.

'The show must go on, sir,' I insisted.

'It will, Neil,' he cruelly replied. 'One of the other boys will play Hamlet.'

This was not the first such incident during my time at Sutton Park. I had previously received seven stitches after someone struck me over the head with a chair during a fight in the library. And the Mayor of Dublin's son, a classmate of mine, had blown the skin off his face in a bomb-making experiment involving gunpowder extracted from fireworks while his friends looked on

7

shouting words of encouragement. When a pupil was expelled for a sexual assault in a classroom my parents, fearing that it was only a matter of time before one of their offspring ended up dead or in jail, decided it was time for us to change schools once again.

Thus, at the beginning of the 1975 autumn term, Stella, Ivan and I lined up for assembly at Mount Temple. A progressive establishment that had opened only three years before, it was the first State-subsidized, co-educational, non-denominational school in Dublin. A thin, rigid old man who identified himself as the headmaster, John Brooks, delivered a speech about enabling us all to fulfil our potential. Standing among a throng of unfamiliar faces, I felt nervous yet optimistic about the future. Perhaps, down these dusty corridors, my destiny would, at last, begin to unfold.

If some time traveller from the future had told me then that, one day, Mount Temple Comprehensive would become a legendary institution in the annals of Irish showbusiness, I would not have been remotely surprised. And if they had informed me that among this generation of students were four individuals who would become the most famous Irish exports since Guinness, why, I would have shrugged bashfully before looking around at my schoolmates to try to work out who were the other three.

2

Paul Hewson was in my sister's class, a year ahead of me, but we soon established something that was more than a nodding acquaintance if less than a friendship, falling into conversation at choir practise and morning assembly and during brief encounters as we made our way to separate classes. It was a passing relationship fuelled by one characteristic we have always had in common: a capacity to talk about anything as if we were experts on the subject, no matter how limited our actual knowledge.

My rapport with Paul did not much impress my sister, who was proprietorial about such matters and did not think I should be fraternizing with any of her contemporaries. Indeed, in normal circumstances, there tended to be little socializing between pupils from different years. When you are young, even a year in age difference is usually perceived as an unbridgeable chasm. But, long before the days of his A-list celebrity, Paul was already something of a star in the school corridor, known to one and all.

Even now, I think of Bono as the Man Who Knows Everyone. His visage is inescapable in modern media. Open a newspaper or magazine and there he is, standing shoulder to shoulder with world leaders and political agitators, poets and pop stars, showbusiness legends and flavours of the month. I've seen him pictured with his arms around presidents, glad-handing prime ministers, quaffing wine with Nobel Prize winners and swapping sunglasses with the Pope. Mention his name to movie and music stars and you are almost guaranteed to hear an amusing anecdote about their friend Bono, with a coda about what a nice guy he is.

He was always a gregarious charmer, loping about Mount Temple like a stray dog, sniffing out interesting conversations and activities, making sure he was part of whatever was going on. There was a lot of mischief in his smile and he had a stubborn, jaw-jutting, bull-headed streak that emerged whenever he felt put upon, but at his core there was a tangibly gentle, compassionate aspect that made him popular with girls (who always seemed to be fluttering about) and tolerant of younger pupils, such as myself. You felt honoured when Paul spoke to you.

He could often be found hanging out in our common room because Paul was engaged in a vigorous, amorous pursuit of Alison Stewart, one of the most beautiful and universally admired girls in our year. Alison had thick, black hair, smooth, olive skin, dark, warm eyes and deliciously curled lips. Being a hormonally charged fifteen-year-old boy, I could not help but notice these things. She was also smart, kind, good-humoured, strong-willed and, frankly, way out of my league. Actually, at that stage in my adolescent development, pretty much any member of the opposite sex seemed out of my league. But with some, at least, you felt you might have half a chance. Alison had a sort of aura of impermiability about her. I never really felt she belonged in the same world as an ungainly youth like me. On principle, I was against older boys going out with girls in our class, since their seniority and bullish air of experience seemed to grant them unfair advantage, but Alison and Paul seemed to fit. He wooed her over the course of a long year, until, when you saw them nestle intimately among the stark arrangement of chairs and lockers in the common room, it became apparent that they were an item.

One of our principal topics of conversation at that time was God (the existence or non-existence thereof); and, indeed, this was to remain a subject of vigorous debate between us over the next twenty-five years. My personal problems with the deity had not subsided, but my confidence in challenging the religious order imposed by Irish society was growing daily. To be fair, religious education at Mount Temple was a very different proposition than under the Christian Brothers. A consequence of it being the only non-denominational State school in mainly Catholic Ireland was that most pupils were drawn from Dublin's Protestant minority. The school itself, however, toed no sectarian line, offering RE classes characterized by a kind of woolly Christian liberalism, presided over by a well-meaning but – as far as I was concerned – drippily ineffective young teacher named Sophie Shirley. There would be Bible readings and class discussions in which Jesus took on the character of a beatific hippie while God seemed to be personified as an avuncular old geezer who only wanted the best for his extended family – if that was the case, I wondered, why was I being kept awake at night wondering if the torments of Hell awaited me when I died? I would fire this and related questions at my long-suffering teacher but I never received satisfactory answers, just platitudes about Jesus loving me.

While the school's official policy on religious matters seemed nebulous at best, there was a curious, almost fundamentalist, born-again style subculture among a section of pupils known as the Christian Movement. Loosely organized in an unofficial capacity by Miss Shirley, they held regular prayer meetings to which a sign on the door announced that everyone was invited. Everyone except me, that was. One day I stopped by to see what was going on and was informed by a literally holier-than-thou classmate (one of Miss Shirley's leading disciples) that my confrontational approach to matters of the spirit meant I would not be welcome at their mysterious jamboree.

'That's very Christian of you,' I commented as he barred my way at the door.

'Ah now, Neil, don't be like that,' said my flustered classmate. 'You know you'd only sit at the back making trouble.' Which was, to be fair, my intention, but I still felt it hypocritical not to give me the benefit of the doubt.

Excluded from an organization I had no intention of joining, I made it my business to antagonize them at every opportunity. The thing that really perplexed me, and indeed intellectually infuriated me, was that the group's members included many of my closest friends, not to mention some of the most attractive girls and coolest guys in the school. Paul and Alison occasionally attended the meetings, where they apparently studied the Gospels, unencumbered by secular ritual, and found solace, harmony and truth there. Yet when I read these same books I found nothing but illogic and contradiction, fairytales passed off as history. The apostle I identified most with was Doubting Thomas. While his scepticism about the appearance of the risen Christ was presented to us as a weakness of character, I always thought that insisting on poking his fingers through his ghostly leader's stigmata was the only sensible course of action under the exceedingly strange circumstances.

I was genuinely baffled as to how such a dynamic and evidently intelligent individual as Paul Hewson could be so committed to these ancient myths. He never became infuriated by my regular challenges to his convictions, however, but would always indulge my penchant for argument. 'I like a good fight' was one of his mantras. 'It's good to ask questions,' he told me once. He would listen to my barrage of misgivings and criticisms of Christianity in all its guises and try to persuade me that the leap of faith required to open yourself up to God was worth it. 'When you look around,' he insisted, 'you see the oceans, you see the sun, you see a storm, a beautiful girl; don't you think there must be something above man? Apart from women?!?!' He would keep coming back to the issue of faith, although he himself was not immune to doubt. He didn't like organized religion or empty ritual and seemed to be engaged in a struggle to quell his own demons. Paul had a temper which could suddenly flare up, his face going red with rage, although I never felt it directed towards me. In the aftermath of his mother's death the year before, there had, apparently, been little explosions in class, with tables being tipped over and chairs kicked across the room. He told me once that there was a period of two weeks about which he could remember nothing. He had a total blank. He was undergoing some kind of existential crisis and almost buckled under the psychological pressure. 'I faced ideas of suicide,' he admitted. 'I was very unhappy; my mind was speeding.'

The school's response had been exemplary. Paul was told he could attend whatever classes he wanted, could come and go as it suited him until he found his feet again. One teacher in particular made himself available to talk and listen: Jack Heaslip, a counsellor to the pupils and responsible for overseeing classes in career guidance and social issues. Heaslip was a gentle, thoughtful, soft-spoken, bearded man with strong spiritual leanings, who would eventually leave teaching to become a Protestant minister. Now Paul evidently had some strong childhood experience of 'otherness', a sense that there was something bigger than mankind. He once told me he had been full of questions about existence and had called out, as he put it, and a voice answered from inside. But it had not been enough to change his life. 'I just wandered on,' he said. 'I refused to believe in God. Why should I? I'd go to church and there just seemed to be people there, singing psalms of glory but they didn't seem to feel anything – it seemed all wrong.'

The death of his mother was undoubtedly what tipped the balance. 'It shocked me into the insignificance of human life,' he said. 'One minute you can be alive, the next you're gone. I could not accept that people would just disappear. If life meant being on the earth for sixty or seventy years, I'd rather go now!' It is an argument that never impressed me. The notion that there has to be a God because there's no point otherwise is emotive rather than rational. But I hear myself saying this and I can see Bono gently smiling, chiding me about my preference for logic over faith. Somehow Paul had made a huge leap of faith and found himself standing on a rock of belief. He didn't have to question the past. He didn't have to let his own mind chase him round in circles of torment. He could pick himself up and move forward. God, in a sense, became the defining ground to his character.

Oddly enough, my RE teacher was unable to demonstrate quite the same sense of equable conviction. I would sit at the back of the class, flicking through a Bible, seeking out anomalies to bring to her attention. Miss Shirley would be in the middle of some happy-clappy sermon when my hand would shoot up. 'Miss! Miss!' She would visibly stiffen while my fellow denizens of the back row stifled their giggles.

'Yes, Neil?'

She had a way of saying my name that conveyed both long-suffering irritation and nervous apprehension. I never got the impression that she much enjoyed the cut and thrust of scriptural debate. One day, faced with another unanswerable contradiction from the good book on which she had based her life's work, she simply burst into tears. We all sat staring at her in stunned silence, a few of my more devout classmates casting dirty looks in my direction. Miss Shirley eventually managed to control herself enough to say, 'If you don't want to be here, Neil, you should feel free to spend these periods in the library.'

Well, cast thee out, Satan! I didn't know whether to feel triumphant or disappointed, because I did actually enjoy the hurly-burly of these classes, where I got to pit my sceptical wits against a member of the religious establishment, however lowly. On the other hand, a free library period every week was not to be sniffed at. I gathered up my books and made for the door. Whereupon the malcontents from the back row started sticking up their hands and asking if they could go too. 'Anyone who wants to spend RE in the library should feel free to do so,' declared Miss Shirley sharply.

One by one we filed out of the class, leaving a rather forlorn-looking teacher preaching to the converted, all six of them.

I spent a lot of time in the library, and not just because I was a voracious reader who had been dismissed from RE classes. I was also excused from Gaelic, which was a relief: under the nationalistic ordinances of the era, if you failed your Irish exams you failed everything.

The library is where I became properly acquainted with Dave Evans, the boy who would become known to the world as iconic guitar hero, musical boffin and the coolest bald man in rock'n'roll: the Edge. Having been born in London of Welsh parents, Dave had also managed to wangle his way out of Irish classes. Though his family had relocated to Malahide, north of Dublin, when Dave was aged one, so strictly speaking he should have been trying to get to grips with the ancient language of Eire along with the rest of the poor native suckers, Dave somehow convincingly masqueraded as a Welshman, born and bred.

I have to say, there was nothing particularly Edgy about Dave in those days. He had hair, a big, dark mop of it as I recall, but this would not have been considered worthy of note at the time. We all had hair, most of it pomped up in appalling, blow-dried seventies bouffants that made our heads look twice the size they actually were. Dave was quiet and somewhat studious, more inclined to use his library time to do his homework than to sit and argue with me about whatever was the latest controversial concept percolating in my hyperactive brain. I remember him being respectful to adults, poised and serious, but with a quirky and sometimes cutting sense of humour. We were civil rather than intimate. I was probably too rebellious and argumentative for his disposition, while, for my part, I felt intimidated by his perpetual air of intellectual superiority. I felt certain that he took a dim view of many of my antics, such as my prank of loosening the library bookshelves so that they would collapse whenever somebody returned a weighty volume. Dave's scepticism towards me was probably not much helped by the fact that he held strong religious beliefs and was close to the school's Christian Movement, with whom I, for some reason, had a bad reputation.

Dave and I were rivals for the affections of certain schoolmates of the female persuasion. He caused me considerable torment when he succeeded in snogging Denise McIntyre, the unwitting object of my adoration, whom I made a point of sitting next to in most classes. My distress when Denise blithely informed me of their brief encounter was only mildly mollified by her appraisal of my rival as a 'sloppy kisser'.

Adam Clayton arrived at Mount Temple in 1976 and made an immediate impact. There was his dress sense for one thing. The school did not have a uniform policy but among the pullovers and anoraks that passed for teen fashion in Dublin in the late seventies Adam's long Afghan coat with shaggy trimmings and decorative stitched flowers certainly stood out. He would, from time to time, sport a kaftan beneath this beloved garment and went through a phase of wearing a yellow workman's helmet on top of his mop of blond curls.

Adam was a gangly, upper-middle-class English boy with an

insouciant line in *faux* sophistication that seemed to implicitly suggest he had already 'been there, seen that, done it' at the age of not-so-sweet sixteen. He had certainly been to more places and seen and done more than most of his contemporaries at Mount Temple, arriving at school fresh from a holiday in Pakistan, where he had hung out with hippies, smoked joints and engaged in a torrid romantic affair (or so he claimed). Adam had a rebellious, confrontational attitude towards authority that was only mildly disguised by his broad smile and impeccable manners. He carried a flask of coffee around with him, from which he would pour himself cups during lessons. When asked by exasperated teachers what he thought he was up to, he would politely explain that he was having a cup of coffee, always remembering to add 'sir' or 'miss' where appropriate. Adam was unfailingly courteous but determined to go his own way – which was often straight to detention.

The last of the future superstars was Larry Mullen. He was in the year below mine, and was a handsome, self-contained blond kid who, at that stage, simply did not register on any of our consciousnesses. But Larry was the start of it all.

In autumn 1976, during my second year at Mount Temple, a notice appeared on the board in the Mall, the corridor that ran the length of the principal school building where we used to hang out. 'Drummer looking for musicians to form band. Contact Larry Mullen, third year.' At thirteen, my brother was a year below Larry, but, as the proud possessor of a Teisco Stratocaster-copy electric guitar, Ivan was invited to audition. On Saturday 25 September 1976, he turned up at Larry's modest semi-detached house in Artane along with Paul, Adam, Dave and his elder brother, Dick Evans.

So that's Ivan McCormick, right? Despite spending most of his life as a musician, being present at the early rehearsals for the group that would become U2 is Ivan's sole claim to anything approaching fame. And then a sloppy biographer handed it to his older brother, robbing him of even this footnote in rock history. So I am happy to have this opportunity to set the record straight.

My brother was the loser who let superstardom slip through his careless fingers, not me.

The assembled ranks of would-be rock stars crowded into the Mullens' kitchen to discuss their plans over tea and crackers. It was, as Ivan recalls, quickly agreed by everyone present that they were ready and willing to form a group. The names of groups such as Led Zeppelin, Deep Purple and Fleetwood Mac – all of whom Ivan had only the faintest conception of – were bandied about as worthy influences. Ivan felt nervous and out of his depth, being by some way the youngest person present, but his trump card was that he had the most handsome guitar, clean and modern with a bright white and red body, which everyone admired. Dave Evans, meanwhile, had a small white acoustic which his mother had bought second-hand for the princely sum of £1 (without strings). But, using Ivan's electric, Dave demonstrated that he could play the solo from Irish rock hero Rory Gallagher's 'Blister on the Moon', which put him in pole position for the role of lead guitarist.

His brother, Dick, was the eldest, at seventeen. He had left school the previous year and, as if to signify his adult status, sported an outcrop of facial hair which he unconvincingly attempted to pass off as a beard. He had brought along a strange-looking object with a body shape that was apparently supposed to resemble a swan in flight, hand-painted bright yellow. Dick had constructed this instrument himself in the shed at the bottom of his garden, following instructions in an issue of *Everyday Electronics* magazine. The resulting instrument sounded about as convincing as it looked but at least Dick could play chords and hold down a rhythm. This was more than could be said for Paul, who also had a big, battered acoustic which he tackled with energy and gusto rather than anything approaching skill or finesse. But Paul made up for his lack of musical skills with his sense of passion and conviction, already talking as if they were a band and not just an ill-sorted gathering of schoolboys.

With four guitarists squeezing in between the fridge and the bread-bin, the designated rhythm section comprised Adam (who owned a cheap Ibanez-copy bass, which he couldn't actually play but could certainly talk about) and Larry, who had opened the kitchen doors to create space in which to set up his drum kit, half in the kitchen and half in a small conservatory precariously attached to the back of the house. In these odd circumstances the meeting concluded with a chaotic jam session involving wobbly renditions of the Rolling Stones classics 'Brown Sugar' and 'Satisfaction'. There were too many guitarists, not enough amplification and no consensus as to the correct chord sequences of the songs being played, but none of that seemed to matter. A new star had appeared in the rock'n'roll firmament. For these plucky individuals – well, some of them, anyway – nothing would be the same again.

Ivan returned home on the 31 bus to announce that he had joined a new band. They were going to be called Feedback (allegedly a reference to the whining noise that emerged when Adam plugged his bass into a guitar amp). I noted this news with only a modicum of concern. If the name was anything to go by, this lot were going to be even less impressive (if perhaps more audibly so) than Electronic Wizard.

My thespian career was advancing, albeit at a much slower pace than I would have liked. I attended drama classes on Saturday afternoons and experienced a moment of encouragement when I won an acting competition known as the Father Matthew *Feis* (pronounced 'fesh', Gaelic for 'entertainment'. I have no idea who Father Matthew was but presumably he liked to have a good time). It was a hideous affair, characterized by rampant overacting, with starry-eyed juveniles racing energetically about every inch of the stage as if convinced the theatrical arts were a branch of the Olympics. When my turn came I stood stock-still in the central spotlight. I would like to say that this was a carefully contrived dramatic device, but actually my legs were trembling so much I was afraid that if I moved I would fall over. It was my first time in front of a large audience and when the applause began my ego took a direct hit from a bolt of lightning. I staggered off dazed with happiness, physically buzzing from the adrenalin rush. This was everything I had ever dreamed about, especially when the results were announced and I was beckoned back on stage to receive a medal for first prize. The principal judge, an obscure drama critic whose authority was undisputed simply on the grounds that she had come all the way from England, whispered to me that my performance was the only interesting thing she had seen all day. Could it get any better than this? Well, yes, actually. On the citation I received she had written: 'A performance of powerful understatement and great control. This boy has immense talent – please look after him.'

But nobody did look after me. Nobody would ever look after me. Not that I guessed that then, otherwise I might have had the good sense to jack it all in and concentrate on my technical drawing or some other useful subject. I remained convinced that stardom was my destiny, although I was a little disillusioned to discover that a commendation from Father Matthew counted for very little in Hollywood.

Ivan continued to attend rehearsals for Feedback in the school music room after hours. He was tolerated by the older boys primarily because of his guitar, which Dave would liberate him of for the duration of the sessions, leaving Ivan to strum inaudibly on Dave's cheap acoustic. Dick had been told he could stay in the fold on the proviso that he got himself a decent instrument, preferably one not constructed in his garden shed. Adam had his bass and therefore his position was assured – all he had to do was learn how to play it. But Adam, at least, had attitude, confidence and all the right buzz-words. With a cigarette dangling from his bottom lip, he would talk about sorting out some 'gigs' by making the right 'connections'. They needed 'good management' and to 'go on the road', apparently, if they were ever going to 'land a deal'. It all sounded good to the others, even if they had only the vaguest idea what he was banging on about.

Paul was another matter. He was really a frustrated musician. He simply could not get his guitar to do anything he wanted it to do, so would usually abandon it and instead expend his considerable energy attempting to almost magically summon, coax and cajole music from the others. During an endless jam of Deep Purple's 'Smoke on the Water' (a song Ivan was hearing for the first time), Ivan was astonished to see Paul get down on his hands and knees in front of Dave as he played the famous riff, holding his fingers in front of Dave's fingers, as if he was trying to play the guitar himself without actually touching it. Paul assumed the role of organizer, telling everyone what they were going to play and how they would tackle it yet actually contributing little himself. He would sing along as best he could, struggling to find the right notes, but without a microphone his vocal limitations were not immediately apparent to anyone other than himself. As the biggest character in the group he began to assume the role of frontman.

Excited about the band, Ivan decided to invest in a new amplifier and blew his entire savings of £12 on a second-hand Falcon Combo. That very evening, as he sat at home fiddling with his new purchase, sending feedback howling through the house, he was summoned to the telephone by our mother. Apparently there was a very well-spoken young man on the line who urgently needed to talk to him. It was Adam. He wanted to know if Ivan had bought the amp because of the group.

'Yes,' said Ivan.

'I wish you'd spoken to me first,' said Adam, improvising wildly. 'You see, the band has got a gig . . .'

'That's great,' said Ivan, enthusiastically. On the road at last.

'The thing is, it's in a pub,' said Adam. 'And, you know, you're too young to get into pubs.'

'Oh,' said Ivan.

'In fact, all the gigs we'll be getting will be in pubs,' said Adam. 'And you won't be able to play any of them.'

'I see,' said Ivan.

'I knew you'd understand,' said Adam. 'Look, no hard feelings, eh?'

Even at thirteen, Ivan knew when he was being given the elbow, however diplomatically. He put the phone down in a state of utter dejection and went back to his guitar and amp, turning the volume up to the max and losing himself in a wall of noise.

There was, of course, no pub and certainly no gig. The group could barely string a whole song together, so attempting to deliver an entire set would have been premature to say the least. But, as rehearsals began to illuminate everyone's strengths and weaknesses, so the band began to settle into a core line-up of Larry on drums, Adam on bass, Paul on vocals, Dave on lead guitar and Dick on rhythm guitar. In fact Dick, too, was not really wanted by his bandmates, but he simply ignored any intimations that he might be surplus to requirements and continued to attend rehearsals until he had established himself as a member.

His pride wounded, Ivan neglected to inform the family of this new development. The truth did not emerge for weeks, until Stella asked Paul how he was getting along with her little brother and Paul, rather embarrassed, admitted they had kicked him out.

'Why didn't you tell us?' asked my astonished father.

'It doesn't matter, anyway,' said Ivan, defensively. 'They're crap. I'm going to start my own group.'

My acting career was not progressing any better. My parents like to proudly tell people that their son was once in a play in the prestigious Gate Theatre with the venerable Irish thespian Cyril Cusack. What they neglect to add was that after two performances I was sacked for missing my cue. I thought the part was beneath me, anyway. I had no lines and was really a glorified stage-hand whose sole purpose was to move furniture for the other actors. As far as I was concerned, anybody could have done it (well, anybody apart from me, it would seem). I craved the physical rush of performing in front of an audience, the ego buzz of recognition by other human beings allied to the strange sense of power that coursed through your body as you held strangers in your spell by sheer force of will. I wanted to utter speeches that resonated in my soul and made sense of my complex internal world. 'To be or not to be?' That was the question I wanted to ask, almost the only question that mattered. I wanted to be Hamlet. But I couldn't even land a part in a burger commercial, when it was deemed that my mixed Scottish and Irish accent might be confusing to viewers. The director was not impressed when I suggested that the phrase 'Mmm, deeeee-licious!' would have sounded equally lame in any accent.

I resolved to solve my casting problems by writing plays myself. As the 1976 autumn term drew to a close it was announced that a talent contest would be staged in the school gymnasium. This, I decided, would be the ideal opportunity to demonstrate my writing and acting skills. And so, with a couple of friends, I concocted a short comic play, which involved our teachers being put on trial for crimes against humanity. The parts were filled by various classmates, with the juicy role of judge being kept for myself. Banging my gavel to sentence unpopular teachers to a variety of extravagant punishments was sure to prove a crowd-pleaser. We had a run-through the week before for our avuncular form tutor, Mr Moxham, who was sufficiently impressed to schedule our production as the grand finale on the condition that we went gently on his character and removed certain of our more cruel and tasteless gags.

I gathered with my small cast at the side of a makeshift stage of jammed-together tables as a succession of pupils larked about, singing, dancing, playing accordions, telling jokes. The large audience of schoolkids heckled the performers mercilessly but most took it in good humour, shouting back insults. Mr Moxham cheerfully patrolled the gymnasium, patting pupils on the back, uttering words of encouragement.

'Ready for your moment of glory, lads?' he inquired of my little crew.

'We're ready, sir,' I reported.

'And you have made those changes we discussed?'

'Do we really have to lose the gag about Mrs Prandy's dog, sir?' I asked.

'Only if you want to live through another term,' replied Mr Moxham.

Four members of Feedback stood around their amps and drum kit, waiting to make their live debut. Dick was absent, since he was not a pupil at the school, but Paul, Dave, Adam and Larry were going to do a ten-minute set, scheduled as the penultimate act, just before our play.

'All right, Dave?' I asked, feeling every inch the seasoned professional comforting a nervous débutante. Dave looked as if he was going to be sick from stage fright, clinging to his guitar and staring anxiously at the crowd. The others appeared considerably more at ease. Larry had played plenty of shows before, albeit with such less-than-rocking outfits as the Artane Boys Band and the Post Office Workers Band. Adam lounged about, affecting his usual seen-it-all-before cool. Paul was practically jumping up and down with anticipation, firing encouraging smiles and nods at his colleagues.

When their slot came, the group started to hoist their equipment on to the stage. It took them about ten minutes to set up, an extended period of inactivity in which any last remnants of discipline in the room evaporated. Kids were running about the gym in all directions, yelling at the tops of their voices, climbing the climbing-frames. I was marshalling my cast, instructing them that as soon as the band were finished we were to get on to the stage and launch straight into our play. I really had no idea what was coming.

An electric hum began to sound in the room as the amps were turned on. Paul stood centre stage at his microphone, guitar slung around his neck, looking defiantly over the boisterous crowd. Dave and Adam stood either side of him. Larry clicked his sticks together and the group launched into a coarse, speeded-up version of seventies pretty-boy rock star Peter Frampton's 'Show Me the Way', kicking off with a roaring D chord that sent a shockwave through the room.

With the wisdom of hindsight, I know this debut performance of the group who would one day rock the world must have been, in truth, a fairly dubious affair. There was nothing remotely cool about their selection of songs, for a start. They played, of all things, a tongue-in-cheek version of the Bay City Roller's pop anthem 'Bye Bye Baby' and a Beach Boys medley.

They had no sound-check, no experience, nothing to go on but hope and desire. But I was completely stunned. Absolutely floored. This was the first live, electric band I had ever heard and a rush of adrenaline shot through my body, apparently disabling my central nervous system and rearranging my entire molecular structure. At least, that's what it felt like. Dave's guitar was splintering in my ears. The pounding of Larry's drums and Adam's bass shook the tables they were standing on and seemed to make the whole room vibrate. I had listened to records in my room, headbanging in headphones, but nothing prepared me for the sheer visceral thrill of live rock'n'roll. When Paul stomped across the shaky stage, grabbed his microphone stand and yelled, 'I want you . . . / Show me the way!' the little girls from the junior classes started screaming.

And that was it for me. I turned to my fellow would-be thespians and announced that there was absolutely no way I was going on after that. It was quickly and unanimously agreed that our play should be cancelled. Mr Moxham, as I recall, seemed quite relieved.

Feedback belted through their bizarre set and then stood there, stupid grins plastered across their faces, as the crowd roared for more. Their repertoire being rather limited in those days, they had to resort to a repeat version of 'Bye Bye Baby'. The gym was in complete uproar, with kids singing, yelling, screaming, clapping, dancing. I looked about me in a daze. A new vision of my future was forming in my feverish adolescent brain.

Forget about becoming a fabulously famous, multi-hyphenated actor-writer-director.

I was going to be a rock star.

3

Ivan and I decided to form a band. There was something inevitable about our hitching together our ambitions. We shared a bedroom for much of our childhood and would lie awake at night conjuring up fantasies of fame and fortune. I don't know if I infected him with my own delusions of grandeur or whether it was something in the competitive dynamic of our family, but we seemed equally convinced that stardom was our birthright as we role-played the parts we believed we would make our own. It was a relatively small journey from Bill and Ben to John and Paul.

Our relationship was a complex mix of filial loyalty and sibling rivalry. We had many qualities in common, not all of them appreciated by those closest to us. It was often remarked that we had the same sense of humour, an observation rarely offered as a compliment. Our jokes could be rather cruel (and were rather too often directed at other members of our family), underpinned by a mutual streak of rebellious irreverence. We both exhibited powerful creative drives and were motivated by a sense of ambition out of all proportion to our circumstances, but our endeavours were often hampered by a ridiculously fierce rivalry. We made short eight-millimetre films together but still fought about who should be credited as director. My sister used to say we thought we were better than everyone else, and that included each other.

For our first songwriting session, we sat on my bed, him with his guitar, me with a pen and pad. 'What should we write about?' he wanted to know after strumming aimlessly for a while.

'I don't know,' I confessed. 'What do people write songs about?'

I wonder if Lennon and McCartney ever had this problem? Our chosen subject matter in the end was rather mundane, reflecting the priorities of two bored teenage boys. It was a twelve-bar blues entitled 'Pass the Pepperoni Pizza', the chorus of which went:

> Pass the pepperoni pizza
> Pass the pepperoni pizza
> Pass the pepperoni pizza, baby
> And another slice of apple pie

Neither of us was particularly impressed with our efforts, so the group project was sidelined for a while.

Music was playing an increasingly important part in my life. In 1975 I had discovered the Beatles, somewhat later than the rest of the world, admittedly, but with much the same devastating effect on my psyche. In an effort to catch up with my peers, I was working backwards in my musical education and one day decided to invest my pocket money in their blue 'best of' collection, *The Beatles 1967–1970*. What a revelatory purchase that turned out to be.

Having returned home with my new acquisition, I sat in the living room and listened to the whole double album on headphones. It was an ecstasy-inducing, quasi-religious experience. I was lost in the swirling psychedelic colours of 'Lucy in the Sky with Diamonds', cast adrift in the awe-inspiring depths and lonely floating vocal counterpoint of 'A Day in the Life' and left battered and bewildered by the surreal epic drama of 'I Am the Walrus'. When it came to the 'nah nah nah's at the sentimental conclusion of 'Hey Jude', tears filled my eyes. I sat there, blubbing uncontrollably, emotionally overwhelmed by pop music for the first time.

I studied the slightly mysterious black-and-white photo of the band on the inner sleeve. These four people had made this whole magical world that seemed to open up new chambers in my brain. They looked impossibly wise and cool. From that day on, I became a voracious consumer of all things Beatle. I investigated the albums gradually, over a long period of time, savouring each record for as long as possible before moving on to the next, fearing that the pure joy of listening would evaporate when I eventually reached the final album. What I learned instead was that great records have strength in depth, expanding rather than retracting with repeated listens.

By the time I saw Feedback I was ready to crumble, falling head first into what would turn out to be a lifelong love affair with rock'n'roll. The Beatles led to other groups: the Animals, the Dave Clarke Five, the Kinks, the Who, the Zombies. I became interested in beat groups, unexpectedly aided by my maternal grandmother, who turned out to have a stash of rather hip sixties vinyl that some lodger had left behind. I was fascinated by David Bowie (who had collaborated with John Lennon on 'Fame', a song I loved for pathetically obvious reasons) but progressive rock bands of the seventies such as Yes and Genesis held no interest for me. Their music seemed tricksy, overelaborate and devoid of wit or emotion. It belonged, in my perception, to the long-haired older kids my sister hung around with. As far as I was concerned they could keep it. Sixties music seemed far more fresh and urgent. With typical arrogance, I was already becoming a snob about something I barely knew anything about.

In 1976, just going on seventeen years old, Stella was too young to be a real hippie chick but this was certainly the pop-cultural status to which she aspired. Her friend Orla Dunne wore her hair in long neoclassical ringlets, dressed in swathes of gauzy material and walked about with two enormous, shaggy Afghan hounds. Stella and Orla listened to soft rock of the seventies (the Eagles and the Moody Blues were great favourites) and chased boys who had long hair and droopy moustaches and smoked dope. They liked to sing and were good enough to be included in the Temple Singers, an elite school ensemble which included past pupils and the pick of the regular common-or-garden choir (of which Paul, Dave and I were undistinguished members). After choir practise one day, the girls were approached by Paul with a proposition.

Adam had managed to blag Feedback a Saturday-night support slot in the hall of my old school, St Fintan's. Encouraged as they were by the positive reception to their first performance, the group felt they had to take things to a more professional level. It was suggested that a couple of sexy female backing singers might add some class and Paul (who seemed to know most of the girls in Mount Temple) said he had just the right girls for the job. And so my sister became the second McCormick to join the group who would become U2.

Although they were in the same year at school, Stella did not know Paul particularly well. He was in Orla's class but, since he didn't conform to the girls' rigidly defined concept of 'dishiness', he had never been of great interest. They both remarked, however, on how amusing he could be, a facet of his character which actually rather puzzled Stella. At the behest of another classmate, Stella attended a couple of the Christian Movement meetings. She watched with growing incredulity as, during prayers, several participants started babbling animatedly in gibberish – or rather, as they would have it, 'talking in tongues'. They were heartily congratulated for these performances by their fellow believers, who claimed to recognize the dialect as ancient Hebrew, albeit delivered, according to Stella, with a distinctly Dublin flavour. Stella found the participants to be a rather ridiculous bunch who managed to be weird and dull at the same time and were all a bit too pleased about their personal relationship with their maker. Paul, however, was different. For a start, he did not check his sense of humour at the altar. 'You finding it a bit hard on the head?' he had asked her, sympathetically, as she watched her schoolfriends roll their eyes and commune with the Holy Spirit. 'It's all very uncool. God doesn't seem too interested in helping you look your best to your mates, that's for sure.' Stella was amazed that somebody could actually be funny, irreverent and devoutly Christian at the same time.

Rehearsals were held at Adam's house in Malahide during a week's break in the winter term. Stella and Orla would turn up at midday, with Adam usually answering the door in his dressing-gown, sleepily rubbing his eyes, having just emerged from bed. In the sizeable living room, the rest of the band would assemble and start tuning up, while Adam slowly got himself together with the aid of coffee and cigarettes. The first afternoon, he wandered about with his dressing-gown flapping open, his prodigious member occasionally poking through. Having had limited exposure to the male sexual organ, Stella and Orla sat debating the strange purple colour and lumpy texture of Adam's underpants until it finally dawned on them that he wasn't wearing any. They burst into giggles while Paul instructed Adam to 'put it away before you frighten somebody'.

The sessions were good fun, with Paul acting as ice-breaker, cracking jokes and filling the room with his energy. While Dave was initially very quiet and Dick seemed to the girls intimidatingly older and somewhat detached, the atmosphere lightened as Paul hustled proceedings along, making sure everyone was involved. To add to their Peter Frampton and Beach Boys numbers, Feedback were rehearsing an eclectic bunch of popular rock songs, including some Rolling Stones, Neil Young's 'Heart of Gold', the Eagles' 'Witchy Woman' and the Moody Blues' 'Nights in White Satin'. As well as angelic harmonies it was decided that the latter would feature a flute solo by Orla. The group were having some problems, however, getting the instrumental interlude to work. Or rather, to be more specific, getting Adam to come in on time.

After the second chorus, the song broke down for a few bars of strummed guitars and flute (played by Orla) before a little bass lick presaged the rest of the band kicking back in. Except, to the initial amusement and eventual exasperation of everyone present, Adam missed his cue every time. His absence of rhythm became a running joke, amusing to all but the bassist himself. At the appropriate moment, everyone in the band would shout 'Now!' and Adam, startled, would come in half a second behind. Nothing could solve the problem. It became Larry's responsibility to cue Adam. 'Just watch me,' he'd instruct him before they played the song. It made not a whit of difference. Adam would come in late and the song would bump awkwardly along till everyone fell in with the laggardly bassist.

Years later, Stella watched U2's documentary *Rattle and Hum*. The band, now considered the most popular and important rock group in the world, were waiting in the wings of an enormous American stadium, preparing themselves to play before a crowd of 80,000. As they walked towards the stage, Stella was astonished to see Larry turn to Adam and repeat the phrase he had employed all those years before: 'Just watch me.'

'I thought, *My God*,' Stella told me afterwards, 'he still can't do it!'

The hall at St Fintan's was a cavernous affair, a concrete shed that acted as school gymnasium cum theatre, ill suited to the acoustics of rock'n'roll. It was the venue for a regular Saturday-night disco, which, in Ireland in 1976, meant a pasty-faced DJ playing a well-worn selection of prog- and heavy-rock records (Zeppelin, Rory Gallagher, Yes) while boys in denim jackets head-banged energetically. The limited numbers of girls who had been persuaded to attend would hug the wall and wait for a slow song (usually Zep's 'Stairway to Heaven' or something equally unromantic by Eric Clapton). The headline band, Ratt Salad, were a typical Dublin covers mob, pumping out twelve-bar boogies with lots of lead solos and lyrics name-checking American cities the participants had, in all likelihood, never visited.

This was all new to me, however. I had never been to a disco before, let alone one with live bands, and I wasn't sure how I was supposed to behave. I walked down to St Fintan's with a neighbourhood pal, Ronan, and we huddled against a back wall, shoulders hunched, the collars of our bomber jackets pulled up around our faces, waiting for something to happen. Experience had taught us to be wary of the older local boys, who would seek out eye contact only to challenge you to a fight. 'What you lookin' at?' was a question from which you were unlikely to escape unscathed, so mostly we just looked at our feet.

A very small crowd from Mount Temple had turned out to support the band and we acknowledged each other with the wariness that comes with being on hostile territory. Alison was there, along with Bono's out-of-school gang, a close-knit group of misfits from Ballymun who called themselves (for reasons lost in the mists of childhood self-mythologizing) Lypton Village. I found the Village, with their stance of self-conscious weirdness and plethora of dryly delivered in-jokes, a somewhat intimidating presence. They were friendly towards me (particularly after I received a welcoming pat on the back from Paul) but I was so out of my element I sensed danger everywhere. If a fight was going to break out, it was likely to be between the Village and the locals – and thus I judged it better just to pretend not to know anybody. I waited for the gig to start in a state of quiet agitation, an undercurrent of fear heightening my sense of anticipation.

Feedback's second show was an almost unmitigated disaster. The sound was poor, with the drums echoing off the back wall and the instrumental mixture criminally out of balance. The cover versions were hackneyed and lumpen, lacking both the finesse of faithful reproduction and the energy of inspired reinvention. While members of the Village threw themselves about in front of the stage in a physical display of support, the rest of the denizens of the hall stood frozen in sceptical silence, gauche teenage boys determined to project seen-it-all-before machismo. Eager to bridge the gap opening up between band and audience, Paul responded by talking too much, babbling away between songs, determined to elicit a response. The response he got, however, was not especially encouraging. 'Play the fuckin' song, ya eejit!' someone yelled after a particularly verbose introduction.

And then they played 'Nights in White Satin'. The girls launched heartily into their oohs and ahhs but couldn't hear themselves through the PA. Neither could anyone else. When Orla began her flute solo, it at last became clear that the backing microphones had mysteriously ceased to function. Paul, guitar slung around his neck, dragged his mic and stand across to Orla and, after a few bars of complete musical confusion, Dave recommenced playing the instrumental section for the second time while Paul crouched in front of Orla, holding the mic to her flute. Then, just as the band seemed to be finding their groove, everyone turned to Adam for his all-important lick, whereupon the startled bassist commenced playing, late and out of time. Despite the exaggerated applause of the Village, there were no encores. Stella felt like crying. All that practise only for the performance to be such a mess.

Years later, Bono told me that the girls had thought the band could be good without him, and tried to persuade the other members to kick him out. My sister, however, vehemently denies it. 'I never thought they could be any good,' she insists.

Probably the only person who walked away from the St Fintan's gig in a state of high excitement was me. I hadn't seen or heard enough live rock to be any judge of quality but my ears were buzzing from the volume, my heart was pounding from the release of tension and I was more convinced than ever that I had to get my own band together. I even liked Ratt Salad.

In a post-mortem of their performance, Feedback agreed that the experiment with backing singers had been a failure. Paul, however, remained inspirationally upbeat about the group's prospects. He had seen a 'spark' and was convinced that the group could build themselves around it until they would set their world ablaze. Concerns, however, were raised about the band's name – which, it was gloomily pointed out, could be construed as a joke at their own expense, suggesting a less-than-professional standard of musicianship. Adam (whose musicianship was perhaps the most suspect) proposed that they become the Hype. It was a word he had come across reading the British music papers, where journalists frequently accused the music business of 'hyping' bands, essentially creating a publicity storm out of all proportion to the band's actual abilities. As a group name it seemed modern, knowing and aspirational, an ironic comment on the music scene. It certainly suited a band whose ambitions currently far outweighed their actual abilities.

Something was happening in the music scene, an urgent new movement taking shape in the rock underground of the UK, the faintest of reverberations being just about distinguishable across the Irish Sea. You had to be almost psychically alert to detect the signs. You had to be hungry for something new. You had, in essence, to be a music-obsessed, Anglophile, neophyte teenager in the grip of an identity crisis with existential overtones. But, amid the sonic soup of corny showband schmaltz, ersatz country and western, earnest folk ballads, self-aggrandizing heavy rock, slushy pop and chintzy disco that formed the soundtrack to Irish life, the first subtle hints of a brutally pared-down, compellingly aggressive rock revolution could be detected.

There was no national pop radio channel in Ireland but if you lived in Dublin, on the east coast of the country, you could tune in through the static to the late-night John Peel show on BBC Radio One, broadcast from transmitters across the sea in Wales. Peel played an eclectic concoction of recordings from the outer limits of the musical stratosphere, to which I somewhat masochistically subjected myself as part of my ongoing musical education. I would lie in bed, in a state of baffled incredulity, listening to portentous, meandering, fey-psychedelic instrumentals and dissonant, distorted experimental metal epics by bands with names that sounded like mystic invocations to some mad old God of music, driven by a conviction that there was something going on here that I was just too young and inexperienced to understand. I listened intently, passing through waves of amusement, frustration and irritation, all the while searching for a key to unlock the door to this arcane world.

And then, one wonderful night, spitting out of my tinny transistor came a sound that almost physically jerked me to attention. A high-pitched squall of keening, angry vocals spilled asymmetrically across an urgent, rhythmic bass and drum barrage, swamped in a thrashing blur of overdriven guitars. '*I am the anti-KRRIST-a! / I am an anar-KYST-a!*' I felt like I was listening to the aural equivalent of an avalanche. '*Don't know what I want but I know how to geddit . . .*' The lyrics invoked an almost incandescent, fearfully righteous anger at the state of the world. '*I wanna destroy the PASS-A-BOY . . .*' Something physical seemed to shift inside me. This, I knew instantly, was *my* music, before I even knew what kind of music it actually was. In his characteristically understated fashion, Peel announced that we had just been listening to the debut single from the Sex Pistols, a group at the vanguard of the punk-rock scene. And so it was that, at fifteen years old, I discovered that I was a punk. Now all I had to do was find out what a punk actually was.

If you read the rock-history books, they will tell you that punk rock was either: a) a sleazy New York pop-art scene of the mid-seventies; or b) an aggressive, sociopolitical London youth movement *circa* 1976. Whatever, punk's originators and instigators, jealously guarding their role at the core of the phenomenon, tend to argue that it was all over bar the shouting, spitting and pogoing by 1977. Well, it might have been over for a tiny King's Road elite. But for those of us out in the sticks, far removed from the pulse of the metropolitan underground, it was just getting started.

I initially approached with great caution. The (very) few punks occasionally featured in slightly bemused TV reports or hysterical tabloid newspapers looked a dissolute bunch: spotty oiks with the dress sense of psychotic hobos. The whole punk aesthetic was designed to provoke, annoy and upset and those elements of society inclined to knee-jerk reactions were duly twitching away like demented Cossacks. My own principal concern at that early stage was from the perspective of a hormonally active teenage boy: would girls go out with me dressed like that? Not that they were exactly queuing up to run their fingers through my curly locks or make admiring comments about the cut of my flares. But, in 1977, the only people who did not seem to find punks stomach-churningly disgusting were other punks. And, frankly, there weren't a lot of them about in Dublin. A few of the older blues bands (notably the Boomtown Rats) swapped their denim for leather, shaved off their moustaches and played their songs a bit faster, but that was about it. Punk simply had no real presence in Ireland. It was not played on radio or television. It could not be heard in the discos. The groups were not welcome in the show-band halls. And even if they had been I would have been too young to gain entry. Apart from tuning in to John Peel's show, the only place I could actually hear punk rock was in Advance Records, a dingy, independent basement record shop in the city centre, where I would sometimes hang about for a few hours on a Saturday afternoon, staring at the posters and listening to the latest releases on the in-store speakers until the owner told me to buy something or fuck off.

My first purchase was the Ramones' debut album. With their power-chords and floppy fringes, the Ramones to me were irresistible, like a buzz-saw Beatles. Afraid my parents would disapprove, I hid the sleeve under my bed and slotted the precious vinyl into the back of a Don McLean album my granny had given me.

Despite punk's cultural invisibility in Ireland, there was one invaluable source of information: British weekly the *New Musical Express*. You could not buy this periodical in the local newsagents, so I had to make a bus trip into the city centre to pick it up. It was worth the journey. The *NME* (and sometimes, if that was sold out, its rivals *Sounds* and *Melody Maker*) was my gateway to a parallel universe populated by bands with strange names and stranger haircuts. I read it from cover to cover, running my fingers over pictures of snarling young men in leather jackets splattered with painted slogans and girls in torn fishnets and badly applied make-up, their faces apparently held together by safety-pins. My weekly engagement with alternative rock culture was an almost visceral, physical experience for me. People used to refer to the British music papers as 'the inkies' because by the time you had finished reading them your hands and face and anything you might have touched was usually covered in black smudge. I slavered over the ornate prose, rabid sloganeering, speculative philosophizing and outlandish polemic of writers who treated rock'n'roll as if it was not just another strand of showbusiness but a matter of life and death.

It would be an exaggeration to say that everything I know about music I learned from the *NME*, but not much of an exaggeration. I followed the careers of groups whose music I had never heard and revelled in an arcane insider language I barely understood. Such was the plethora of acronyms employed that at first it seemed to me to be written in code. It took me a while to decipher the meaning of terms such as R'n'B (rhythm and blues), AOR (adult-oriented rock), MOR (middle of the road) and woofers and tweeters (I still have no clear understanding of these). For an inordinately long time I thought a BOF was some kind of extremely clever boffin (and not, as it turned out, a Boring Old Fart) and that 'gobbing on' was slang for 'chatting with' – embarrassingly, I didn't grasp the latter until I was fully immersed in the local live rock scene and suggested to a friend during a gig that we should go and gob on a rather attractive girl in the corner; naturally, when he explained that this would involve covering her in spit I pretended that that was exactly what I'd meant.

In school, there was a handful of fellow travellers and we were beginning to identify each other, exchanging scraps of largely bogus information. We followed the careers of groups we had never seen and passionately debated the merits of records we had never heard. It was almost better that way. Reviews were written in such vivid, passionate, evocative, polemic prose that just to read them was to hear music in your head, an imaginary sound of almost apocalyptic scope, make-believe compositions that could alter your very sense of reality – when in fact, more often than not, the records were just some tinny, speedy, three-chord, pub-rock thrash with someone yelling cheap revolutionary slogans over the top. Punk excited every fibre of our teenage beings because the very idea of it mirrored the changes our bodies and minds were going through, a physical revolt into the independence of adulthood. That the music all too rarely lived up to that promise hardly mattered. We imagined it did, and that was enough.

A new school term commenced in September 1977, the final year for my class, with the dreaded Leaving Certificate exams ahead. The pressure was now on to buckle down and work, and this seemed to me like incredibly bad timing. My results up till then had been good but, at sixteen, my innate rebelliousness was becoming even more pronounced, fuelled by my identification with punk. Just when it was supposed to matter most, I lost all interest in school. I had other things on my overactive mind – such as the meaning of life, and how to impress girls.

One day in September, I was surprised to come across Paul Hewson in the school corridor. Being in my sister's year, he should have departed for university that summer. It transpired, however, that he had failed the crucial Irish-language exam that every schoolkid in the country was expected to pass, and consequently his place to study for an arts degree at University College Dublin had been withdrawn. So Paul was back at Mount Temple for another year, with nothing to do but study Irish. He didn't seem to mind too much. He had the group, he had Alison and he had the chance to make some mischief.

With typical boldness, Paul was the first to physically cross the line and appear in school dressed in the new garb of punk rock. Having raided his older brother Norman's wardrobe for some second-hand sixties clothing, Paul turned up one day in creased, tight-fitting purple drainpipes, a sharply cut, thin-lapelled suit jacket and a pair of scuffed black Cuban heels. He had a fresh, tightly cropped haircut that was, in itself, positively shocking in an era when attractiveness corresponded with hair length; and to top off the whole outrageous effect he was wearing a thin chain that stretched from an earring to a safety-pin through his mouth.

The response was electrifying. As he strode purposefully through the Mall, a gaping crowd, simultaneously fascinated and abhorred, retreated shrieking before this strange vision. Teachers emerged from the staff room to see what the fuss was about and stood in open-mouthed horror. 'Hewson, what do you think you're doing?'

'Nothing, sir.'

The lack of dress code at Mount Temple meant that they were left spluttering ineffectively as he continued his walkabout. He cheekily approached Alison and asked for a kiss. She was all too aware of her boyfriend's propensity for pulling stunts, but his new look genuinely upset her. 'Get away from me,' she yelped, repelling his advances. 'What have you done to your face?'

I watched all this activity with a surge of pride. Punk rock had finally reared its ugly head in Mount Temple. Attempting to escape the hullabaloo, Paul ducked into the prefects' room. I followed.

(Neither of us were prefects but the room was considered an ideal hang-out by the more insubordinate pupils, the experience being immensely enhanced whenever a prefect tried to make us leave.) 'Where did you get that?' I said, admiring his chain. I had seen such things in the *NME* but it was hard to believe that someone would actually mutilate their cheek for the sake of fashion. 'Dandelion Market,' said Paul. 'Look.' He winked at me and removed the safety-pin, demonstrating that you did not actually have to pierce your skin to keep it in place. Listening to the calamity outside the door, he seemed mightily pleased with the response his appearance provoked. Except for one thing. 'Ali's finished with me,' he revealed.

The romance was patched up later the same day, when Paul promised to leave safety-pins for babies' nappies. His flirtation with punk as an anti-fashion movement was short-lived. (As the Edge remarked to me years later: 'Bono was never a punk. He just looked like one 'cause he didn't know how to dress!') Likewise, the Hype never became a fully fledged punk band, but punk certainly affected their music. They arranged a gig on a Friday night in the unlikely environs of the Marine Hotel, a posh beach-side establishment at Sutton Cross (close to St Fintan's). This was their first proper headline set for their own crowd, performing on the floor of a small bar packed with inebriated teenagers. The atmosphere was like an after-hours party, with gangs of schoolkids, unleashed from the restraining influence of authority, scooping down pints with an urgency born of the fear that at any moment the barman would realize they were under eighteen and turn the tap off. Alcohol held no appeal to me but I watched with nervous amusement as my contemporaries melted into drunkenness, lurching about, slurring words and apparently delighting in their growing clumsiness. Everyone was determined to have a good time.

The group had been practising every Saturday in the school music room and were growing in confidence and ability. Dave's guitar playing was becoming sharper and this imbued the shy boy with new confidence on stage, where he would whirl his arms and throw rock'n'roll shapes. Paul was coming into focus as a frontman, pouring every ounce of his excess energy into performance. This crowd was already on his side and he fed off their goodwill, urging his band on. Alongside the usual rock standards, their set included tougher material by Thin Lizzy and David Bowie and a host of punk covers, including the Ramones' 'Gimme Gimme Shock Treatment' and Tom Robinson's rabble-rousing '2-4-6-8 Motorway'. Paul waved his arms about and stomped his feet as he bellowed the chorus, leading a noisy singalong. They played their first original composition, an incongruous country rocker called 'What's Going On'. They banged out the Sex Pistols' 'Anarchy in the UK', a ridiculous song for an Irish band to perform, but with Paul aping Johnny Rotten and the band hammering away at the power chords, the effect was exhilarating. Stella and Orla and the soft-rock trimmings were gone. Instead, Paul's friend Fionan Hanvey, a sometimes scarily intense character from the Village, stepped up to deliver unpolished backing vocals on a furious, high-speed version of Bowie's 'Suffragette City'. 'Hey Man!' he drawled as Paul countered, 'Oh leave me alone, ya know!' Paul was still playing guitar on many songs, not always making the same chord changes as his bandmates but thrashing away so hard that he cut one of his fingers. Blood streamed down the body of his guitar. This was rock'n'roll. The room was in a frenzy. As the band finished their set, a pretty blonde in a blue dress, absolutely sodden with drink, staggered into a plate-glass window separating the bar from the hotel swimming pool, collapsing in a heap of broken glass. Kids gathered around to gape at the blood and wreckage. The management had had enough. They shut the bar and began ushering the rowdy teens out of the establishment. An ambulance was on its way.

I hovered on the edges of a throng around Paul, who was sodden with sweat, basking in the praise and admiration of friends, a huge, gormless grin stretched across his face. He looked dazed, lost in the emotion of the moment. Something had been born that night. Something true and undeniable. Everybody in the room could feel it. Oh, how I longed to be part of it.

4

Perhaps still feeling somewhat guilty about the manner in which they had dismissed Ivan from their ranks, Larry approached my brother one day in the school corridor. He was accompanied by a friend and classmate, a tall, gawky fellow with short, choppy hair and dark, sorrowful eyes, wearing a T-shirt with a loosely knotted school tie hanging incongruously in front. 'You two should get together,' Larry genially suggested. 'You both play guitar. You could form a group.'

'I'm Frankie Corpse,' announced the gawky kid as he shook Ivan's hand.

Actually his name was Frank Kearns but, as a demonstration of his allegiance to punk rock, Frank had given himself a new identity. He was not alone in this. One boy in my class, Garret Ryan, insisted on being referred to as Garret Rancid and did everything possible to live up (or down) to that name. The various members of the Lypton Village gang invented names for one another, which once decreed could not be rejected. Fionan Hanvey became Gavin Friday. There was also Guggi, Strongman, Pod, Dave-Id and Reggie Manuel the Cocker Spaniel (also known as Bad Dog). Paul Hewson showed up at school one day wearing a Lypton Village badge, which he insisted had miraculously appeared on his black polo-neck overnight. Henceforth, he revealed, he was to be known as Bono Vox (a name that could be pidgin Latin for 'Good Voice' although it was in fact appropriated from a hearing-aid shop in O'Connell Street). Truth be told, it took a while for this name to catch on but, in the interests of narrative clarity, Bono he shall be from this sentence forth. Bono, in turn, named Dave Evans 'the Edge', apparently on account of the shape of his head, though I don't know how he could have detected any edges underneath the tangled mop that passed for a haircut in Dave's schooldays.

Personally, I wasn't overly keen on this pseudonymous business. The name I wanted to see up in lights was my own. That aside I was becoming an ever-more committed member of Dublin's small punk-rock fraternity. I went to see the Boomtown Rats perform a free concert at St Fintan's. Enraptured by Bob Geldof's outrageous exhibitionism, I rushed into town to buy their single, 'Looking After No. 1', the first great Irish punk record. My album collection was expanding weekly, to include the Clash's eponymous debut, Elvis Costello's 'My Aim is True', the Jam's 'In the City', the Vibrators' 'Pure Mania' and the Sex Pistols' 'Never Mind the Bollocks'. Having become bold enough to leave the record sleeves out in the living room, I was starting to become mildly irritated by how unperturbed my parents were about the whole punk phenomenon. When I announced that I was going to cut my hair short, my dad proposed that, instead of wasting money at the hairdresser, he would do it for me. Given his lack of skill in this department, he easily achieved the requisite chop-top effect, but, still, there was something not quite right about this parental endorsement of teenage rebellion. My mum even took in my flares on her sewing machine (straight-leg trousers being an essential component of the punk look) and helped me dye various items of clothing lurid shades of green and red. When I came home one day to find my dad listening to a Ramones album and nodding his head in approval, I was silently fuming. What did a guy have to do to get a reaction around here?

Ivan and Frank began practising together. I would arrive home on Saturdays from drama class to find the pair hunched over Ivan's guitar amp, both clutching guitars, with Ivan painstakingly teaching Frank the chords to 'House of the Rising Sun' and 'Johnny B. Goode'. Not very punk rock, I know, but Frank was still a novice and dependent upon Ivan's repertoire of rock standards. His passionate advocacy of punk was beginning to have an effect on Ivan, however, who adopted Frank's sartorial style and gave himself a punk name: Ivan Axe (a terrible pun revolving around rock slang for guitar). Despite the fact that there were only two of them, they began to refer to themselves as Frankie

Corpse and the Undertakers. I felt a stab of envy when I heard that. But given that they needed at least another two Undertakers to make a full set, the question was broached about whether I would join. The fact that I had no musical ability was never even a consideration. This was punk rock, after all.

I asked Adam Clayton how I could go about buying a bass guitar. 'I'll sell you mine, man!' he responded, with an undisguised delight that should have raised my suspicions.

The reasons I chose the bass guitar were prosaic. Drums held no appeal, on the grounds that drummers tended to sit at the back of the stage, obscured by their kit. I wanted to be at the front and I wanted to sing. Keyboards seemed like too much hard work. Not only were there all those black and white keys, there were knobs and switches to consider too. The bass guitar, however, had only four strings, each of which was thick and easy to get your fingers around. And anyway, from watching Adam play, I reckoned at least two of those strings were superfluous. I chose bass because I thought I could just about get away with it.

The Hype were becoming legends in their own lunchtime. During noon break one day they played a gig in the sixth-year common room. It seemed like every kid in the school tried to crowd in, the overspill jamming the corridors as the group hurtled through a breakneck set, including a punked-up version of a popular television superhero theme, with Bono leaping into the air to yell 'Batman!' at the apposite moments.

They were starting to look like a rock band now. Bono wore black polonecks and black jeans and affected a sleek, new-wave look. Dave Edge had taken to sporting stripy T-shirts and red jeans, offset by a ludicrously outsized black blazer, complete with naval insignia. Adam had always looked like a rock star and Larry was so pretty-boy handsome it didn't matter how he dressed. The younger kids in school treated them like celebrities, following them around the corridors, giggling and pointing.

I went along to the Hype's next weekend rehearsal. The school was eerily deserted as I strolled in, with just the strange echo of distant electric guitars and the clatter of drums rising up above the playground. They were in full flow in the music room, guitar and bass amps positioned either side of Larry's kit, everyone ranged in a circle so that they could watch each other play. Bono, who had by now abandoned attempts to play guitar and had assumed the role of lead vocalist, was the centre of attention, a whirl of energy and activity, one moment frantically waving his arms as if conducting the Edge's and Dick's guitars, the next squeezing his eyes tightly shut to extemporize vocals, as if summoning them from the ether, talking in tongues like his friends in the Christian Movement. 'Some day . . . Maybe tomorrow . . . New direction . . . Hello . . . Oh, no, no, no . . .' he half spoke, half sang in a Bowie-esque drawl. They were working on a song of their own. It bore scant resemblance to the derivative country rocker from the Marine. This was an amorphous, sprawling rocker, built around fast, punchy bass and drums with Dick scratching a choppy rhythm while the Edge concocted a spiralling lead. Bono, meanwhile, groped about at the centre of this often chaotic noise, grasping for words. The phrases that emerged were elliptical, elusive, barely making sense. 'I walk tall, I walk in a wild wind . . . I love to stare, I . . . I love to watch myself grow . . . Some say . . . Maybe tomorrow . . . Resurrection hello . . . Oh no, no, no, no, no, no, no . . .'

They must have played that song for over an hour, with the groove constantly breaking down and slowly coming back together, interspersed with bursts of excited chatter – mostly between Bono and the Edge – about where it might go next. Sure, the playing may have verged on the shambolic, while the song itself somehow stubbornly resisted their best efforts to manipulate it into shape, but the mood throughout was inspiring: five young musicians struggling to carve out their own sonic terrain and discover what it was that they wanted to express. The chorus itself was revealing, Bono repeating a single phrase over and over: 'Street missions . . . Street missions . . . Street missions . . . Street missions . . .' I could picture Bono as a preacher, standing on his soap-box in the park, trying to bring his message to the world. First he had to work out what that message was, of course. Whenever in doubt, he would sing, 'Hello, oh no, oh-oh-oh-oh.' I think those phrases could be found somewhere in every one of the group's early songs.

Afterwards, Adam cheerfully sat down to show me his bass guitar. It was a shit-brown Ibanez copy, physically ugly and of piss-poor quality. Not that I knew the difference. He told me that he would reluctantly let it go for £70, just to help me out. This was probably twice what it had cost him but sounded plausible to me. I was completely out of my depth, a fact that I am sure had not passed Adam by. I sat around and plonked away at the strings, listening to the satisfying low rumble emerging from his amp. Adam took it from me and, cigarette dangling, began to pick out a riff. 'It's got good action,' he declared, encouragingly. 'Yeah, it sure has,' I knowledgeably agreed, wondering where the action was and if there was a switch to control it.

I handed over the wadge of £10 notes. 'A pleasure doing business with you,' smirked Adam. Thirty pounds represented my entire savings, extracted from my Post Office account. The rest had been borrowed from my dad, with the assurance that he would get it all back with interest when I was rich and famous. To be honest, I think Dad was as convinced as I that this was a sound investment.

We recruited a drummer. Keith Edgley was in Ivan's year, a ruddy-faced fifteen-year-old who could usually be located lurking behind the science lab, where self-styled undesirables tended to congregate for quick fags and other acts of private insurrection. He became Keith Karkus, a name that appealed to his inner hoodlum. In keeping with his macabre taste, Frank wanted to call me Neil Nasty, but I was having none of it. 'Nothing really goes with the name Neil,' I said, trying to wheedle my way out of the whole business.

'Neil Down!' blurted out Ivan, while the others guffawed with laughter.

And so it was that, despite my protestations, my rock career was launched as a bad pun.

On a weekend in January, 1978, the full line-up assembled in front of the lace curtains in Frank's tiny living room for the first time. Guitars and bass were plugged into two small practise amps. A microphone was routed through the family hi-fi. Frank's mother floated about, reminding us not to put our feet on the sofa and tutting anxiously as Keith's kit expanded around her three-piece suite. 'Don't break anything, dear,' she fretted, mussing her son's hair.

'Mum!' groaned Frankie Corpse. I knew how he felt. It was hard to be a punk rocker at home.

Ivan had taught me the rudiments of a twelve-bar riff sequence. So, when everybody was ready, Frank shouted out 'One-two-three-four' (the Ramones always counted in like that and so we would too) and we launched into a ridiculous, high-speed version of 'Johnny B. Goode'. Oh, how to explain the thrill of that moment? The drums were clattering away, a noisy collision of messy hi-hat and rattling snare, my bass playing was plonky, frantic and out of time, Frank's rhythm guitar was a fuzzy blur and Ivan was yelling the words of the song in a voice still squeakily unbroken, but when it came to the lead solo we all looked at each other and broke out in grins.

For sheer, adrenalinized, sonic exhilaration, it is hard to surpass the noise an electric guitar makes, especially with the volume turned up full on a valve amp and the mysterious 'gain' switch creating a background bed of distortion. When you hear it buzzing close up and loud, generating strange harmonics amid the random multiplications of colliding notes, it sounds like ten instruments at once, a noise you can never quite capture on a record. And when that seems to be coming from configurations of your own fingers, it is almost impossible not to be transported by it.

That first rehearsal was simultaneously frustrating and exhilarating. We were constantly coming bang up against the limits of our amateur abilities and everything would just fall apart, petering out in a cacophony of twanging strings and flatly thumped drums. But at other moments, even at this most primitive of levels, we would suddenly lock together and the music would just explode and proliferate, becoming something much greater than the sum of its rather humble parts. Such is the wonder of amplification. The primal force of rhythm. The divine glory of melody. And the simple beauty of three-chord rock'n'roll.

Believe me, I am under no illusions about what the first rehearsal of Frankie Corpse and the Undertakers actually sounded like. But I know what it felt like. And it felt good.

We would rehearse whenever possible, usually at home in Howth (where the parental regime was more favourable to teenage punks) but sometimes at school, putting in a couple of hours on the Hype's superior equipment. At Frank's behest, we started off by learning 'Glad to See You Go', which was track one, side one of the Ramones' latest album, *Leave Home*. Having mastered that (or at least a frantic approximation of it) we moved on to track two, 'Gimme Gimme Shock Treatment'. We were having problems with this one, until the Edge kindly offered to write out the chords. The trouble was, following his instructions didn't make the song sound any more authentic. 'He's got the right chords but in the wrong order,' Ivan finally worked out. 'Look, he's going A to G instead of G to A, see?' We tried it and, lo and behold, Ivan was right. The Hype, who also included 'Shock Treatment' in their set, were playing the song back to front.

I think we all felt a little glow of professional pride over this discovery, as if it somehow put us on the same level as our more experienced schoolmates. It does throw an interesting slant on the oft-remarked originality of the Edge's guitar playing. But the Hype were beginning to move beyond covers now, anyway. Adam was hustling support gigs by ringing venues and, in his sophisti-cated English tones, presenting himself as the manager of a hot, up-and-coming band. They travelled sixty miles to the market town of Mullingar to play in a bar for a sum that would barely cover petrol costs, only to be confronted by a local demanding to know what was the point of coming all that way to play bad cover versions. 'If we wanted to hear cover versions,' he sagely remarked, 'there's plenty of bands round here who can play them just as badly.' At least, that is the story the Edge told as he attempted

to persuade his bandmates that the only way forward was original material.

They were debuting new songs in rehearsal at a fairly prodigious rate – although, given Bono's extemporizing process of
composing lyrics, the material rarely seemed completely finished,
with lots of 'oh-oh-oh's being sung over Edge's slippery chords.
Bono's imagery tended to the abstract, even when his subject
matter reflected the sometimes banal realities of teenage life.
'White walls, morning eyeballs / A thousand voices echo through
my brain / School daze, new directions,' he sang on a blustery
little number apparently based on his unhappy experiences in the
Leaving Cert. The chorus was constructed around an appalling
pun comparing school to the Nazi Holocaust, all delivered in a
jerky, hiccupping new-wave style: 'C-C-C-Concentration Cramp!
Ha ha ha!'

'The Fool' was more promising, a yearning epic that quickly
caught my attention. I loved the opening lines, although I had
no idea what they meant (and I am not convinced Bono did
either): 'Alive in an ocean / A world of glad eyes . . . Insane /
Walk a wall backwards / It's all just a shameful game'. The chorus
had Bono bullishly declaring, 'I break all the rules / They call
me a fool'. He spoke excitedly about creating a character he
could portray on stage, someone to represent the outsider, an
idiot savant capable of piercing illusions. 'Just a fool, a street jester,
the hero of society,' he sang over the song's rambling end piece.
'Just a fool, a street jester / Look at me, now can't you see?' It
wasn't exactly subtle but it spoke volumes about the grandiosity
of his ambition.

Meanwhile, Frankie Corpse and the Undertakers set about
learning another Ramones' song. It was gradually becoming clear
that Frank's idea for the group was to learn the whole of side
one of Leave Home and then, when we had accomplished that,
move on to side two. Frank loved the Ramones.

To be fair, the Ramones were ideal start-up material for a
young rock band: their chord progressions were simple and
arrangements essentially boiled down to everyone playing the

same notes at the same time as hard and loud as possible, yet the overall effect was fantastically dynamic. Joey Ramone had a gulping, weeping voice that could break your heart even when he was singing about murder and mental illness. I heard entire symphonies of electric sound in the buzzing of Johnny Ramone's guitar. Their songs made me laugh and rage and jump around my bedroom, punching the air. At sixteen, I was so enraptured by the whole Ramones' oeuvre that I never even questioned their comical self-mythologizing, taking it on trust that Johnny, Joey, Tommy and Dee Dee were, indeed, the inbred bastard spawn of some mutant geek family from the industrial wastes of New Jersey who had stumbled across the secret essence of rock'n'roll but were actually too dumb to ever fully comprehend their own worth. I was devastated when I learned from the *NME* that the Ramones were not actually related. It was like a child discovering that Santa Claus never existed: your whole inner world tips on its axis for a moment, as you are compelled to realign to a harsher and more banal reality. I felt betrayed, cheated, abused and utterly foolish . . . for about five minutes, anyway. Then I just started pretending I had known all along, making myself feel better by puncturing other people's illusions, starting with Frank. 'What? You thought they were really brothers? Come on, Frank, how gullible can you be?'

Anyway, Frank needed to be put in his place. He was starting to behave as if he was our leader. 'It's Frankie Corpse *and* the Undertakers,' he declared one day in an attempt to settle an argument, as if having his name out front entitled him to an extra vote. He was quickly disabused of that notion. His attempts to install himself as lead vocalist were also given short shrift. After a particularly gruesome rehearsal, Ivan and I quietly discussed how we would break the news to Frank that his vocals had all the tunefulness of a deaf dog howling for his supper. In the event, we decided to give it to him straight.

'The thing is, Frank,' my brother said nervously, 'you can't really sing.'

'It's punk rock,' he replied.

This was Frank's answer to everything. His wholehearted commitment to the cause was inspirational to us. We had each of us been harbouring secret dreams of stardom for so long it was an incredible relief to be able to share them. Just to speak our desires aloud without fear of being mocked created a powerful bond. Together Frank, Ivan and I could dare to believe that we could make something of our music. But there was no getting around the fact that if Frank had been charged with singing for our supper we would all have starved to death.

In a display of band democracy we elected to share vocal duties, although that didn't turn out a great deal better. We were a ridiculous triumvirate. I'd start off the song, which was definitely a bad idea. My timing was abysmal, my pitching not much better, and, although I could just about hold a tune, once I had located the key (which usually took me a couple of bars), I really didn't have much idea what else to do with it. Then Ivan would come in for the next verse with his squeaky pubescent voice, sounding like a choirboy on helium. And then Frank would round things off with some indecipherable barking, sounding like he was singing something else entirely, in a completely different key to the rest of us.

So Ivan and I wrote a song especially for Frank, geared to his distinctive vocal inadequacies. It was titled, without irony, 'Punk Power'. Over three simple power chords, the chorus went:

I'm a punk, I'm a punk
And I'm blasted on junk
Won't take no for an answer
And I can't stand the funk
I'm a punk, I'm a punk, I'm a punk
Oh, I'm a punk

To be fair, there aren't a lot of words that rhyme with punk. I wasn't actually entirely sure what 'junk' was but I knew it was slang for something nasty that you could, apparently, get 'blasted' on. And as for being unable to 'stand the funk', we had gleaned from the *NME* that punk stood in direct opposition to disco – but, unfortunately, disco didn't rhyme with punk.

Frank loved it, howling through rehearsals with a passion we all found preposterously impressive.

The Hype arranged a gig on a Friday night in February, 1978, in a basement room in the old school building, a gothic, orange-brick monster that loomed over the modern complex where we attended lessons. We were invited to play support. Mysterious posters started appearing around the school, bearing the legend 'THE UNDERTAKERS . . . are coming to take you away' beneath cartoons of four severed heads. OK, they weren't really that mysterious. I was drawing them in art class, to choruses of mocking from my classmates. 'Is that supposed to be you?' But there was an atmosphere of excited anticipation on the night. Attending a rock concert in school seemed impossibly exotic, with the air of real, grown-up entertainment.

There was a stage at one end of the low basement room where the Hype set up their equipment. There were even some coloured disco lights. I suppose we did a sound-check. I really don't remember. We were all so nervous everything went by in a haze. In the hours we had to kill before the actual performance, Frank, Ivan, Keith and I went for a stroll in the winter evening and ended up walking miles from school, down to the windy seafront, chattering in the cold as the sky grew black, talking about our hopes and dreams for the future, reminding each other of musical cues, geeing one another up.

When we got back the place was full, with a mobile disco entertaining the audience. We slipped into an upstairs room where instruments were being stored and sat with the Hype, waiting to go on. They were relaxed and chatty, discussing set lists and plans. We were nervous and withdrawn. Mr Moxham appeared at the door. 'Good crowd tonight,' he boomed cheerfully. 'You ready, lads?' I thought I was going to be sick.

We trooped down and pushed our way through the crowd, clutching our instruments, clambering on to the stage to plug in. In the glare of the spotlights, everything was, quite literally, a blur to me. I am incredibly shortsighted but I hated the big, ugly glasses I was compelled to wear. Moments before going on stage, I suddenly decided I could do without them and instead borrowed a pair of cheap children's blue plastic toy sunglasses from Garret Rancid. Consequently I was shrouded in an out-of-focus, blue-tinted world. We had all adopted Frank's T-shirt-and-tie combo, the uniform of punk rock, and in addition I was wearing a pair of tight jeans (specially adjusted by my mum) and a tiny blue corduroy jacket that had shrunk in the wash. There was an expectant cheer that sounded to me as if it might contain a hint of sarcasm. Amps buzzed into life. We plunked strings, making sure we were in tune. Frank stood up to the mic. 'Wan-two-tree-faw!' he yelled.

And we were off, in a blizzard of thumping bass strings, thrashing guitars, clattering drums, playing the Vibrators' minimalist thrash 'Yeah Yeah Yeah'. The shot of adrenaline to my system was dizzying. We were jumping up and down, scissor-kicking, colliding with one another as we rushed about the stage, constantly swapping position to take our turn at the front and yell into the mic. The gig went by in a flash. A planned half-hour set was over in about twenty minutes as we shot through songs at double speed. I am sure the whole thing was a ridiculous mess but the crowd was cheering, the amps were cranked up loud, my heart was pumping and my head felt like it might explode in ecstasy.

There was only one major cock-up. In the middle of the set, we played 'House of the Rising Sun' (the punk version). This had been added at the last minute, to pad things out. The problem was, I had never actually learned it. In rehearsal, I watched Frank's fingers move up and down the fretboard and I would play the root note of whichever chord they landed on. Of course, in rehearsals I was wearing glasses. On stage, I couldn't see a thing, so (living up to my nickname) I had to kneel in front of Frank, face shoved as close to his guitar as possible, screwing up my eyes to try to make out what he was doing. If that wasn't bad enough, my proximity panicked Frank, who began playing open chords.

Now I was in uncharted territory, just plucking random strings that I hoped approximated his chords.

But none of that seemed to matter. Like me a year earlier, most of the people in the room had probably never seen a live rock band before and were simply enthralled by the noise and spectacle. The crowd went mad. We ended the set with 'Punk Power', for which we had prepared a theatrical conclusion. During woodwork class, Ivan had made a thin plywood guitar body, painted to look like a yellow Stratocaster. Frank swapped his guitar for the fake, pretending to play as he barked the words of the song.

At the climax, with Ivan coaxing feedback from his amp and Keith trying to demolish the drum kit, Frank started to trash the fake guitar, banging it repeatedly off the stage until it splintered and broke, screaming all the time 'I'm a *punk*! I'm a *punk*!' He tossed the broken remains into the crowd, who were screaming encouragement. I came off the stage, dazed and dripping in sweat, my schoolmates patting me on the back as I pushed my way towards the dressing room. If there had ever been any doubt in my heart, now it was all over. It was rock'n'roll for life.

'That was fantastic,' Bono declared magnanimously as we entered the room. 'Well done! Well done!'

We flopped down, exhausted, laughing with relief and joy.

'Sorry about the kit,' said Keith to Larry. 'I think I knocked over a couple of cymbals.'

Larry rushed from the room, looking like he could commit murder.

The Hype went out and really rocked the crowd. I stood at the back of the room and watched them, full of admiration. As a group, they were still in flux, playing cover versions of songs like Thin Lizzy's 'Dancing in the Moonlight' followed by their own odd creations, sharp-edged, yearning mini-epics, full of quicksilver guitar bursts from Edge and stammering, elliptical vocals from Bono. He was not the singer he is today, his thin, young voice hiding in the folds of the songs rather than staking a claim to be heard, up front and loud, yet he was already compelling to watch, jabbering away as much between songs as during them, trying to reach out, and always holding eye contact, staring at the audience as if daring us to look away first. His desire was transparent, his energy undeniable. He seemed heroic to me.

Afterwards we sat around talking in the dressing room, enthusiastically complimenting each other's performances. I was still on a high, my mind dizzy with possibilities.

'I like your bass style, man. Simple and direct,' said Adam, kindly. He was probably just happy to have discovered a bassist even worse than him.

'Yeah,' I said, nodding in agreement. 'I don't go with all that fancy stuff.'

'Me neither,' said Adam.

This was the life! Just a couple of pros, sitting around, shooting the breeze.

5

Adam was kicked out of school in February 1978. He had to go quite far to upset a broad-minded regime who had tolerated his cheerful insolence, apathetic approach to schoolwork and deliberate flaunting of convention. The day he turned up for classes in a long, flowery dress, he was merely told to go home and change. But streaking naked down the Mall finally did for him.

I don't think exclusion particularly bothered him. The group still practised in the music room and Adam could frequently be spotted around the premises. He assumed the role of manager and was busy trying to get them gigs. Adam developed a habit of casually dropping the names of significant figures from the local music scene into conversation, mentioning chats with members of the Boomtown Rats and Thin Lizzy.

The truth eventually emerged: that he was cold-calling people, often drawing them into conversation by pretending to be someone else. But we were nonetheless impressed.

Membership of the rock fraternity bonded us all. We were allies, united by a common cause, like a secret resistance group working behind the enemy lines of the conservative Irish cultural scene. I remember a party in Howth when a large group of us just gathered around the record player, listening with startled awe to Patti Smith's newly released *Easter* album. Her astonishing lyrical flow was admired and discussed, with individual lines seized upon and dissected in an attempt to expose their secret meaning and, perhaps, bathe us in their magical power. The cover, showing the elegantly gaunt, androgynous figure of Smith with bare arms raised to reveal large sprouts of body hair, was held up by Gavin Friday as if it were a religious object. 'She is the epitome of all that is beauty,' declared Bono, in half-comic, half-serious veneration. 'The ideal of femininity! Behold the power of woman!' Other disgruntled partygoers would nervously approach to suggest changing the record, complaining they had heard this screeching banshee wail four times already and wondering if it wasn't time for a bit of Queen or *Saturday Night Fever*, but they were given short shrift. 'Be off, Howth Pigs!' snarled Gavin, putting the needle back to track one, side one as the petitioners retreated. I was terrified of the Village and their deliberate provocations, uncertain how much of their pantomime alienation was a humorous pose, but as long as I was with Bono they tolerated my presence.

The rare visits of international punk bands were major occasions for punk's growing local fraternity. I saw the Buzzcocks, the Clash and the Jam, guitars drilling right through my head, losing myself in the reverbations of the huge speaker stacks. In the heart of the crowd watching the Ramones, I experienced a moment of real epiphany, the realization that there is community in the audience of a great rock gig, a blurring of interpersonal boundaries, unity in a song, the sense that, in this moment, right here, right now, everyone is experiencing exactly the same thoughts and emotions. We are all one. 'Gabba gabba we accept you, we accept you, one of us,' as we all chanted with Joey during 'Pinhead'.

One weekend, when my parents were away, my sister threw a party, giving me express instructions beforehand not to monopolize Bono. 'I don't want the two of you sitting in a corner all night talking about music!' she decreed. 'And stay away from the record player!' Bono's home did not actually contain a record player, only a large, old-fashioned reel-to-reel tape machine, so he never passed up an opportunity to explore other people's record collections. Sure enough, come one a.m., Stella was casting me dirty looks as Bono, Edge and I crowded around the hifi, sorting through my expanding collection of records, forcing her friends to endure a steady diet of new-wave weirdness. 'Ah, now, Stella,' Bono said, with a cheeky, seductive grin, when she tried to wrest back control of the stereo. 'You can dance to the Buzzcocks, see!' He got up and did a comical little pogo. At least Adam was mingling, guzzling wine and regaling Stella's friends with stories of his rock-star acquaintances. Mind you, Adam had been quite specifically not invited, Stella having expressed the fear that you never knew when he was going to do something to upset people, like getting his penis out.

I noticed that Bono was sporting a new badge on his jumper, identical to one on Edge's blazer. It was a large white disc featuring the mysterious alignment of a single letter and single digit in green, computerized script: 'U2'.

He tapped it proudly. 'That's us,' he said. 'We're changing the name of the group.'

I was incredulous. 'U2? What does that mean?'

'Whatever you want it to,' shrugged Bono.

I shook my head discouragingly. 'The Hype's a great name for a band. I love the Hype! U2 just sounds like an old submarine! Actually, it's like something you'd see stencilled on the side of a container. "Stick that over there, between U1 and U3!"'

Bono was not to be discouraged. The new name had been coined by Steve Averill, who operated under the punk alias Steve Rapid. He was the former lead singer of one of Dublin's first significant punk bands, the Radiators from Space, and a prime mover in the tiny alternative rock scene. More significantly, as far as Adam was concerned, he was an alumni of Mount Temple. Steve had been dragged along to watch the Hype play a support slot in a pub and had seen enough to convince himself they were an interesting prospect. The name, though, had to go. Steve thought it cynical, old-fashioned and dreadfully affected, striking an ironic pose in direct contrast to the band's passion and idealism. U2 was . . . Well, what was it? Vagueness was a bonus, the band decided. The name had connotations of inclusiveness (You Too) but it did not pin the group down. The audience could bring to it whatever they wanted.

'It'll look good on a poster,' said Bono confidently. He was an admirer of my Undertakers' posters, new variations of which kept appearing throughout the school. Graphic art was one of my private obsessions – not the high and mighty terrain of the fine arts, but the film posters, album sleeves, book covers, comic strips and advertisements of the commercial world. I considered myself something of an artist. My cartoons and caricatures of teachers and pupils adorned the covers of the annual school magazine, which I had renamed (over protestations from members of staff) *The Ugly Truth*. I planned to go to art college, primarily because that was what John Lennon had done when he left school. So I was flattered but not surprised when Bono asked me to design a poster for the band.

My heart wasn't in it, though. I really didn't like the new name. The concept I came up with was so lame I was embarrassed to even show it to Bono and the Edge, who gathered around one day in the art room. On an A3 sheet of paper I had drawn a picture of a German WWII U-boat submarine and put a big red X through it. Next to it there was a drawing of an American U2 spy plane from the Cold War with a big red X through that. I left a space where, I explained to Bono, we would stick a photo of the band with a big red tick and the legend: U2: The Rock Band. 'Very funny,' said Bono, who evidently thought I was joking. Edge just looked at me sympathetically.

Who knows where life might have taken me had I risen to the task? Steve Averill, who had a day job in an advertising agency, eventually lent a hand, coming up with a simple but quite fantastic poster: a high-contrast, black-and-white image of the group over a huge, bold, red 'U2' on a stark white background. It looked sleek and modern and cool and stood out from the run-of-the-mill band posters you could see plastered all over town. Steve has done most of U2's graphic work ever since, designing all their record covers. He now runs his own highly successful graphic agency, Four 5 One, in Dublin. But hey, some you win . . . and some you are happy to have lost. That I never made it to the top as a world-beating graphic artist is not one of the great regrets of my life.

The name change was celebrated with an extraordinary gig in Howth in March that served notice of U2's ambitions. The smart new posters had gone up all along the lampposts of the Howth road but the show, in a small, out-of-the-way church hall, was sparsely attended. The Village were all there, dressed in their usual misalignments of fashion, standing out among a few heads from school and a smattering of locals. My friend Ronan and I stood in the middle of the dancefloor, in a display of loyalty, but I could feel the space around us, with most of the thin crowd hugging the walls.

The five-piece Hype opened the show, performing a set of cover versions. Stones, Neil Young, Lizzy: the familiar rockers warming up the audience. At the end of the set, to the strains of 'Glad to See You Go', the bearded figure of Dick Evans bade farewell, leaving the stage and the band. Bono announced that the Hype were no more. But they would be back, later, as U2.

Like Ian Stewart, the unlucky piano player with the young Rolling Stones whose face just didn't fit, Dick had never quite looked the part. More seriously, perhaps, with his younger brother's guitar style developing to fill up sonic spaces with ever-more inventive flourishes, Dick's rhythm guitar was increasingly extraneous. Displaying tact and timing, Evans senior opted to leave before his role really became an issue. He claimed he wanted to concentrate on his studies at Trinity College, although it was only a matter of weeks before he resurfaced as guitarist with U2's dark alter egos, a band that would develop from the Howth gig's strangest performance.

On to an empty stage, to the backing of odd, disconcerting sound effects, strode Gavin Friday, in a raincoat and smoking a cigarette. Misapplied eyeliner streaked his face. He walked up to the microphone, eyeballing the audience with a sense of almost indifferent disdain. His coat fell open to reveal that he was wearing a dress. He took a long drag, blew some smoke then leaned forward to say just two words. 'Art. Fuck,' boomed from the PA.

Now, they might have been used to this kind of thing in the alternative cabarets of London, but to an audience of Irish teenagers who had come to see a rock band Gavin's appearance was genuinely perplexing. Still, this being Dublin, it was inevitable that some wag would let him know what they thought. 'Fuck art!' someone bellowed, to a ripple of laughter.

Adam took up a position stage left and began banging out a propulsive line on his bass guitar. The Edge appeared stage right, contributing sudden shards of electric. Between them they were concocting an odd, spacious, disjointed, disconcerting sound, far removed from U2's own brand of taut, melodic, hard rock.

The favoured term of the era was 'new wave', a phrase that was supposed to suggest rebirth: out of the fiery cauldron of punk, bathed in the spittle of Johnny Rotten, sonic warriors would emerge to create fresh vistas of sound, adhering to the modern principles – lean, mean, independent, creative. At least, that was the dream. While punk fell into the hands of shouters and skinheads, the vanguard was moving on with astonishing rapidity in a multitude of directions, experimenting with the reggae rhythms of ska and dub, rediscovering the tribalism of rockabilly and mod, embracing the icy electronics of Kraftwerk and detuned guitars of a new art school. Enthused by the achievements of their friends in U2, the Village were keen to embrace the new freedom rock music promised.

The blond, androgynously handsome, glammed-up Guggi joined Gavin on stage in black stockings, torn lingerie and too much make-up. The Village yelled encouragement as their representatives began to roar and rage at the baffled onlookers, colliding and hugging each other in homo-erotic frenzy before breaking apart and turning vituperatively on the audience, screaming 'Art fuck!' over and over. This went on for an uncomfortably long time, degenerating into a blizzard of white noise and verbal abuse from the audience. Then it was done. We had just witnessed the birth of the Virgin Prunes, a group who would become one of the prime movers in the Irish underground rock scene, polarizing opinion and dividing critics, the negative reflection of U2's bright optimism.

Adam, demonstrating previously unsuspected versatility, remained on stage to play with Steve Rapid's new synth band, the Modern Heirs. A tinny drum machine provided the beat while Adam's individual sense of rhythm brought a little bit of quirky humanity to the dry, dystopian sci-fi muzak. It left me cold, which was probably the point.

And then it was the turn of U2 to perform to an audience who had grown distinctly restless. The stripped-down four-piece attacked an all-original set with rabble-rousing vigour, playing as if they had something to prove. Dynamic, melodic, upbeat and gloriously aspirational, they swept me away once again. Edge was developing a distinctive, chiming guitar sound. Larry and Adam were tight and fast. Bono was all over the place, hyperactive in his attempt to get hold of the audience, clambering on the equipment, striking odd poses, pouring heart and soul into everything. They performed a juddering, slow-burning ballad of spiritual awakening, 'Shadows and Tall Trees', over the conclusion of which Bono demanded: 'Are you out there? / Can you hear me? / Do you feel in me anything redeeming? / Any worthwhile feeling?'

I was lost in the rapture of the moment when a commotion broke all around me: fists flailing, boots swinging, shouts and obscenities. With the alertness of a skinny boy used to dodging bullies, I scooted to the far side of the hall as some local hard lads, offended by what they had witnessed, tangled with the Virgin Prunes. If they thought Gavin and Guggi were going to be pushovers because they wore stockings and make-up, they were mistaken. The Village were used to fighting for their right to be different and all piled in. Bono, visibly dismayed, appealed for calm. 'We didn't come here to fight!' he pleaded. 'We came to play music!' When his exortations fell on deaf ears, however, the peacemaker jumped off the stage to join in the mêlée, hustling the thugs out of the building in a rain of kicks and blows.

Walking home along the Howth seafront at night, Ronan and I debated what we had seen. U2, we concluded, really were something special. But as for the Virgin Prunes . . .

'Are those two fellas into each other, you know what I mean?' Ronan wondered.

I knew what he meant. Officially there was no homosexuality in Ireland. Along with no contraception, no divorce, no abortion and (if the Catholic church had its way) no sex for any unmarried person not engaged in the procreation of good Catholic babies. 'I don't think so,' I ventured. 'They just like to wind people up.'

'Why?' asked Ronan. Which seemed fair enough.

'To get a reaction.'

'Well, they got a reaction tonight,' laughed Ronan. 'Half the audience fucked off and the other half tried to kick the shit out of them. They were crap.'

He had a point. Over time, the Virgin Prunes would, perversely, become the focus of the local rock scene's resentment towards U2, attracting the kind of elitist audience who sneered at U2's populism. Yet at that gig in Howth, I saw the Prunes emerge from the womb of U2, the bastard offspring proclaiming autonomy and scampering away into the night. The connection between these two camps always baffled the uninitiated. They were like yin and yang, opposite sides of the rock'n'roll coin. On one side you had a primal, four-piece guitar band reaching for the sky and trying to carry their audience with them and on the other were a gang of performance-art provocateurs, breathing fire and brimstone in an effort to shock audiences into reacting – positively or negatively; the Prunes didn't seem to care which. Bono would joke that it was like having God and the Devil on the same bill, but it did not always serve U2 well, since they often had to play to a crowd who had been completely alienated by Gavin and Guggi's antics. But for Bono it was about embracing extremes: the Prunes ventured into places U2 couldn't or wouldn't. Not for another decade anyway.

That gig gave me food for thought. Rock music was entering a period of flux, there was room for sonic experimentation and artistic exploration but, despite my allegiance to the supposedly revolutionary aesthetic of punk, I began to realize that it was really the traditional musical virtues to which I adhered. I liked melody and lyrics, not noise and rhetoric. I wanted soul and substance, not pretension and provocation.

U2's growing creativity was rewarded with the first signs of local recognition. I was strolling down Nassau Street (home to

Advance Records) one Saturday when I was hailed by Bono, who had in his hands the latest issue of the *Hot Press*, a fortnightly broadsheet magazine covering the burgeoning home-grown music scene under the banner: 'Keeping Ireland Safe for Rock'n'Roll'. 'Have you seen this?' asked Bono. In the corner of one page were four tiny, artily black-and-white head shots of my schoolfriends, over the comically banal headline 'Yep! It's U2'. A few short paragraphs by Bill Graham, the magazine's leading critic, suggested that U2 might be 'a band for the future', although, quaintly, he revealed that they would not be around for inspection for a while as they were 'currently studying for their Leaving Certs'. Bono was proudly showing it to everyone he knew.

The appearance of U2 in print seemed revelatory to us at the time. *Hot Press* had been running for about a year. It may have been amateurishly laid out, badly printed and full of typographical errors, but, by celebrating the achievements of a handful of Irish rock icons (Van Morrison, Thin Lizzy, Rory Gallagher, Horslips and, latterly, the Boomtown Rats) alongside reviews of local concerts, it legitimized the native music scene, helping to shrug off the sense of inadequacy that pervaded Irish pop culture. To be written about in *Hot Press* was proof that your band existed in the wider world, not just in an imaginary scene consisting of friends.

As the school year drew to a close, U2 were invited to perform an outdoor concert during a Mount Temple open day, and once again invited us to support. A problem soon developed, however, when Frank demanded to play the four-note guitar riff kicking off the Sex Pistols' 'Pretty Vacant', which we had just learned.

'No way!' insisted Ivan, asserting his right as lead guitarist to play the lead guitar parts.

'Maybe you could both play it,' I suggested.

'No way!' Frank and Ivan chorused.

This went on for days. Larry was called in to try to break the deadlock. 'Lads, lads,' said Larry, reasonably, 'it's just a riff.'

'But it's my riff,' said Ivan, stubbornly.

Frank declared that if we didn't let him play the intro he wasn't going to play anything at all. 'I'll just have to leave the band.'

I realize that this might not seem a particularly significant incident in the annals of rock history but to me it felt as cataclysmic as the break-up of the Beatles. I had pinned a lot of hope on our little band of brothers, constructing elaborate hypotheses of our imaginary futures. Would it really all be over before it even began? In an instant, I could see how naïve my whole conceit about this group had been.

Ivan grumpily caved in. Frank could play the intro, then, if it really mattered so much to him. Frank cheered up immediately. We were all friends again, as if nothing had ever happened.

But something had. At seventeen, there are moments when you really feel like you are accelerating towards adulthood. Tiny revelations flare like fireworks, leaving their after-image burning in your mind. With a blush of something approaching shame, you sense the innocent illusions you have maintained throughout childhood being suddenly stripped away. I knew then that we were just rank amateurs, schoolkids playing at being a band, and that if we were ever going to achieve anything we would have to raise our game.

There was a meeting in the changing rooms of the school gymnasium before the show. A stocky, watchful man in his late twenties was quietly seated in a corner as U2 and the Undertakers discussed running times and set lists. I assumed the interloper must be an elder sibling of one of the band. Bono was doing all the talking, which was not unusual, until the conversation turned to the schedule for our half-hour set.

'Half an hour is out of the question,' the interloper quietly but firmly interjected.

'What?' I spluttered, struggling to understand what one of U2's relatives could possibly have against us.

'Guys, this is Paul McGuinness,' said Bono. 'He's our manager.'

With a friendly smile that belied his firm, no-nonsense tone, McGuinness ran through the afternoon's schedule, explaining that (due to time pressures) we had to be on stage by three o'clock and off by three fifteen. 'We've been practising a half-hour set,' I muttered sullenly.

'Sorry, fellas,' said McGuinness, not looking sorry at all. 'You're here because you're friends of the band. It's U2's show, U2's equipment. There has to be a little give and take.'

So that's how it was going to be, then. 'We'll just have to play faster,' said Frank.

At the appointed hour we took our positions on a makeshift stage on the low, flat concrete roof of the boiler room, overlooking the school car park. Frank started picking out the opening riff to 'Pretty Vacant'.

For us, this was an apocalyptic anthem of sneering teenage-outsider attitude but (despite the enthusiastic pogoing of three of our punk allies) the smattering of parents spread about the car park seemed largely unimpressed. There is something very dispiriting about yelling your heart out into a microphone to be confronted by the sight of onlookers chattering among themselves, sticking their fingers in their ears with pained expressions on their faces or, worst of all, drifting off to see if there is something more interesting going on elsewhere. When we finished – with a snarled 'And we don't care!' – our efforts were mortifyingly greeted with polite applause.

As we kicked into 'Sheena is a Punk Rocker', I was fighting a losing battle with my bass guitar, struggling to stay in time with drum beats enveloped in multiple echoes off the back wall of the school building. I stared at my fingers with horror. I could count the beats in my head but somehow I could not communicate the information to these rebellious digits at the end of my own hands. Even our loyal fellow punks were looking confused and had halted their desultory attempts to jump up and down in time. When it came to performing the Buzzcocks' 'Fiction Romance', I did something that had been at the back of my mind for some time. 'What are you doing?' hissed Ivan as I put down my instrument. 'Just start the song,' I insisted. It was a complicated bass part which I had never really mastered and, in front of all these critical gazes, it finally dawned on me that I was never going to. Indeed, that I did not even want to. I did not belong in the fraternity of bass guitarists, the backroom boys of the band! I was here for one thing only. Lights! Music! Action! It was rock stardom or nothing! So, while

Frank and Ivan concentrated on the interaction of their jagged guitar parts, I grabbed the microphone and started singing.

Now this was more like it!

'Fiction romance! Fiction romance!' I yelped. I bent the microphone stand and leaned out to the audience, snarling and whining and roaring the lyrics of the song. I waved my fist at the disinterested faces. I grabbed the mic and prowled the stage. I held my arms aloft. I demanded attention!

As the song came to a tinny, bass-less conclusion, Paul McGuinness appeared in the corner of my vision, making a vigorous chopping motion with his hands. It quickly dawned on me that this was not applause. 'That's it, lads,' he mouthed, imperiously waving us off.

'We've only played three songs!' I protested. But Adam was already unplugging our leads while Edge was plugging in his effects units. The urgency of their actions suggested they were afraid that if we played any longer the car park would be completely empty by the time U2 went on.

'Well done,' said Bono, kindly, as we trooped off.

There was a smattering of applause from the corner of the car park where our families were gathered.

As U2 launched into a smart, professional set, Ivan and I exchanged a look that communicated more than words ever could. Edge's guitar chimes floated over our heads. How come we hadn't been able to make a noise like that? Bono was putting on the moves, Larry was pounding out the backbeat, even Adam was swinging his bass around like he was playing Shea Stadium not a half-empty school car park. There was a chasm between us and them . . . And they weren't anywhere. So where the hell did that leave us? We actually started to laugh as our parents approached.

'That was lovely!' announced Mum with all the cheerful goodwill she could muster.

Ivan and I guffawed helplessly.

'What's so funny?' Dad wanted to know.

'Nothing,' I said, giggling with the insane relief of a disaster survivor, standing among the wreckage of shattered illusions.

6

School was over. Summer and adulthood stretched ahead. What a strange few months: a little interlude between distinct phases of existence, the calm before the storm of life.

I was having a fantastic time. I may have given you the impression that music was all I cared about but, of course, that is not strictly true. There were girls, for a start, but (oh, my aching heart) let's leave them out of it for the moment; they were the one thing that could have spoiled my whole summer, all that raging desire locked behind a barrier of self-consciousness. But my teenage psyche was so pliable and amorphous that it could be entirely consumed in the fabric of the moment, reshaped on a whim. I could thrash around my bedroom dreaming of being the first rock star to play a gig on the moon and conducting imaginary interviews with journalists at ground control while floating in zero gravity ('As David Bowie pointed out so eloquently, fellas, planet earth is blue. Unlike Major Tom, however, I do know what to do!') then sit down with my sketchpad and decide that actually I was born to be an artist. This was not your staple Van Gogh or Picasso fantasy of misunderstood, revolutionary genius, however (although I was attracted to the idea of living in a garret full of naked life models). I wanted to be a comic-strip artist. I spent huge swathes of time drawing detailed pen-and-ink studies of square-jawed spacemen grasping phallic sci-fi weaponry surrounded by scantily clad female aliens and erotic robots with armour-piercing nipples, pouring all my sexual frustration on to the page. I actually sold a couple of cartoons to *In Dublin*, a listings magazine, including a pen-and-ink caricature of Elvis Costello, who was my new musical hero, principally on account of all those twisted couplets detailing his miserable romantic life. But don't get me started on romance, for pity's sake.

I got a job running Howth's municipal tennis courts (which essentially entailed putting the nets up in the morning and taking them down again at night) and harboured brief fantasies of representing Ireland at Wimbledon, practising my lethal backhand against any poor sucker who turned up without a partner until two schoolgirls punctured my illusions by whupping me and my friend David Hughes in straight sets. But never mind those floozies. I went sailing, crewing with various friends who raced two-man dinghies in front of Howth harbour. I never dreamed of being a famous yachtsman, however. The sea was too cold and wet for my tastes. The only thing I liked about sailing was the post-race dances held at the Yacht Club, where I could cast longing looks at the pretty, posh girls who would hardly deign to talk to me because I didn't even own my own boat. Ah, but let's not get into that! Rather, let me recall my great triumph at the Malahide races, crewing for a fellow Mount Temple rebel, Gordon Maguire. We won every race in our category, despite raising the judges' hackles by insisting on playing Sex Pistols songs on a ghetto blaster as we crossed the finish line, the sound of Johnny Rotten's howls floating surreally across the bay, rising above the flapping sails and colourful pennants until his keening voice became lost among the hungry cries of the seagulls. Gordon went on to become Ireland's most famous sailor, an internationally renowned yachtsman whose assignations with page-three models we followed in the pages of the tabloids. But I already knew what a sneaky seducer he was because the bastard went and got off with Grace Anne, my friend Ronan's sister, who I had coveted all my life but never built up the confidence to kiss. I had even taken her to the final school dance, where Bono turned up accompanied by Gavin Friday dressed in a silver glitter outfit and perilously high platforms on which he staggered around all night, getting outrageously drunk, leering at everyone and uttering inscrutable remarks. I, meanwhile, wore a dismal blue tuxedo with wide lapels and mooned around after my beautiful date. As the night came to an end I manoeuvred her out into the hotel gardens to make my move – only to discover that my dad was already there, smiling helpfully. He was concerned that we wouldn't be able to get a taxi and so had come to drive us home, a ride spent listening to him mutter inane platitudes of the 'I hope you kids had a good time' variety. *Kids*, for fuck's sake! But let us draw a veil over that episode. Missed opportunities and girls aside, it was summer and I was young and free and ready to take on the world.

In the diaspora of Mount Temple pupils, bits of information would drift back. I heard that Bono had finally passed his Irish exam and been accepted at university. Actually, I heard he got someone else to sit the exam for him, but I have never been able to get to the bottom of this rumour. But it wouldn't have mattered anyway, because he never did take up that place. U2 played a gig at McGonagles, Dublin's premiere rock club, and Ivan and I trooped along to see them.

It was a scruffy little establishment, dim lighting barely conceal-ing the decrepitude of the peeling black paint job. The un-impressive dimensions of the narrow stage were further reduced by the band having to share space with incongruous plastic palm trees left over from the venue's previous incarnation as a disco. I seem to remember a glitterball. U2 were supporting Advertising, English exponents of power pop, the latest new-wave subgenre. Essentially it was souped-up sixties beat music, replete with harmonies and hooklines, but dashed off with a bit more speed and aggression than would have been fashionable before punk. 'Ah, they're nothing special,' said Bono, who refused to be impressed by their status as recording artists. 'We're gonna blow them off the stage!' Bono had a competitive streak in him, driv-ing him towards greater achievements, and that night his confi-dence was high. U2's set was growing in internal coherence and musical drama. They had a new song, 'Out of Control', written around the time of Bono's eighteenth birthday in May, which proved a bit of a show-stopper, an anthemic, soaring articulation of teenage epiphany, the moment you realize that life is bigger than you will ever be and your fate is not necessarily in your own hands: 'One day I'll die / The choice will not be mine,' roared Bono. 'Will it be too late? / You can't fight fate! / I was of the feeling it was out of control, the crazy notion I was out of control . . .' There was plenty of space left in the lyrics for Bono's usual 'oo-wee-ooo's and 'oh-ey-oh's but the song communicated his inner turmoil with impressive conviction.

Advertising were polished and sterile by comparison and later I thought I detected a smug grin on Bono's face as he watched the headliners from the shadows, Alison on his arm, various members of the Village gathered around. 'They're good,' he said, his natural generosity reinstated by his own warm reception from the audience. 'Tight. Musical. I can see what they're trying to do.' Was there a hint of condescension there? Because what Advertising were trying to do was make pop music that reached towards art, celebrating its own superficiality. Bono wanted to make art that reached towards pop music (only he would never use the word pop. Pop was for kids. To Bono, it was always rock, with all the connotations of serious, hard, grown-up sensibilities that implied). Bono felt that U2 were starting in a place already some way beyond the superficial. They may not have been as well drilled and musically accomplished as Advertising, but they had soul in abundance and, in front of an audience filled with local movers and shakers, they had more than held their own against the pros from across the water.

'What's going on with your band?' Bono inquired.

'There've been a few changes,' I said, glancing guiltily across to where Frank was chatting with Larry. Ivan and I hadn't actually kept our fellow Undertaker informed of all the latest developments. Like the fact that we had changed the name of the group, recruited a new bassist and decided Frank's particular talents were surplus to requirements.

After the débâcle at school, we decided it was time to get serious. We spent long hours listening to records, studying the *NME*, struggling to write songs, enthusing, dreaming, plotting, arguing. Lots of arguing, though mostly with Frank. Ivan and I were very taken with the Jam, whose new mod sensibilities tied into our mutual fascination with the Beatles and the sixties. To Frank (who concurred with Bono's preference for things that rocked), it was all power pop, a genre which he considered a girly dilution of punk's principles. And for that matter, he informed us, the Beatles sounded suspiciously like power pop to him.

Now Ivan was rapidly becoming even more of a Beatles obsessive than me. He was currently engaged in a mammoth effort to learn every Beatles song on guitar, in alphabetical order, just because that's the way they were printed in *The Complete Beatles* songbook. Indeed, it would get to the point where the Beatles became a kind of plumb line he would drop into conversations to assess depth of character. If you were not intimately familiar with the Beatles' oeuvre, Ivan would just give you a withering look of contempt, as if to suggest that your lack of taste precluded further fraternization. So when Frank said he preferred the Stones, his fate was sealed. It was agreed we'd dispense with his services. We carelessly neglected to inform him of this, however, preferring the cowardly option of making lots of excuses about missing rehearsals and suggesting, what with it being such a busy summer and all, we let things lie for a couple of months.

And so Frank became the first of many musicians to part ways with the McCormick brothers. Which was probably a stroke of luck for him. Like almost everybody else we ever played with, he would go on to have a more successful musical career than us (it would be hard to have a less successful one), eventually forming a short-lived but acclaimed rock band called Cactus World News who released one well-received album on MCA in 1986 and got to number one in the US college chart. Frank now owns and manages Salt recording studio in Sutton, Dublin. We run into each other occasionally, usually backstage at U2 concerts, where we both get the measure of our actual status in the music business.

Since I'd insisted that I was going to be frontman, we recruited a neighbourhood friend of mine, John McGlue, to play bass. John's distinguishing characteristic was his big Afro-style curly hairdo, a look never really displayed at its best perched atop the head of a skinny white Irish boy. John was exceedingly proud of it, however. He thought it made him look like Phil Lynnot (bassist and frontman of Irish rock legends Thin Lizzy) and I guess there must have been enough of an association in our eyes for us to take a chance on someone whose musical skills, to that date, extended to being just about able to tell one end of a guitar from another. John's sole recommendation was that he was desperate for stardom and pronounced himself willing to do anything to be in a band, including learn an instrument. I somewhat grandiosely promised I would teach him everything I knew; when he had mastered that in half an hour, I told him to take my bass home and work the rest out for himself. John fancied himself as a bit of a ladies' man ('They go for the hair,' he would explain), so was strangely flattered when we gave him the punk name Johnny Durex. His only concern was that it might upset his mother. 'Your mother doesn't know what a Durex is,' I assured him. 'Otherwise you wouldn't be here.'

'Up yer hole, McCormick!'

'Fuck you, McGlue!'

As you can probably tell, we were close friends.

Choosing a name for a new group is a task charged with excitement, anticipation and not a little tension. It carries with it a burden of responsibility to the future, like giving an identity to a baby before it is born, the very act of naming making the intangible appear solid and real. The name has to be capable of carrying the weight of dreams.

'The Taxmen.'

'That would really inspire people to come out and see us. Remind them how much money they owe to the government.'

'How about the Axemen?'

'No way. Guitarists don't get their names out front. How about Neil Down and the Shin Pads?'

'Neil Brown and the Shit Heads, more like it.'

'Johnny Durex and the Premature Ejaculators.'

'Fuck off!'

'Fuck off. I like it. Fuck Off tonight in McGonagles. Fuck Off and buy the record!'

Vast amounts of rehearsal time were taken up with conversations like this. We made huge lists, then spent hours arguing the cases of our favourites and deriding each other's suggestions. We eventually settled on the Modulators, based on something Ivan had seen written on a keyboard in a music shop. To be honest, we had absolutely no idea what a modulator actually did but we were entranced by its inbuilt association with the currently fashionable mod movement.

Keith was still officially the drummer, though he would never actually turn up to rehearsals but would phone at the last minute with a series of increasingly lame excuses. Ivan and I remained focussed on the task in hand, meanwhile, and wrote songs at a prodigious rate (sometimes knocking out two or three in a session) — the quality of which can be deduced by the fact that when I look at the titles absolutely nothing comes to mind: no lyrics, no riffs, no melody, no rhythm (this may well be an accurate reflection of the songs themselves). In Frank's absence, however, we did learn two Beatles songs, 'Twist and Shout' and 'Revolution'.

When we felt we had enough material for a gig, we went to see Rocky De Valera. Rocky's real name was Ferdia MacAnna. He was a bit of a star in the Howth firmament, a spidery six-foot-something rock'n'roll fan with a black leather jacket, blue suede brothel-creepers and a louche manner learned from studying early Elvis Presley films. 'Rock on, Rocky!' the kids would chorus whenever they saw him hanging about on a street corner. 'Ah, feck off, ye little bastards!' he'd reply, assuming (correctly) that they were taking the piss. Rocky had a sidekick called Jack Dublin, an enormously overweight bassist. 'It's a glandular condition,' he would explain, and everyone would nod seriously. No one took the piss out of Jack for fear that he might flatten them.

Despite fronting a band called Rocky De Valera and the Gravediggers (a name considered in some quarters to be a slanderous insult on the saintly patriot President Eamon De Valera, a cranky survivor of the 1916 rebellion), Rocky was not a punk. He favoured old R'n'B standards, which he would deliver with maximum showmanship and the minimum tunefulness. Although sceptical about any musical style developed post-1959, Rocky and Jack were amenable to the idea of encouraging local talent and lent us microphones for rehearsal and dispensed lots of free advice. 'Forget this punk-rock power pop whatever ya wanna call it new-wave shite,' they'd say. 'Stick with the classics. That's all Irish audiences wanna hear. You can't go wrong with good old-fashioned rock'n'roll.'

The Gravediggers, who were quite successful on the Irish pub circuit, occasionally performed all-ages shows in the large hall at Howth Community Centre. Despite their scepticism about our oeuvre, the Modulators were invited to make their debut as a support act in September 1978.

It wasn't a huge surprise when Keith called to say he couldn't make it to the final rehearsal before the gig, since he hadn't made any of the other rehearsals either. But his prolonged absence was plainly becoming a serious issue, especially in the light of our forthcoming concert. 'You've got to make the gig, Keith!' we said, our sense of desperation precluding us from the usual threats and abuse. 'We're counting on you.'

'I'll be there, lads, I swear,' he assured us.

The morning of the gig, he duly called to say he couldn't make it.

I'll spare you the expletive-laden insults and increasingly pathetic entreaties that greeted this announcement. At least for once he had a good excuse. Indeed, he finally explained what had been going on the whole summer. Apparently he'd got into unspecified trouble with the local constabulary and had probationary restrictions that forbade him leaving his area. I am still not sure if this story was true, but it did contain a crucial ingredient for a middle-class new-wave group: street credibility. Our drummer had fought the law! And now the law was going to stop us playing a gig! Well, there was just no way we were going to let that happen. The man could not keep us down! Yeah! Fuck the pigs!

Once we got that out of our system, we called Larry Mullen.

'No problem, lads, I'll sit in for you,' announced U2's drummer. Larry, however, seemed to consider himself a pro helping out a bunch of amateurs (Us?! *Amateurs?!* Wherever did he get that idea?) and there were limits to how much effort he was prepared to make. 'I don't want to come down and rehearse. I'll just see you at the gig. We'll busk it.'

Since we had never even rehearsed the set with Keith, this arrangement was perfectly acceptable to us.

'See you there,' said Larry. 'It'll be nice to catch up with Frank.'

I put down the phone. Shit! We hadn't even told Frank he was no longer in the group, so it was hardly surprising that his friend didn't know. It was perhaps time to address this situation. I called Frank.

'Hey, Neil! Long time no hear! What's going on?'

'Uh, this and that, you know. I'm just calling to tell you we've got a gig tonight.'

'Hey, man, that's great! But, fuck, don't you think we should practise first?'

I took a deep breath. 'The thing is . . . we have been practising,' I admitted.

I felt like a heel. Groups cohere around intangibles like taste and ambition, often the most fragile points of contact, and are held together by a kind of unspoken code of loyalty. You put your trust and faith in each other, nurturing a sense of interdependence that can quite quickly create a gang mentality and, over time, a powerful sense of family. Groups, like U2, who get the line-up right early on exhibit an inner strength that allows them to face down whatever hardships life throws their way. It is called togetherness, I suppose. United they stand. Musicians who get into the habit of chopping and changing band line-ups will rarely ever find that kind of familial coherence, perhaps because they always see the option of addressing a problem by change of personnel rather than drawing on their shared resources. I knew nothing of such things back in 1978 but I did know that we had treated Frank shabbily. At least he took the news well. 'It would never have worked anyway,' he grunted. 'You and your brother are such a pair of fuckin' pains in the bollocks to be around. You've always gotta have things your own way. I suppose you're playing that Beatles shite now? I pity the poor sods you get to do your bidding . . .' And plenty more in that vein.

'No hard feelings, eh, Frank?' I said, when I sensed he had run out of invective.

'Ah fuck you, ya bollocks!' said Frank.

Larry turned up at the community centre about an hour before we were due on stage, with his motorcycle crash helmet under one arm and some drumsticks in a bag. Of course, the first thing he asked was, 'Where's Frank?'

'He didn't tell you?' I said, feigning surprise. 'Frank left the group. Said he wanted to do his own thing.'

Larry looked at me sceptically, perhaps unconvinced that his friend would have made such a move without relaying it to him. In those days, Larry was a boy to me, even though he was actually only seven months my junior. He had a brooding but quietly confident presence, with the emphasis on quiet. Larry seemed to occupy a silent space of his own while his lovely girlfriend, Ann Acheson, a skinny blonde who had been immensely popular in school, would do all the chatting and socializing. I thought of Larry as a solid character but not as particularly interesting. While most of us involved in music tended towards artiness and rebellion, Larry seemed to have a very straightforward, working-class approach to life. At sixteen he'd quit school to take a job as messenger boy, viewing employment as more practical than further study, and his attitude to music seemed equally workmanlike. Adam wanted to be a star. Bono and the Edge were reaching for the stars. Larry just seemed to like hitting things. In retrospect, he may have been more grown up than most of the rest of us, and certainly more interesting than I gave him credit for. Larry never acted like he had anything to prove but instead adhered to a steady, internal course. He prized loyalty and integrity and other uncomplicated values. And he was always as good as his word. So, while he may have suspected us of double dealing, it never occurred to him break his end of our agreement. He stuck around to play drums.

And Larry could play. In the early days of U2, he was certainly the most accomplished musician in the group and his power-house style gave the Modulators' first gig a kick start. Without rehearsal, there was little room for subtlety and nuance but, frankly, there wasn't much of that kind of thing in our set anyway. It was four-to-the-floor, fast-and-furious, power-chord rock'n'roll. Ivan would shout quick instructions, kick off with a solo four-bar intro to set the tempo, Larry would come battering in and we were up and running.

Well, I was running. And jumping. And high-kicking. And doing everything else I had ever seen a frontman do: racing about from one end of the large stage to the other, scissor-kicking, twisting the microphone stand, tossing the mic, standing on the monitors, leaping in the air, jumping down into the crowd to whirl about among the gaping onlookers. I felt no nerves about assuming the role of frontman. I felt like I belonged up on that stage. I felt in command. I can't vouch for my singing, which was probably weak and strained and frequently flat. Sometimes I may well have even been in the wrong key entirely. But at least I had some moves.

The audience in the community centre appeared utterly divided by what they were witnessing. Some of the older crowd hung back sceptically, probably wondering what was the point of a band who couldn't even do a Led Zeppelin number. Some (especially the youngest members of the audience) went wild, pogo-ing about, yelling encouragement and generally behaving as they thought they ought to at a rock concert. And some, many of them teenagers our own age, were absolutely incensed, hurling abuse and insults. It may have been late 1978, but for many in Howth this was the first live exposure to a musical genre they had only dimly heard about – and what they had heard was not good. They seemed enraged at the very idea of our group. One local hard-lad, perhaps mimicking something he had read about punk rock but more likely just showing off to his friends, forced his way to the edge of the stage and spat, a huge gob of phlegm arcing through the air and attaching itself to John's bass guitar.

John looked down in horror. The spittle was running down the neck. As the band ground to a halt he pulled his guitar off, holding it away from him as if afraid of infection. Then he stepped forward to the edge of the stage and suddenly swung the guitar at his assailant, banging him across his head. The guy staggered back, dazed and shocked, as John put his bass back on and indicated that we should carry on.

Rock'n'roll!

I felt like a star leaving the stage. My head was spinning with the attention. People milled about, a swarm of human beings pushing and shoving, but there was something different about the way the crowd ebbed and flowed around me. I could tell I was the centre of attention. Kids stepped up to have a closer look. Strangers patted me on the back. Friends congratulated me. Rocky De Valera shook my hand and muttered words of encouragement. And then it was as if the crowd parted and there, standing directly in front of me, was the last person I wanted to see. Frank. Oh fuck.

He stepped forward, a cheesy grin on his face.

'That was fuckin' ace, man,' he said and gave me a hug.

Could the night get any better? It could! I found myself talking to a girl called Mary, who wore a black beret that implied, to my teenage mind, a Gallic sense of erotic awareness. And here was the thing. I didn't have to chat her up. I didn't get all gawky and awkward or find myself trying to be hypersmart and cool. Mary led me into the corner of the community centre and, while Rocky and his crew banged out their set, shoved her tongue down my throat. By the end of the evening we were rolling about on the dirty floor, my knee was pressed between her legs and my hand was inching down from her neck to her . . . What was that curved shape beneath my fingers? Oh, just her shoulder. I must have been kneading that shoulder for fifteen minutes. Never mind. The advance continued, down, down, to the promised land. And lo, two hours after coming off stage on my debut as a frontman, I got my first grope of female breast.

If I had any lingering doubts about my future, that was what finally did for me. After that there could be no going back.

7

Having been sent into paroxysms of delight by my first, fumbling palpation of a female breast (inside the shirt but outside the bra, if you must know, fellas), it was not long before I found myself growing strangely jaded by the sight of naked flesh. Girls would drop their clothes on command, bend over, bend backwards, bend whichever way they were asked. Women of all shapes and sizes displayed their fleshy wares for my contemplation, from the athletically lithe to the grossly overweight. Sometimes I actually preferred the fat ladies: there was something about the undulating curves and folds that held my eye. Sometimes it was men who would shuck their pants to let my eyes feast on their members, flexing their muscles and adopting the required position. Gender was not an issue. Sometimes I enjoyed the experience. But often, contemplating the ever-changing array of nipples and buttocks and loins, my eye would drift to the clock and I would find myself wondering when I could get out of there and go home.

I had not turned overnight into a promiscuous lothario. In autumn 1978 I began attending art college, where the regular life-drawing lessons were proving disappointingly short of anticipated eroticism. My friends in Howth would pore over the drawings I brought home, apparently incredulous that I actually managed to stand in the same room as a naked woman without spontaneously combusting. But the truth was that I was finding the whole art-student experience lacking in something. I was impatient to get on with life. To get things moving. I was being encouraged by well-meaning tutors to find myself when what I wanted was for the world to find me.

I guess I made a peculiar art student. For one thing, all of my contemporaries were actually interested in art. I was interested in graphics. The foundation year divided between those who liked to paint flowers and landscapes and lovely things and those who would stick a matchbox to a blank canvas then spend hours explaining what it meant. And then there was me. I argued vociferously with anyone who would listen that art should have a functional purpose, that art had to earn its living, that art should court popularity, that all great art had been made for money (wasn't Michelangelo commissioned to paint the ceiling of the Sistine chapel?) and that there was more great art now being produced in advertising agencies than there was in all the garrets of the world. My fellow students could all starve themselves in pursuit of masturbatory visions no one else cared about. I was interested only in art that made money.

I spotted an advertisement in *Hot Press*, for a graphic designer with an interest in music. That was me! I duly arranged an interview for the part-time post of assistant to the art director at the rock magazine, and dressed for the occasion in a leather jacket covered in badges (Mods, U2, Sex Pistols, Ramones, Jam), torn grandfather shirt held together with safety-pins, a pair of self-dyed luminous-green straights and some red suede winkle-pickers. This, I was sure, was a look my fellow rock aficionados would appreciate. The offices were located in Mount Street (just a short walk from the National College of Art and Design), a wide Georgian boulevard popular with Dublin's prostitutes, one of whom opened her coat to flash her naked body at me just as I reached the door. If she wanted to make an impression, she should have picked on somebody who hadn't just spent all day staring at naked women. 'No thanks,' I said politely.

'Whassamatter, punky boy?' slurred the big-breasted harpy. 'Can't get it up?'

I ventured inside to be greeted by the sight of a goat in the hallway, idly munching on a stack of magazines. As we gazed at each other, my expression of incredulity being met by the goat's dumb curiosity ('Are those green trousers edible?' I imagined it to be speculating), a beautiful hippie woman came hurrying down the stairs. 'There you are! Bad boy!' she said, in a soft, chiding voice, apparently addressing the goat, not me. She introduced herself as Colette Rooney, *Hot Press* secretary, as she led the goat and me upstairs, taking some pains to explain that the animal was not a permanent resident, she was just looking after it for a friend.

What kind of place was this? I had imagined magazines to resemble the newspaper offices of Hollywood movies: cutting-edge steel-and-glass constructions, crammed with desks, hacks banging away on typewriters, secretaries scurrying to coffee machines, men with rolled-up sleeves and visors shouting 'Copy!' *Hot Press* occupied just four rooms on the upper two floors of a tatty house, with torn rock posters tacked to the walls, disorderly piles of magazines stacked along the stairs, albums and books perilously heaped in every corner and (in an L-shaped converted attic) a mismatched assortment of cheap desks arranged at odd angles, all overflowing with notebooks, opened envelopes, stacks of paper, black-and-white photos, torn record sleeves and random bits of stationery equipment. A handful of people were apparently responsible for this incredible mess. At one desk sat a man with long greasy hair and wild, jagged eyebrows, smoking furiously and slurping from a coffee mug while all the while grunting to himself and muttering random words aloud as he scribbled frantically on a jumbo notepad. 'Provocation as parody . . . Ah . . . ah . . . ah . . . heavy-metal hooliganism . . . divergent streams . . . Uhm . . .'

'How's the copy coming, Bill?' inquired Colette. So this was the legendary Bill Graham! He looked up with an expression of glazed distraction, as if his mind was occupying quite another plane of reality. 'I'll have another page for you any minute, Colette,' he finally announced, once he had identified the source of this interruption to his mental process.

'Sure, I've waited ten days, I can spare another couple of hours, Bill,' replied Colette, with warmth rather than sarcasm.

Then Bill focussed his suddenly rather penetrating gaze on me. 'Have you seen the Virgin Prunes?' he asked, firing the question like an interrogator ready to beat the truth out of his subject.

'Yeah,' I replied, cautiously.

'Ah!' said Bill, with almost childlike glee, a grin spreading from ear to ear. He proceeded to fire off what I could only vaguely grasp as some complex theory about the roots of the Prunes' art terrorism, punctuated with raised inflections where I surmised that I was expected to nod agreement, all delivered at such high speed that it verged on incomprehensible babble.

'Don't be disturbing Bill when he has to work,' snapped a small, sharp-featured, bespectacled woman wearing a neck brace. This was the production manager, Mairin Sheehey. I subsequently learned that the brace was the result of a car accident, although nobody was entirely certain if the whiplash Mairin claimed to be suffering was genuine. The generous compensation paid out by the insurance company, however, was currently all that was funding the impoverished magazine's payroll and so it was deemed best that Mairin never remove the brace lest insurance investigators might be lurking. Mairin's job was to keep everything ticking over, not easy in an underfunded organization staffed by rock'n'roll hedonists, and her approach to management oscillated unpredictably between supplicatory good humour and parade-sergeant bursts of bad temper. It was commonly held that her bark was worse than her bite, but her bark was generally bad enough to discourage anyone testing the truth of that particular cliché.

'I . . . I . . . I didn't say anything to him,' I protested to Mairin, who scowled at me sceptically.

'Bands aren't allowed up here,' announced Mairin. 'You can leave your flyers or whatever it is you've got downstairs.'

'The goat'll take care of them,' cracked a scrawny, mop-topped figure in his early twenties, to much laughter. This was Liam Mackey, another writer and sub-editor.

'I'm not here about my band,' I protested. 'I'm here about the job.'

'Jesus, Mary and Joseph, you don't look old enough to trust with a paper round,' sighed Mairin, to more general amusement.

I was rescued by the appearance at the door of the adjoining room of a man with the longest hair I had ever seen, huge cascading waves of hair that reached to his waist. This was editor and publisher Niall Stokes. Surely, I thought, this hippie could not be responsible for keeping Ireland safe for rock'n'roll? 'Back to the grindstone now, Bill, we're all waiting on you,' he instructed his star writer, winking at me cheerfully as he ushered me into his inner sanctum.

I had brought along a portfolio full of cartoons, life drawings, some Modulators posters and a portrait of Johnny Rotten as a crucified Jesus, none of which, it became increasingly obvious, were remotely relevant to the job on offer. 'Are you familiar with Letraset?' Niall wanted to know. 'Do you know anything about copy-setting?' 'Have you got any layout experience at all?' To each question I glumly replied in the negative. Niall did not seem unduly perturbed, however, and just quizzed me on my taste in music. I told him about the Modulators and raved about U2's recent performance supporting the Stranglers at the Top Hat Ballroom.

'What did you think of the Stranglers?' inquired Niall.

'They're just a bunch of old farts pretending to be punks,' I declared.

'How old are you, anyway?' laughed Niall.

'Seventeen!' I responded defiantly. 'Old enough!'

So there you had it. I was young, inexperienced and full of shit. They gave me the job on the spot. Years later, I asked Niall why. 'You were so obnoxious I thought you had to have something going on,' he replied. But crucially, he explained, I was a teenage punk and practically everyone else working for the magazine was a twentysomething remnant of the hippie era. He felt he needed an injection of new attitude if *Hot Press* was going to keep up with the times. So while I was hired to assist the art director, a sharp Canadian rocker called Karl Tsigdinos, I was encouraged from the outset to share my views on music, no matter how ill informed. 'Horslips? Horseshit, more like!' I quipped about Ireland's leading folk-rock band. 'All that diddly-aye crap sounds bad enough without having to hear it whacked out on an electric guitar.' 'You're not thinking of putting Eric

Clapton on the cover?' I grunted in horror. 'Slowhand is right! He could fall asleep playing those solos and nobody'd notice. That's 'cause most of the audience would have already passed out by then.'

My coworkers would shut me up by putting on classic albums in the office and insisting I listen before I speak. I had a lot to learn but *Hot Press* was a great place in which to learn it, surrounded by some of the most articulate and knowledgeable music enthusiasts in the country. After one particular diatribe against Bob Dylan ('Why would I want to listen to an old hippie who sounds like a dog being dragged through barbed wire?'), Niall sent me home with a copy of *Highway 61 Revisited* and the reprimand that Dylan was a punk before punk had even been invented. I spent the night in my room playing 'Ballad of a Thin Man' over and over, revelling in the way this strange hipster with the twisted tongue heaped passionate, surreal scorn on the straight world. My introduction to Dylan was a mind-expanding experience akin to my belated discovery of the Beatles, kicking off a lifetime's fascination.

In terms of the actual work, I was even further out of my depth. Before the modern era of computers and desktop publishing, magazine layout was a hands-on process, made even more complicated by *Hot Press'* lack of resources. Raw copy came in from journalists via the editor, often in the form of near-illegible handwritten tracts in biro on bumper pads. We were then supposed to instruct the typesetter on the point size of the lettering and the dimensions she should set the copy to. As the reams of copy arrived, we would cut them up with rulers and scalpels and adhere them to pages of A3 tracing paper (placed over a grid) with a sticky substance known as cow gum. Headlines would be laboriously scratched out with Letraset. Graphic touches would be added by hand. We would calculate the dimensions of photographs and leave blank spaces while the original pictures were sent off with the pages to the printers to be transformed into print-ready coagulations of dots, known as bromides. Colour overlays and specific instructions were added (in black) on a second sheet of tracing paper. It did not help that the printers, chosen on the basis that they were the cheapest in Ireland, were based hundreds of miles away in Kerry so there was no opportunity to examine pages and correct mistakes before the magazine went to press. All of this was new to me but I decided to bluff it. For the first few months I felt like I was walking a tightrope and that I could be blown off balance by the slightest gust. My progress was painfully slow but I covered up with chat, all the while trying to obscure (from Mairin in particular) how little I was actually getting done. I worked evenings and so, when everybody else left, I would volunteer to stay on, finish a few things off and lock up. Then, in the empty office, I would sit and labour alone for hours, ensuring I got my page rate up to an acceptable level. It was often so late by the time I finished that I would just sleep on the floor of the office, arising after a few hours' uncomfortable rest to walk down to art college and start my day there. When college finished, I wandered back to *Hot Press* to begin another evening session. The second time I did this, I prepared for the long haul by taking a packed breakfast into work with me. It did not occur to me that cereal and milk might disintegrate overnight. When I opened my Tupperware dish in the morning, I was so disappointed by the soggy mess inside that I tossed the whole lot out the window. That evening, I listened to much bemused chatter about how a solicitor whose offices were located below *Hot Press*' had been complaining that his third-floor window was plastered with soggy cornflakes. I didn't say a word.

'He's never been the same since the goat ate his files,' sighed Mairin.

Eventually I started to get the hang of things. I enjoyed being part of the witty, passionate team who put *Hot Press* together. Life in the office was endlessly fascinating and amusing, work being carried on with much creativity and good humour under the calm, nurturing auspices of Niall, who facilitated the whole fragile enterprise with an impressive combination of warmth, wisdom and goodwill. After a while, even Mairin (Niall's partner in life as well as work) started to be nice to me. I felt as if I had gained entry into the very crucible of Irish rock culture. I could get into gigs for free and take home advance copies of the latest records. Sometimes I would answer the phone to find myself talking to an Irish rock legend. 'Could you tell Niall Rory Gallagher's returning his call.'

I would stare at the handset sceptically. 'Rory Gallagher?' I'd say.

'That's right.'

'Rory Gallagher the guitarist?'

'Just put Niall on, will you, for fuck's sake!'

I couldn't wait to get back to Howth and tell my friends I had been chatting with Rory Gallagher. The exact nature of the conversation hardly mattered. He was a star. And he was talking to me!

One day Bono and the Edge came into the office, plugging their latest gig. They did a double take at the sight of an old classmate sitting in this hallowed ground. 'What are you doing here?' Bono inquired with evident puzzlement.

'I work here,' I grinned. 'I should be asking you that question.'

'Bands aren't allowed upstairs,' snapped Mairin.

'It's OK,' I said. 'They're with me.'

Conversation quickly turned to music. The Modulators were gigging consistently, performing most Friday nights in the support slot at the community centre. We hadn't really solved our drummer problem. We did one gig with a local stoner called Hopeless Eric, a moniker which turned out to be sadly apposite. He smoked dope all through rehearsals then freaked out on stage, shaking with nerves and fleeing immediately afterwards, never to be seen again. After that, Paul Byrne sat in on drums. He was a neighbourhood friend and the best young drummer in Howth but insisted we explain on stage that he wasn't actually a band member. 'Don't want any girls out there thinking I'm a punk,' was his reasoning.

I was enjoying my growing local celebrity but soon learned that fame could have its down side. Walking up Howth Hill one day I was attacked by two boys my own age who kept knocking me to the ground with judo moves, swiping my legs from underneath me every time I tried to stand. 'You can play guitar but you can't fight!' yelled one of my assailants.

'I can't even play guitar,' I protested. Obviously I had been mugged by mistake. The one they really hated was Ivan.

I related these tales to Bono and Edge to much laughter. But U2 were hardly strangers to the problems facing young bands. Edge told me about a Crofton Airport Hotel gig, for which only six people turned up, three of whom thought a different band were playing. 'That's the worst we've ever played,' he reported.

'But look on the bright side,' said Bono, 'only six people know about it.'

The biggest débâcle, however, was U2's support slot for the Greedy Bastards' December gig at the enormous Stardust Ballroom. The Greedies were a part-time outfit featuring members of Thin Lizzy and the Sex Pistols and so this was the hottest ticket in town. Everybody who mattered in the Irish music business and every hip punter in Dublin was there, but the Greedies' disorganization resulted in U2 going on without a sound-check. They tried to cope by walking on one at a time to twang and bang away for the sound-man's benefit on an extended opening to 'Out of Control', but the audience were cat-calling even before Bono started singing. Ivan and I watched incredulously, failing to comprehend how a group we knew to be dynamic and inspiring could be made to sound like rank amateurs. Maybe there was hope for all of us!

'Everybody's gotta fall flat on their face sometimes,' said Bono afterwards. 'The important thing is to pick yourself up.'

I knew how that felt. John announced he was leaving the Modulators, uttering the immortal line: 'I don't think I can handle the rock'n'roll lifestyle.' I looked at him incredulously. What was it that he found particularly difficult to cope with? We weren't exactly fighting off groupies, there were no drugs and only the occasional gig in the local community centre. We found out soon enough that John was actually doing to us what we had done to

Frank. He and Paul Byrne were forming their own band, Sounds Unreel, playing prog rock, a genre where John's Afro and Paul's blow-dried bouffant would not be so out of place.

We recruited a new bassist, David Parkes. He had a distinct advantage over everyone who had held this position before in that he could actually play an instrument. Not bass, mind you – that would have been asking too much. But he was an accomplished classical guitarist and Ivan set about teaching him what he needed to know to transfer his talents from six strings to four. Then, through an advertisement in *Hot Press*, we procured a drummer who didn't have probation restrictions, suffer from dope-induced paranoia or require us to make disclaimers before every performance. True, Johnny McCormack (no relation, thank God) was a Dublin Jack-the-lad who was quite a bit older than us (he must have been all of, oh, twenty-two or twenty-three, which seemed positively ancient) and with whom we had absolutely nothing in common, but he was willing to play drums in our band and (beggars, choosers and all that) that was enough to seal the deal.

By summer 1979, we were ready to rock. Or perhaps that should be ready to pop. Our ideas of what we wanted to achieve were starting to coalesce and Ivan and I agreed there was something inherently limiting about the rock genre. It was full of bands who seemed to take themselves terribly seriously and who relied for effect on a form of sonic pummelling. We liked songs: verses, choruses, middle eights and all. Our heroes were the Beatles and we wanted to create a musical platform that would ideally allow us room to explore a multitude of different styles. And, in our fierce ambition, we really wanted to be popular, the key word that lay at the very core of our vision of pop music.

'It's all pop music,' I said to Bono after a gig one day, expanding on ideas that tied into my rejection of artistic elitism. 'It's about what's popular, what the audience chooses to hear, what people listen to and sing to themselves even when the band isn't there. You're making pop music.'

'Up yer bum, chum, with a big bass drum!' retorted Bono, aghast at the very idea. 'U2 is a rock band.'

'I'm talking about the Jam, the Boomtown Rats, the Ramones, Blondie . . .' I rattled off (perhaps pausing for a moment to contemplate the vision of Debbie Harry, new wave's most appealing pin-up). 'It doesn't all have to be flashy disco and Eurovision mush. This is the new wave of pop. Its got snap and crackle!'

'You want to sound like a breakfast cereal?' laughed Bono, incredulously. 'That is the problem with pop! It's like pre-packaged tins of music. Rock doesn't fit on the supermarket shelf.'

'Of course it does. When rock becomes popular then it's pop music by definition.'

'Calling us pop is like an insult to me,' countered Bono. 'It's such an insubstantial thing. Pop! The bubble bursts . . . and then it's gone. But a rock will still be there no matter what. There could be storms, waves pounding, nothing is gonna wear it down . . .'

We could go on like this at great length (and frequently did). But while we agreed to disagree, Bono invited the new-look Modulators to make their debut supporting U2 in McGonagles. They were planning a month-long residency known as the Jingle Balls, which they advertised as 'Christmas in June!' in a gimmicky attempt to stir interest. Christmas decorations were draped all over the stage with a row of Santa masks hanging at the rear. The idea was to offer a cornucopia of delights, with special guests and other surprises every week. I don't know how much of a surprise the Modulators were to the assembled throng, but our central-Dublin debut was a storming success for us. We tore through a set mixing originals and covers, encoring with a hugely silly, extended riff on the Ramones' 'Kill that Girl', complete with a mock-preacher-style rock'n'roll call-and-response heavily influenced by Rocky De Valera, in which I practically testified to my homicidal intentions. In retrospect, perhaps there were a few issues regarding my summer of rejection by the opposite sex that I still had to deal with.

We got our first review in *Hot Press*. 'The Modulators (who demonstrated more enthusiasm than polish on their "first" gig) boast a very fine lead vocalist who will undoubtedly establish himself as a major local force.' It was written by my boss, Karl, but who was I to question his taste and judgement?

U2 were in another league. I could sense what they were becoming, even then. At a series of six Saturday-afternoon gigs in a disused car park next to the Dandelion Market and then over the month at McGonagles I watched all that promise suddenly bloom before my eyes and ears. They were a white-hot modern rock band, forging their identity in the blast furnace of performance. The Edge was just mind-blowing, playing through a set of effects that he would trigger with his foot, reverbs and repeats and delays transforming his guitar into a six-string orchestra as he layered up power chords and pinging harmonics to produce swirls and flashes and flares of bright electric sound. Adam and Larry thundered behind him, building up a booming wall of rock. And there was Bono, in a string vest and black-and-white Pierrot trousers (he was never anyone's idea of a fashion icon), hair clamped to his forehead with sweat, always exhorting, cajoling, roaring his heart out, surrendering himself to the music and the audience.

There was a white screen set up at the side of the stage with lights projecting on it from behind. During 'Stories for Boys', a snappy song about male-fantasy role models, Bono dragged Alison on stage and they disappeared behind the screen, where their silhouettes groped and snogged one another. It would be a long way from this shadow play to the hi-tech displays of Zoo TV but U2's multimedia ambitions were present even in those earliest days.

We supported them again at Howth Community Centre in August. This was our territory, the hall was crammed and the Modulators played a blinder. Then U2 came on and ripped the roof off the place. They played a furious new-wave rocker called 'Cartoon World' (written, so I gathered, by the Edge, which might account for why it had finished lyrics rather than relying on lots of 'oo-ee-oo's). Against a chunky, stop-start guitar, Bono delivered droll depictions of ordinary lives where the characters seem to be increasingly dysfunctional, climaxing with the memorable couplet: 'Jack and Jill go up the hill / They pick some flowers and they pop some pills!' With Bono roaring the punchline with maximum showmanship, hands aloft as the Edge's guitar kicked in the chorus, the crowd went absolutely wild. These were Beatles-in-the-Cavern experiences for me. I was getting used to seeing all the big names who came to Ireland, but U2's gigs were always the most special.

Afterwards, Alison (or Ali, as everyone now called her, so Ali it shall be) approached me as I was chatting with some of local fans, all of whom happened to be female (these were, to be honest, the only kind of fans I was remotely interested in).

'I'll have to keep my eye on you, McCormick,' she said. 'Everytime I see you you're surrounded by girls.'

'It's your boyfriend you should be watching out for,' I said. 'Bono's gonna be a big star.'

'Ah, never mind him,' said Ali. 'He's always thought he was a star. It's my job to keep him down to earth.'

My adolescent awkwardness around girls had more or less evaporated now. Being onstage was feeding my ego, until my natural self-confidence was in danger of becoming overcharged. I had a new girlfriend, Barbara McCarney, a fellow art student with whom I first made eye contact across a crowded life-drawing class, catching a twinkle that made far more impact on me than the nude model seated between us. She was a lovely, oval-faced, curly-haired, red-cheeked, sweet-natured, giggly girl, a million miles from the kind of rock vixens who occupied my fantasies, but over the course of a year studying together I became absolutely smitten. I courted Barbara for months and finally jumped on her on the very last day of college, prompted by the fear that I might otherwise not see her again all summer. She physically leaped back when I kissed her, and I thought, 'Uh oh . . . Could I really have misjudged all those signals?' Then she smiled and reciprocated, whispering, 'You took your time, boy.'

'Lordy,' I thought, 'I'm sure I'll get the hang of this sooner or later.'

I finally lost my virginity at an anti-nuclear rock festival in Carnsore, on the southwest coast of Ireland. I would like to state for the record that I actually disdain the notion that one can 'lose' virginity. I don't consider myself to have lost anything. Rather I gained something special when we surrendered to our natural desires in a tent in a muddy field while the din of rock music echoed in the background. But 'losing' your virginity was a major psychological and sociological issue among my peers at the time. In a patently misguided effort to stop the single people of Ireland fornicating like beasts of the field, the Catholic lobby had succeeded in making contraception illegal. Condoms were traded like contraband on the black market and so it was that I managed to score a packet of three off a drug dealer at the festival. 'Are you sure you don't want a bit of hash to go with that?' he muttered seductively. 'It'll heighten the whole experience, believe me.'

'No, no, just the Durex, thank you,' I mumbled, blushing furiously. Romeo and Juliet never had to put up with crap like this.

I wrote a song with Ivan about that, called 'In Your Hands', a torturous but rather poetic account of the fear and guilt and twisted sense of defiance that was loaded by the church on to the simple act of making love. Our songwriting was definitely improving. And with it an artistic goal was crystallizing. I wanted to write about the realities of teenage life in Ireland: the frustrations of desire in a nation where law seemed to make young love illegal; the gnawing fear of mortality set against the bland succour of an atrophying religion; the obstacles placed across the path to fulfilment by repressive adult society. I wanted to fill the songs with practical details only a teenager would know, writing about the frustration of having to leave my girlfriend's house every night to catch the last bus home in the prosaically titled 'Last Bus Home'. I wanted to accomplish great things and I believed the Modulators could be my vehicle.

We were getting paying gigs at last, with Johnny negotiating an £80 fee for supporting a show-band at an illegal strip club known, rather unattractively, as Sweaty Betty's. Anticipating that the audience might not be particularly open-minded, we learned a raft of rock'n'roll classics which we duly played at our usual breakneck speed. The place went wild, with one rather elderly fellow jiving on the table-tops to our hyped-up 'Peggy Sue'. Afterwards he came up to congratulate us. 'So this is what they call punk rock, eh?' he said. 'It's not so bad!'

We made our television debut on *Young Line*, a well-meaning but ridiculously stuffy and amateurish youth programme on RTE, Ireland's only TV station. I walked into the studio wide-eyed, spinning around to take in the cavernous room with its thick hanging drapes and the multitude of lights suspended from a latticework over our heads. I took my position on stage and watched as the huge cameras rolled silently about, their lenses turning like blank eyes towards me. I stared boldly back, as if trying to see through the looking glass and out into the world of TV-watchers. Here I was: inside the magic box at last! I felt entirely nerveless. This was where I belonged. At a crucial juncture of our performance, I did something I used to do at gigs and leaped off the stage to jive about on the dancefloor. Unfortunately, to the viewing public I simply disappeared out of shot. The camera had not followed my flight and now darted around in panic, as if looking for someone or something else to focus on. Then it cut to a presenter wearing a ridiculous multi-coloured knitted pullover and muttering inanities in front of a wobbly silent projection of the rest of the Modulators' performance. It was dreadful. I cringed inside at the sight of all my exaggerated movements and laboured gesticulations. Did I really look like that? And as for my singing . . . I knew my voice was not exactly one of the natural wonders of the world but I was absolutely horrified by its lumpy tone and my gulpy, frog-in-throat delivery. How had I ever convinced anyone to let me front a group?

But in the weeks that followed the power of television kicked in to reassure me that I was on the right path. Kids in Howth would approach, giggling nervously. 'We seen you on TV!' I was a star, if only in my own backyard.

One day in September, I descended into the basement of Advance Records to buy a 12" single. I held my new purchase in my hands with a sense of wonder. It was U2's debut release, an EP featuring 'Out of Control', 'Stories for Boys' and 'Boy/Girl', billed as *U2-3*, and for the sum of £1.49 I had picked up number 16 (written on the sleeve in black felt-tip) in a limited edition of 1000. It is now probably the most commercially valuable record I own – but it has always been valuable to me. Back in 1979, it represented the bridging of a gap between the mundane, ordinary world in which I had grown up and an alternative, fabulously exotic universe of records, rock stardom, glamour and . . . possibility.

The possibility that someone like me could actually cross over into the silver-screen dimension of twenty-first-century dreams. Because some guys I knew had actually made a record! Boys I went to school with! Logically, of course, I had always understood that this was possible. But, like Doubting Thomas, I needed proof. It had to be more than just seeing it with my own eyes. I needed to touch it. To hold it in my hands. To put it on the turntable, to watch it spinning hypnotically around and around and around at precisely 45 (the magic number) revolutions per minute, to let the needle slowly descend until with a soft click and the faintest hiss it dropped into the groove and . . .

. . . there was the metal pulse of Adam's bass. De-dum-dum-dum-de-dum-dum-dum-de . . . How many times had I watched him playing that riff, standing close enough to touch? Then ching-chang-ching! The Edge's guitar riff chimed out. Larry's drums kicked in, racing hi-hats and snappy snare. And here came Bono: 'Monday morning / Eighteen years of dawning . . .'

The record had been made under the auspices of Jackie Hayden, who ran CBS Ireland, a parochial offshoot of the multinational that was not taken remotely seriously by its parent company. CBS had passed on Jackie's recommendation of the Boomtown Rats and so, while they remained unenthusiastic about his latest local discovery and rejected the opportunity to sign U2 worldwide, they did sanction the Ireland-only release of a set of demos produced by London A&R man Chas De Whalley. It was a measure of U2's growing pre-eminence on the Dublin scene that *Hot Press* supported them with a cover feature in October, much to the grumbling discontent of every other local band. Bono and Edge came into the office on the day of publication, to pick up a copy hot off the press (so to speak).

'Looking good!' said Bono, a note of genuine surprise sounding in his voice as he contemplated the cover.

'Well, I look good,' joked Edge. 'I don't know what *you* look like! I told you not to wear that shirt with the paint down the front but would you listen? You look like you've just wandered off a building site.'

Bono ignored him. 'We look like a rock band,' he said, confidently.

Meanwhile Edge, who was in ebullient spirits, turned his mocking attentions to me. 'How's the *pop* group going?' he asked, making 'pop' sound like an insult.

'You didn't hear about it?' I said.

'What?'

'We got fucked by the Pope!'

It had all been going so well. The Modulators played headline gigs in both the big universities (Trinity and UCD), did an art-college dance and put on a massive show in front of 200 high-spirited kids at a packed community centre in the notoriously rough area of Darndale. That would have been judged a great success were it not for a stage invasion at the end of our second encore during which £200 worth of hired equipment got spirited away, leaving me standing on the stage forlornly pleading with the crowd to return at least one of the microphones. And then we had been offered a shot at the Dublin big time: a head-lining slot at McGonagles.

There had to be a catch. We just weren't high enough up the local greasy poll to warrant such billing. Could it have been anything to do with the fact that Pope John Paul II was arriving in Ireland on a three-day visit guaranteed to paralyse the country, culminating in a Mass for an estimated one million people in Dublin's Phoenix Park on the same day as the gig? Well, it didn't bother us. Ivan and I were among a very tiny minority in Ireland completely unmoved by the papal visit. As far as we were concerned, the Pope could play to his crowd and we would mop up whatever irreligious rock'n'roll dregs were left behind. Then our bassist informed us that he had the honour of being selected to be an altar boy for the Pope and, because of the complex logistics of the occasion, would not be available to perform that evening.

I was incredulous. What wannabe rock star in their right mind would put serving God's representative on earth before a headline spot at McGonagles? We bullied, we hectored, we wheedled and flattered to no avail. I pointed out that there would surely be thousands of other altar boys involved in this massive public act of communion and that one would not be missed. But our saintly bassist would not be shifted. 'It is a great honour to be asked to assist the Holy Father,' he said, crossing himself. 'It's a once-in-a-lifetime opportunity.'

'So is headlining McGonagles,' I snapped back. The peculiar thing is I really believed it. To me, this gig was more important than anything going on in Ireland – fuck it, in the entire world – that day. 'You've got to play the gig,' I insisted. After days of relentless pressure, David finally caved in. He would do the Mass then extricate himself in time for a late sound-check, making his way to a street corner some distance from the park, where we would be waiting to pick him up and scoot over to McGonagles.

'Miss this and you're out,' I warned him.

'I'll be there, all right? Don't worry,' he promised.

Where had I heard that before?

I borrowed my dad's car and Ivan and I drove into Dublin on the day of the Mass. The city was dead. Not a person on the streets. Not a shop open. It seemed everybody had gone to the park to see the Pope. The scale of the event finally began to dawn on me. We found one pool hall that had not locked its doors, owned presumably by a fellow curmudgeonly atheist, and so we went in and shot a couple of games, listening to the balls clack together in the empty silence, giggling with pleasure at our blasphemy.

Of course, when the time came to pick up our bassist he was nowhere to be found. We waited for hours, exasperation building to murderous proportions, before making our way back to McGonagles to discover that our drummer (who was proving to have the reliability of Keith Karkus) had got tired of waiting, packed up and split. We sheepishly confessed to the manager, Terri O'Neill, that we wouldn't be able to play.

'Never mind, lads. Nobody's fuckin' turned up anyway,' he said, which I thought was very charitable of him under the circumstances. 'It's dead out there.'

So that is how the Pope broke up my band.

'You better get down on your knees and pray, boy,' laughed Bono, as I finished my sorry saga. 'Sounds like you've got some powerful enemies.'

8

Without a band to burn up all my excess energy, I threw myself into life at *Hot Press*. I managed to persuade Niall to let me take albums home to review. The first time this happened, my opus about some minor-league punk outfit almost filled an entire school exercise book (it was a mark of my age, I suppose, that I chose this particular medium for my labours). I then had to endure the sound of scratching from the editor's office as he struck blue pencil lines through every pretentious sentence, finally emerging to admit defeat. 'There was a lot of interesting stuff there,' he said, encouragingly, 'but, uhm, nothing I can actually print.'

Niall was a great editor, among the best I have ever known. He may have been overseeing something more high-powered journalists would have dismissed as a parochial rag but his passion and commitment raised *Hot Press* far above its natural level. Niall believed that the magazine had the potential to make a difference in Ireland and encouraged his writers to use it as a forum for serious issues and a vehicle for their highest creative ambitions, always encouraging passion and nurturing individuality. And he was an immensely supportive person, with time and consideration for everyone who worked for him, inspiring huge loyalty among his staff. Certainly, he seemed to have identified something in me worth persevering with, and showed immense patience in developing whatever talent I had. He would talk me through the journalistic process, point me to other writers who might inspire me and carefully explain the cuts he made to my naïve early efforts so that I began to understand things like structure and substance.

Of course, for a cut-price operation like *Hot Press*, employing me offered one distinct advantage. Although I received a wage for my graphics work, it did not even occur to me that I might be due extra money for my writing. Even when I progressed to doing cover stories for the magazine, I received not a penny for my efforts. And never thought anything of it. I wanted to write. I begged for the opportunity to write. What kind of ingrate would expect to get paid for it as well? I did the local live reviews no one else wanted to do. Wrote about the albums none of the other critics were interested in. Interviewed the bands no one else wanted to talk to. And considered myself the luckiest guy in Dublin.

There were, inevitably, moments of doubt. Like my first interview, with the Revillos, a band from Scotland who had formed from the ashes of punk-party outfit the Rezillos. In retrospect, they were one-hit wonders whose career was on a rapid downward spiral to oblivion, but that one hit, '(Everybody's On) Top of the Pops', was exactly the kind of self-aware, catchy, unpretentious new-wave pop that fitted my personal manifesto for music, so I repeatedly solicited Niall to allow me to interview them.

The night before I met the Revillos, I watched them perform a show of spirited, silly, day-glo pop that married Shangri-La girlie-group melodies to jerky rock with comical B-movie lyrics. Band leader Eugene Reynolds had the longest quiff in showbusiness, a towering achievement for hair gel that threatened to decapitate his fellow performers every time he turned his head. And singer Fay Fife was a sexy Scots minx, punk's Highland pin-up. Throughout the gig, I was glowing with a secret sense of pride that I (me!) was actually going to meet these stars of stage and TV screen tomorrow (in person!). To everyone else in the audience they would remain objects of distant veneration. I was about to enter their world.

I turned up at their hotel the next day thinking that there must have been some kind of mistake made. I still clung to the belief that anyone who had a record out (certainly anyone who had appeared on *Top of the Pops*) must be fabulously rich and famous, so I was bewildered to find myself at a low-rent boarding house where half a dozen members of the band and crew were sharing a couple of dingy rooms. Without her make-up and stage costume, Fay was sharp-faced, spotty and distinctly ill at ease, her expression shifting between boredom and outright hostility. The strands of Eugene's quiff hung long and limp in front of his face as he sat on the edge of a lumpy single bed, no doubt contemplating with mounting depression the sight of this skinny, opinionated teenager, clearly the most junior member of the *Hot Press* staff, who had been sent to speak to them.

I carefully consulted a piece of paper on which I had scribbled questions. 'How would you define the Revillos' trash aesthetic?' I began, a question designed to show the band they were talking to no ordinary rock hack.

'Whit does that mean?' sneered Eugene in a thick Scottish accent. 'Trash aesthetic? How would *you* define it? Trash aesthetic! It's just two words stuck together to make them sound interesting. It disnae actually mean anything at all.'

'I mean . . . uh . . . What I mean by that is . . .' I began to fear he might have a point. What did I mean by 'trash aesthetic'? 'I mean the aesthetics of trash, ehm . . .' I would have to do better than that.

'Trash as in "rubbish"?' asked Fay. 'Trash as in "garbage"? Are you saying we're garbage?'

'What I'm talking about is finding beauty in something other people might think of as disposable rubbish.'

'Ach, yer talking shite, man,' snarled Fay.

'Next question,' ordered Eugene.

I struggled on, but even as I read them off the page I could see that the questions I had worked on so lovingly were convoluted and pretentious. Soon the pauses were growing so pregnant they could have gone into labour. Eventually Fay broke the embarrassing silence. 'Yer not much of a journalist, are ye?' she said.

I returned home in a state of abject despair. My deadline was Monday, so I had the weekend to rescue this humiliating travesty. I laboured at my typewriter (no more school exercise books for *this* aspiring professional) in my bedroom for forty-eight hours with very little sleep, writing and rewriting, tearing things up and starting again, slowly and painfully crafting a piece about the illusory nature of pop music and the sometimes painful gap between fantasy and reality. It was a kind of coming-of-age piece, concluding not with disillusionment but with new acceptance of the contract of the imagination between performer and listener.

I left it on Niall's desk then listened fearfully outside his door for the next half an hour, ears peeled for the sound of the dreaded blue pencil. But there was nothing, not a scrape, not a scribble. Finally the editor emerged. 'It's excellent,' he pronounced. 'I'm sending it down to the typesetter.'

The despondency I felt a few days before was transformed into delight. I had cracked it! This was a profound moment in my interior life. I knew there and then that I could actually do this. That I could write. That I could express myself in print. The process was no mystery to me any more. I was a journalist.

Usually I was entrusted with only the most boring *Hot Press* pages, but Karl allowed me the honour of laying out my own maiden interview. I went to town on it, with a wacky font for the headline, a large photo set at a zany angle and, topping it all off, an overlay of a comic-strip zig-zag across the whole page, with instructions to print it in bright yellow.

'That'll look cool,' said Karl encouragingly.

Well, it might have looked cool if it had been printed by someone who knew what they were doing. When the magazine came back from the presses in Kerry I contemplated my work with horror. The overlay had been printed jet-black. A huge inky zig-zag ran through the middle of my piece, randomly obliterating huge passages of painstakingly crafted prose. The article was illegible.

'Wow!' said Liam Mackey, with mock awe. 'Is that the kind of thing they teach you at art college? Remind me to make sure Karl lays out my next feature.'

To be honest, I am not sure what kind of thing they were supposed to be teaching me at art college, since I was rarely there. In order to reach the required eighty per cent attendance, I had to get Barbara to sign me in. Although I was now on a special-ist graphics course, I was increasingly bored with the lessons. I felt I was learning more practical skills on the job at *Hot Press*. When I tried to talk to tutors about print-ready artwork and four-colour separations I saw a look of blank fear creep into their eyes. Not for the first time in my life, I became convinced that I knew more than those responsible for my education.

As much as I was caught up in life at *Hot Press*, I was posi-tively itching to get another group started. I was about to turn nineteen and there was still no sign of my destiny arriving with all bells ringing and lights blazing. In February 1980, as if to emphasize the expanding gap between us, my classmates played the National Stadium in Dublin. This was an extraordinary event by local standards. The 2400-seater arena (calling it a stadium was always somewhat fanciful) was the preserve of top inter-national acts. U2 had by now released a second CBS Ireland single (the uplifting but woefully underproduced 'Another Day', featuring a rather amateurish sleeve sketch by Bono) and topped five categories of the *Hot Press* readers' poll, yet it was consid-ered by most of their contemporaries to be the height of narcis-sistic folly to think that a home-grown new-wave rock band last seen playing the pubs of Dublin could fill such a large and prestigious venue.

I was on the guest-list that evening. But then, so was every-one else I knew. History records that the gig was a sell-out but I am not convinced. There must have been at least 500 friends and associates and friends of friends and associates of associates with free tickets. There were perhaps 500 paying customers. But the atmosphere was all that really mattered and another 1000 or so people would not have made the slightest bit of difference. The crowd gathered to the fore, loud and proud, roaring support for our boys. With Bono as lightning conductor, U2 electrified audiences, sweeping them away in a landslide of emotion. As far as everyone in that stadium was concerned, the night was a blind-ing, joyous celebration, a valediction for our local heroes – and a kind of farewell, because we all knew there would be no going back after this; U2 would be moving onwards and upwards, taking off from this small island to take on the world.

In the dressing room after the show, U2 were offered a deal by Nick (sometimes known as Bill) Stewart, head of A&R at Island. It was almost unheard of in those days for a British A&R man to actually make the effort to come to the rock'n'roll backwater of Ireland, so Stewart's appearance at the show was a bit like the mountain raising itself up and shuffling over to pay tribute to Mohammed.

I saw Bono at a bus stop in town sometime afterwards. There was another mental adjustment to be made. I thought that record deals were synonymous with limousines, the beginning of the easy life. 'You know, you spend all this time and energy trying to get a record deal,' said Bono. 'Then you get to the end of this whole struggle and find out it's only the beginning. The real work starts now.'

We sat at the back of a 31 bus, talking. He was riding out to visit Ali at her parents' house in Raheny. I was on my way home from work. Bono was in a serious mood, contemplating the future, talking in an urgent, intimate whisper. 'U2 are alone out there. We don't fit in. We're not going to be able to take the usual roads to success. But I really think it's important that we get to where we're going, we get a chance to fulfil our potential. 'Cause music can be a celebration of life. It's a contemporary art form for everybody, working-class, upper-class, never before has there been an art form so versatile. And it's being abused. It's being commercialized. And it's being bent. Punk was about trying to straighten it out but it was just the same old story. Power corrupts and it bent it out worse than it was in the first place. U2 are standing against that. It's one up for the positive side of this culture – the pop culture, as you always call it. If we're on the radio, if we get to number one, we're doing all the people that make that crap factory-produced music out of a job. I think it's important.'

Oh, I was convinced! Bono can be a mesmerizing speaker. He has the poetic language and proselytizing gifts of a preacher, but rather than ranting and raving his delivery is low-key and intimate, filled with warmth, humour and surprising humility. Small-talk is not really his forte. He has a tendency to go straight for the big issues. But he doesn't talk *at* you; instead he puts his listeners at the centre of the conversation, making you feel as if your involvement and agreement is vital. That you are in this together. 'You've got to get your band going again, Neil,' he told me, pressing the notion as if the very future of the music business depended on people like me standing up to be counted. 'You've got a big talent, you've got a part to play.'

Then we were at his stop and he was off, with a last 'God bless'. Why did he always have to bring God into it?

Ivan had been gigging with two friends who used to roadie for the Modulators, Ivan O'Shea (who will be henceforth referred to by his surname, to avoid confusion) and Declan Peat (who shall be known by his nickname, Deco, the basic approach to male nicknames in Dublin being to take the first syllable of the christian name and add an 'o' at the end. Thus I knew lots of people with names like Philo, Johno, Robbo, Kevo and Steve-o. But, funnily enough, only one Bono). They called themselves the Jobbys, a euphemism for noxious waste products expelled from the posterior. 'We're shit and proud of it,' as my brother would say. The basic principle behind the Jobbys' unique sound was that each member was assigned to the instrument he was least competent on. Thus Ivan was drummer, O'Shea was guitarist (though he had never before touched the instrument) and Deco was bassist (ditto). Their songs involved them all changing chords at the same time but not necessarily in the same order, and they performed with buckets on their heads and their backs to the audience. This was all very amusing (to them at least) but it was essentially just a diversion, bringing Ivan and I no closer to our goal of global stardom. It did not pass unnoticed, however, that Deco was threatening the very *raison d'être* of the Jobbys by making swift progress on his chosen instrument. So one day we asked him to accept promotion from roadie to bassist in our new group. Given that we didn't actually have a new group, in reality this represented only a minute step upwards in the band infrastructure, but Deco was so slobberingly grateful you might have thought he was join-ing the Rolling Stones. 'I won't let you down, guys,' he declared in tones of humble conviction.

'That's what they all say,' I countered.

Like all our former bassists, Deco inherited Adam's old Ibanez and required some instruction on how to play it from Ivan, but otherwise his enlistment represented a distinct improvement in our recruiting policy. As indicated by his fandom, friendship and voluntary roadie status, Deco was one of us, sharing an outlook, sense of humour and taste in music. Immediately we began to feel like a unit. Now all we needed was . . .

No, not a drummer. Top of the list of our priorities was a new name.

Things were changing on the band-name front. 'The' was becoming increasingly redundant. From Liverpool, we were listen-ing to a burst of exciting new psychedelia from bands with fanci-ful names such as Echo & the Bunnymen and Wah!Heat. Sex Pistols manager Malcom McLaren was promoting the Burundi beats of Bow Wow Wow, while the extravagant new glam of Adam & the Ants was rising to prominence in the charts. And from the underground were coming whispers of a 'new romantic' movement that wanted to shake off the dourness and negativity associated with punk by emphasizing the fabulousness of fashion and glamour, spearheaded by outfits with names like Duran Duran, Spandau Ballet and Culture Club.

While I tended to be unimpressed by the lumpen dance beats of the new-romantic recordings (my record of the year was Elvis Costello's 'Get Happy', a spirited reworking of sixties Motown music suffused with much romantic misery), I was enamoured of the conceptual thinking behind it, the idea that this might deliver a shot of alternative culture into the mainstream pop charts. I briefly took to wearing gaudy, multicoloured chiffon scarves over a bright-yellow shirt and some baggy, wine-coloured trousers that I thought of as rather piratical. There may even have been, on occasion, a touch of eyeliner, although it would have been hard to spot under my hair, a curly mop-top with an excessively long fringe designed to hide my despised spectacles. This was the cause of frequent disasters, as I had to constantly brush the hair out of my eyes in order to see, whereupon I often caught the edge of my glasses and flicked them off my face. 'I've never known anyone to break so many pairs of specs,' my optician observed one day. 'Don't you think it would be cheaper to get a haircut?'

At any rate, to someone as caught up in the shifting currents of pop fashion as I was, it was imperative that our new name reflect this spirit of adventure. And there would be no room at the front for the definite article.

'What about just Modulators?' suggested Ivan.

'The whole mod thing is over,' I countered. 'It's finished. We'd be dead before we even started. We've got to come up with something fresh, new and original.'

'Bats with Guns and the Third Earth Radio,' suggested Deco.

'Not that original,' I said.

'Lucky Frogs Evaporate,' said Deco, who was reading random words from the pages of a comic.

'Oh God,' sighed Ivan.

'I like it! One big word on the posters. GOD. Live at the Baggot Inn.'

'Amen!' said Ivan.

'That's not bad! Amen! I can see it now, crowds chanting, "Amen! Amen!"'

Eventually, following this convoluted line of thought, we came up with Yeah! Yeah! (complete with exclamation marks, our bold use of punctuation reflecting my growing appreciation of the typographical properties of Letraset). I loved that name, since it suggested a modern interpretation of the spirit of the Beatles, who remained our principal role models. And it got a big endorsement when Bono gave it his seal of approval. 'You can usually tell if a band is going to be any good by the name,' he said. 'I like Yeah! Yeah! already.'

Now it was imperative that we find a drummer. Deco invited a schoolfriend, Leo Regan, to audition. He was a scrawny fellow with outrageous eyebrows: a pair of thick, black, beetley arcs that seemed to have a life of their own. They lent a soulful, almost mournful air to his expression and complemented his intense nature. Actually, the word intense barely does Leo justice. Leo is a kind of emotional and philosophical extremist. When he was young, it was the extremes of hedonism to which he dedicated himself, but, as he grew older and more serious, he became a highly demanding, almost self-punishing artist. We have been friends for life but it wasn't the easiest of beginnings. I identified him straight away as an oddball, but he could play the drums and that was all that really mattered. For his part, Leo recalls a great uncertainty about getting involved with Yeah! Yeah!. He thought that Ivan and I were a couple of egotistic arseholes but he had never met two people so confident and committed to achieving their goals, and decided, on balance, that he might as well come along for the ride.

Ivan and I had a plan. Well, we always had a plan of some kind but this time we had convinced ourselves (and several of those closest to us) that we had a plan that would actually work. We were going to create new-wave pop based on the Beatles' template: melodic, intelligent, singalong songs delivered with wit, panache, passion and invention. And then we were going to practise until we were note perfect before launching ourselves on the scene in a blaze of glory.

And that was it. That was the plan in its entirety. In retrospect, of course, it wasn't really much of a plan at all. It was more like a hopeful punt.

Ivan and I were born in the sixties, children of a class revolution, the spawn of TV and pop culture. We were part of what was probably the first generation to take fame for granted. Everybody is at it now, of course. Something previously represented as available only to the highest achievers in mankind is now seen as a career option. We wanted to be famous. Therefore we would be. It was obvious, wasn't it?

Ivan finished his leaving certificate and entered Trinity College to study for an engineering degree. I suppose he felt he was doing something Dad would approve of but it did not take Ivan long to realize he had made a mistake. There was clearly far too much hard work involved, for one thing. After just four weeks he dropped out, with the solemn undertaking that he would resit some exams and gain the points necessary to study natural science, a course that promised to leave far more time for his real interest, the pursuit of rock stardom.

My parents must have begun to worry that there was a pattern developing when I announced that I was dropping out of art college. Karl Tsigdinos had departed *Hot Press* to oversee a glossy women's magazine, to much derision from his colleagues, who viewed teaching Irish women about the mysteries of the orgasm as a much less honourable vocation than keeping the country safe for rock'n'roll. So, at the tender age of nineteen, I was offered his job. I persuaded my parents that I was better off working as art director of a magazine than studying for three more years to get a degree that might, if I was lucky, get me a job sharpening pencils for someone like me.

Around the same time, I broke up with Barbara. This was entirely my doing. She was the first great love of my life but I was restless and confused, driven by the notion that my destiny lay out there somewhere, in a world as yet unexplored, with people I had not even met. I thought of myself as fearless and yet I was desperately, secretly afraid of becoming tied down in the world of my childhood. So I told her it was over one night, rather unsympathetically breaking the news on the back of a bus. She fled in tears. I went home and wrote a song, 'Tears Turn to Rain', and felt mightily satisfied with my evening's work. Perhaps I should break up with girls more often! A short while later, to my horror, Barbara started going out with my former bassist John McGlue. Conveniently overlooking the fact that I had brought this on myself, I adopted the pose of wounded lover. At night I listened to Bob Dylan's *Blood on the Tracks*, the Everest of break-up albums, with new appreciation. I had discovered this album when I was eighteen and the nearest I had come to heartbreak was not getting past first base with Ronan's sister. Listening to 'Tangled Up in Blue', I wanted to fall in love with a difficult woman who would leave me broke and drunk with lipstick on my collar and whiskey on my breath, rambling the city streets after midnight, ranting at the stars in the sky, just to savour some of these bittersweet sensations for myself. Now here was my chance. I would mope around near McGlue's house every night in the hope of bumping into the new couple, so that they could see by my expression of stoic melancholy and transparently false cheerfulness that I was holding up despite suffering from a badly broken heart. They never seemed particularly pleased to see me, for some reason. I was also churning out lyrics to torturous love songs, with titles like 'Love Is Was', 'I Broke a Promise', 'See My Face', 'Cut It Out'. I began to entertain the rather dangerous notion that misery was conducive to creativity.

U2 were recording their debut album at Windmill Lane studios and one night I paid a visit. The studio, located down Dublin's docks, was like something out of science fiction to me, dominated by what looked like an enormous flight desk covered with a spectacular configuration of little knobs and a sheer glass internal window overlooking a sound booth in which headphones hung from microphone stands, leads trailed everywhere and the Edge's guitars were racked up along one wall. Lights flashed on and off, visual displays showing vertical green bars of dots jumping up and down in time to the music crashing from the two biggest speakers I had ever seen, the sound so rich and deep it made the hairs stand up on my neck. I had never heard anything like this before. The Edge's lush guitar lines cascaded from the speakers like sheet lightning. Adam's basslines were sleek and silvery. Larry's drums an echoey, piledriving forcefield. And Bono. I think he was worried back then that his vocal frailty would be exposed in the studio. He was a frontman more than he was a singer. It was his passion, his lifeforce, that drew people in but, technically at least, he wasn't going to win any singing prizes. His range was limited, his tone stretched and often thin. But context is everything. Under Steve Lillywhite's inspired production, Bono's voice was a vulnerable, emotive shimmer that swam through the songs, lending colour and character, while Edge's waves of guitar provided dynamic focus. The band seemed to have made an incredible leap forward in the studio, ironing out any rough edges.

They were all lounging around, listening to this playback mix with considerable satisfaction. It transpired that many of their established live favourites (such as 'Cartoon World', 'Silver Lining', 'The Speed of Life', 'The Dream is Over', 'Jack in the Box') were not being recorded for the album.

'So what's going to happen to them?' I asked.

'Gone for ever,' smiled Bono.

'Whoosh!' said the Edge, as if watching their old material disappear at high speed over the horizon.

I felt a tug of nostalgia for this music that had meant so much to me over the last couple of years, never to be heard again. 'That's the past,' said Bono. 'We're looking to the future now. I'm already thinking about the next album. I've got a head full of songs that haven't even been written yet.'

'The way you go, they'll never be written,' Edge joked. Bono seemed to have a reluctance to commit his onstage extemporizing to paper. I have a sheaf of old lyric sheets that I once badgered Bono into writing out for me in biro, in big schoolboyish handwriting. 'Stories for Boys', already a live favourite recorded for their debut EP, concluded with the note: 'NB: pop stars, bionic men soon to be featured in verse 3, as yet unknown'. The sheet for 'Speed of Life' just said 'P.T.O.' On the other side Bono had written 'It's gone'.

As the evening progressed, I picked up an acoustic guitar to play the first song I had composed entirely on my own, entitled, prosaically, 'I Wrote this Song'. My ability on the guitar was minimal. I knew only three chords and this song included all of them (for the record they were G, E minor and C). My strumming was restricted to a leaden downbeat but it was a sweet little number that did not need much adornment.

I don't know any real songs
'Cause I don't know what's real
But I wrote this song

And I don't know any love songs
'Cause I've never been in love
But I wrote this song

And it won't stop the leaves from burning
Won't stop the light from turning blue
It won't stop the rain from falling
But take this song
'Cause I wrote this song
For you

Bono was effusive in his praise, which meant a lot to me, but expressed astonishment when I told him I didn't see this song fitting into my plans for Yeah! Yeah!. I laid it all out. We intended to start out with bright, poppy material aimed at winning over a large commercial audience before introducing more complex and personal work as we progressed, taking the audience with us step by step. This was the way the Beatles had done it, after all.

Bono was horrified. 'Oh no!' he declared, with a sudden burst of passion. 'You've always got to do the very best, just play the best stuff you can.'

Ah, what did he know? The peculiar thing is that, as much as I loved U2 and felt convinced they had what it took to become a successful international rock band, I seriously doubted whether they would ever trouble the singles charts. And that is where I saw Yeah! Yeah! heading. I wanted the mass audience. Given the obvious commercial limitations of their high artistic principles, U2 could perhaps reach the level of playing arenas (if they were lucky) but I had my eye set on stadiums. Fuck it. I wanted the planet.

In my mind's eye it was already real to me. This was my plot for the eighties. I would get a major record deal and release a classic debut album of teen-angst pop that would delight critics and teenyboppers alike. My band's first three albums would be melodic, punchy, meaningful and, most of all, commercial. We would make a couple of films that would be the finest synthesis of rock and cinema since *Hard Day's Night*. I was already working on the script for one of these, a story about the meaning of life, the universe and everything, based on an obscure science-fiction novel by Kilgore Trout entitled *Venus on a Half Shell*. My main concern was how to turn the banjo-playing hero into a four-piece rock'n'roll band. I had George Lucas, fresh from his *Star Wars* triumphs, pencilled in as director. At the height of our success we would astound the world by producing a daring, innovative album that would be to the eighties what *Sgt. Pepper's* was to the sixties. A new hi-fi system would have to be built to cater for this recording revolution, which would mix multichoice visuals with sensurround sound. We would follow it up with an on-the-road album mixing live work with studio demos, rehearsals and other off-the-cuff recordings. Critics would write theses about the meaning of my increasingly convoluted lyrics while pop magazines would worry about how weird we were becoming. We would break up acrimoniously, sending suicide rates soaring. My long-time lover, Nastassja Kinski, would leave me and I would retreat to the studio to work out my pain in a solo outing to rival *Blood on the Tracks*. At the end of the decade, the group would triumphantly re-form to play a concert to be broadcast live all over the world from the first moon station. I would be knighted.

But first we had to do some gigs. The St Paul's end-of-year talent contest was coming up again but this year it was to be open to the public and was being held in their massive gymnasium, which was the site of a popular weekly rock disco and had a full-scale theatrical stage. This, we decided, would be the ideal place to unveil the future of popular music on an unsuspecting (but presumably grateful) public. We redoubled our efforts at rehearsals.

In October 1980, *Boy* was released. I held U2's debut album in my hands and marvelled at this proof that the impossible dreams of teenagers could come true. U2 were touring the UK and Bono suggested in a phone call to *Hot Press* that I might like to come over to see them at the Marquee. Having witnessed their very first performance, I would have a unique angle from which to assess their progress. 'It's like the Beatles in the Cavern, Neil,' he told me excitedly. 'It's going so well.'

The only problem was that the U2 gig on Thursday 27 November was just a day before Yeah! Yeah!'s planned debut at St Paul's, so it would have to be an overnight return. Feeling like an international jetsetter, I flew to London. It was already dark when I set off and I remember spending the whole journey staring out the aeroplane window, marvelling at the delicate spider-web of road and city lights flickering in the blackness below.

I arrived at the Marquee in a state of mental agitation. I had travelled by Tube from Heathrow airport, trying hard not to stare at my fellow passengers, people of every conceivable brand of ethnicity. Coming from a white, exclusively Roman Catholic country, I found my head put in a spin by London's overcrowded multiculturalism. The Marquee itself was smaller than I imagined. I had read the name of this legendary venue in the *NME* so often that I had pictured a vast arena, not a crowded club. I negotiated my way to the narrow backstage dressing room to greet the band, who seemed happy to see a familiar face. 'You're going to witness something special tonight,' Bono promised me.

And I did. The place was jammed with sweaty bodies, a capacity crowd of 740 riding U2's tidal wave. I had not seen them play since a secret gig in the Project Arts Centre in July and I realized I missed them. After getting used to the crafted beauty of their debut album it was simply stunning to catch that furious live attack again: hard, rocky, pulsating. Bono did not speak so much any more; he did not exhort the crowd to become involved. He didn't have to. He was preaching to an audience already converted by the album. There was a tiny bit of resentment in my heart towards the hipsters of this foreign metropolis who were roaring U2's name as if the band belonged to them. I could feel that tug of letting go, familiar to everyone who watches their private discovery become public property. But mostly I was ecstatic and amazed. My school-friends had come so far so fast and they were still travelling at hypervelocity, heading upwards and into the ether.

In the dressing room afterwards, Bono babbled with excitement. 'This band isn't gonna stop. You've seen the pits, Neil. You've seen where we've come from. To get from there to here, you'll admit, is rather interesting. To get from here to a gold album in the US is nothing, a small step. I'm serious. We're gonna break America like no British band has broken it in a long time.'

With a sheepish grin, Adam disappeared into the night with some girl who had been at the show. His taste for the traditional rock'n'roll vices was becoming something of a running joke in the band. The rest of us headed back to a flat in Earl's Court rented by Island Records. It was an unimpressive affair, with (as I recall) just one large bedroom containing a number of single beds, where Larry, Edge, Bono and I settled down to talk. They wanted to catch up on news from home, expressing particular interest in what up-and-coming bands were filling the void left by their departure. Then I pulled out a tape recorder to begin the official interview, rustling my notes to assume the role of journalist.

'I suppose we should start with the album,' I said.

'I suppose we should,' said Bono.

'Uhm. Well. What do you think of the album?'

'It's my favourite album,' said Bono, laughing.

'What a question!' said Larry. 'This guy really goes in at the deep end!'

'I think it's lovely,' said Edge.

We talked till all hours of the morning. We spoke about the history of the band, with Bono spluttering whenever I interrupted his sometimes fanciful rewriting of the past to remind him of the often more banal truth. When he tried to assert that the Marine Hotel was the first gig, I raised the spectre of their Bay City Rollers cover versions in the school talent contest. 'Oh please, Neil, you go back. This is like my life passing before me. What have we done to deserve this?'

'At this stage, Bono is taking a coughing fit,' Edge solemnly noted for the benefit of the tape recorder. 'He's looking bad.'

We spoke about the past, the future, their influences and motivation. But most of all we spoke about something Bono and I had often talked about. God. Religion. Faith. For the first time, Bono was uneasy about the subject – all too aware that rumours about the band's Christian commitments were flying around, and fearful that this was an association that could damage them in the eyes of self-consciously cool rock commentators and consumers. 'We don't want to be the band that talks about God,' he insisted. 'Anything that has to be said is in the music or on stage and I don't want to go through the media. I'll talk to you personally about it but I don't want to talk to the world about it because we will face a situation where people will see us with a banner over our heads. This is not the way U2 is gonna work.'

But still we did talk about it. Long after the official interview was over, Bono and I were sitting in our underpants in adjacent beds talking furiously into the wee small hours, while the Edge lightly snored in the corner and Larry grumbled that he was trying to sleep. Faith seemed to me nothing but a panacea for fools. I had examined the Christian religion from every conceivable angle and found it wanting. I felt I had seen through it and called it out, the way the boy shamed the bleating flocks of yes-men in the tale of the emperor's new clothes. Yet here was this guy I thought the world of, as smart as they come, who had apparently gone through the same process of questioning and doubting and reached entirely the opposite conclusion. 'I don't understand how you can find faith in religion when you see all the damage it's done, especially growing up in a country like Ireland,' I argued.

'I'm not into religion,' Bono countered. 'I am completely anti-religious. Religion is a term for a collection, a denomination. I am interested in the personal experience of God. When I was fourteen I called out and asked God to show me a direction, and I wondered whether there was any direction or not, and then I saw it happening. I saw the band taking shape and being pointed in that direction and it gave me an insight.'

'But you were part of that Christian Movement in school,' I said. 'All those happy-clappy people, they used to do my head in.'

'I found that very hard on the head, too,' he insisted. 'I found them very uncool. But I realize now that that is their beauty. Because God's values are not the values of this world. They're not the values of cool. It says in the Bible that it's harder for a rich man to get into the kingdom of Heaven than it is for a camel to get through the eye of a needle, and we are rich men. We are people who are rich in intellect or personality and we tend to judge people by our values. God doesn't judge people by our values so it's usually humble people who find God. But at that stage I couldn't handle those people, so I left.'

'I'm baffled about how someone as intelligent as you can think you can find all the answers in a centuries-old book,' I said.

'I'm still finding my way,' he replied. 'I don't have all the answers, I haven't got everything sussed. It's not easy being a Christian. When you discover Christianity, you discover other things as well. You tend to experience a darker side of life. You experience great temptation. Becoming a Christian you go into battle. Because of what this band stands for, 'cause of where we are in the business, you wouldn't believe the pressures we're under. I mean spiritually. We get up early in the morning and we work against it. Every day is a battle, every moment is a struggle, and it's the same struggle other people have in life if they're looking for an answer. It's the same struggle you are going through.'

'But I'm not trying to force anyone to live their life a certain way. I'm not on a crusade.'

'I'm not on a crusade, Neil,' Bono asserted. 'If there is a God and Jesus Christ died on the cross and if there is any value in what He says, it should be shown in our lives. We're not puritans. We're not saying this is the right way and you are wrong. But if people come up to me and say, "I'm asking questions", I'm willing to share my experience. If they want to follow that through, that's fine, but I wouldn't lay it on anybody. Look at Adam. He is as free as any individual. He honours our commitment. He realizes that it is a very important source of inspiration. But he rejects it himself. That's the way the world should be. I'm not going to hit somebody over the head if they don't believe.'

'To me the Bible is all arbitrary rules and regulations based on unsound supernatural principles,' I said. 'It's all about surrendering your own will and giving up responsibility for your own existence. There's so much in life I want to experience and I'm not gonna be stopped by all that Catholic guilt they tried to foist on me growing up.'

'A lot of people think surrendering to God means giving up all the "good things". I used to believe that, in a way,' said Bono. 'But when you get involved, you start to see things very clearly. You start to see what's happening around you. When a guy goes for you with a bottle, you realize what is happening, you realize he's being cheated. It's an insight. It's certainly not puritanical or cowardly. It's not about abdicating responsibility. It's about taking life into your own hands.'

'You're so sure you're right and I'm so sure I'm right,' I said. 'But we can't both be right!'

'You make me smile, Neil, because I know you are looking for answers, you are looking for God, and it's all right at the end of your nose!' said Bono.

'Go to sleep!' grumbled Larry from his bed.

'Better do what he says,' suggested Bono. 'Big day tomorrow.'

'Yeah,' I agreed.

'Hope you've said your prayers,' joked Bono.

'I don't need to pray,' I countered. 'I believe in the power of rehearsal.'

9

Yeah! Yeah! rocked the packed hall at St Paul's, playing three original songs and dancing away with first place, an outcome that had never been in doubt (in our ranks, at least).

A leading pirate-radio DJ was on hand to present the prizes. 'I'm Gerry Ryan,' he declared in a breezy, mid-Atlantic DJ swagger, winking as he shook my hand, his manner suggesting that we should all know who he was already. I had never heard of him before but tried to cover up my ignorance by asking, incredulously, '*The* Gerry Ryan?'

'That's right,' he responded, with admirable nonchalance.

'I'm *the* Neil McCormick,' I announced, with gleeful immodesty.

What the hell. I was *the* Neil McCormick and who could deny it? I was a teenage member of Dublin's rock elite, the youngest person in *Hot Press*. I had been on radio and TV. And my band was ripe and ready to take on the world. I felt like everything I touched would turn to gold records.

I experienced a rare moment of self-doubt on 8 December 1980, the day John Lennon was murdered. I must have been the last person in the world to hear this news, or at least the last to take it in. I was standing at the layout table, working on the cover of the Christmas edition of *Hot Press*, an elaborate affair that I had been slaving over all day, when Niall came in and said, 'All change! We're going to put John Lennon on the front.'

'Why?' I said, with astonishment. 'Have we got an interview?'

'He's been shot,' said Niall. 'Haven't you heard? He's dead.'

'Oh, fuck off!' I cheerfully responded. Niall encouraged an atmosphere of irreverent candour, so I felt I could say such things to my editor without fear of reproach. As the junior member of the operation I was used to being wound up and, since everyone in the office knew how I felt about the Beatles (and Lennon in particular), I assumed this was just the latest gag at my expense. So I continued working on my original cover while various members of staff trotted up to insist that my hero was deceased, retreating with bafflement when I told them all to piss off and let me get on with my job. It was only when Bill Graham came in, muttering to himself about Lennon's legacy, that I began to have doubts. Bill was too far adrift on his own sea of endless internal contemplation to allow himself to be dragged into an elaborate practical joke at the expense of the art director. I put down my ruler and scalpel and went out on to the street. And there it was, emblazoned across the evening papers in black and white: 'LENNON SHOT DEAD BY CRAZED GUNMAN'; 'BEATLE MURDERED'; 'JOHN LENNON DEAD'.

I sat down on the pavement and started to cry.

In the fantasy world where I spent so much of my mental time, I always thought that I would meet John Lennon. He was the only rock star I really wanted to talk to, up close and in person, not so much to ask him the million and one questions I had about the Beatles and his solo career and not just to tell him, like so many fans before, how much he meant to me, personally, but to look him in the eyes and see . . . What? My reflection, I suppose. To see myself in my hero. To find out if I actually existed in the same dimension as him.

God may have died for me years before but Lennon was my living idol, sitting astride my personal pantheon of rock deities. My bedroom had become a shrine to the cult of rock'n'roll. Elvis Presley, the Beatles, Bowie, Dylan, Johnny Rotten: these were the almost supernatural icons whose images were plastered on my wall. And a whole tier of bizarre lesser divinities besides, from the patron saint of geeks, Joey Ramone, to my Aphrodite, goddess of love, Debbie Harry. But I didn't just want to prostrate myself at their altar. I wanted to ascend the stairway to the stars, where my own psychedelically coloured painting of Lennon held pride of place, cast in the guise of mystic seer, Buddha, Christ and Zeus all rolled into one idealized figure, floating through the universe like *Marvel* comic's Silver Surfer, peering omnisciently through little round spectacles that contained the whole world. Surely the godhead of my psyche could not have fallen too?

I tried not to leave much space for doubt in my life. After all those years of wrestling with the concept of faith, long nights of self-torturing analysis as I questioned every facet of the religion I had grown up with, I knew only too well how those little worms of misgiving could gnaw at the mind, chomping away until there was nothing in there but a black hole of despair. So I crammed them down into one dark corner and bolted the cellar door shut. I relied on confidence to carry me through. I believed in self-belief. But I was shaken to the core by Lennon's murder. If one of the brightest stars in the firmament could be so capriciously snuffed out, what chance was there for the rest of us mere mortals? Suddenly the future seemed a far less certain place. What if I never made it? What if I was just swept away by the random workings of the universe?

Yeah! Yeah! had a gig that week, supporting the Gravediggers. We played 'Twist and Shout' as an encore, ripping the place up. I stood in the lights at the end, riven with emotion, listening to the crowd applauding, thinking, 'I *can* do this. I've got to do this.'

My interview with U2 appeared in the same issue as Bill Graham's moving Lennon obituary. I was a little bit nervous about its reception by the band. Despite Bono's repeated admonitions that U2 did not want to be the band that talked about God, I felt strongly that the spiritual issue had to be addressed. For a start, there were the rumours about the band's religious commitments, with their enemies on the Dublin scene (and there were plenty of those, a motley collection of professional begrudgers and vanquished rivals) depicting them as Bible-bashing puritans, which I knew not to be the case. But, just as importantly, I felt that you could not properly understand the group without taking into account their spiritual imperative. It had been the subject of their first proper song, the unrecorded 'Street Missions' and continued to inform much of the material on *Boy* (what was the album's desperate, driving, optimistic opening track, 'I Will Follow' if not a dedication to God, with its declaration of 'I was lost / I am found'?). A conviction that U2 existed for a higher purpose underpinned Bono's need to reach out and touch his audience, to enfold and encompass their humanity, to be at one with them.

In a rock'n'roll milieu where studied cool was often valued over passion, U2 had always seemed bravely and unfashionably open in their desires and it disturbed me now to think of them trying to close ranks and cover up something so crucial to their identity. 'I don't know what you're going to do with this,' Bono said to me before I left London. 'You have a sort of peculiar understanding of the group 'cause you've been there right from the beginning and I really wanted to talk to you about it. So if you want you can go right ahead and print it all. It's all on tape. But it's a difficult area and we're going to be faced with the consequences. A lot of people will use it as a trap and work it to their own ends. And I really cannot entertain that.'

I was halfway through writing the article when I suddenly decided I simply could not turn a blind eye to the truth, so I dived into an exposition of U2's spiritual evolution (although I did not include Bono's private conversation with me), effectively outing them in the media as Christians. A few days after the issue hit the streets, U2 performed an emotional homecoming show at Dublin's TV club. I went backstage and entered the dressing room with some trepidation. Bono cast me a look of pantomime reproval (pursed lip, raised eyebrow) before breaking into a grin and enveloping me in a hug. 'Now everyone knows what you know,' he said. 'If it bothers them, they'll just have to get over it.'

'If we had to be stabbed in the back by somebody, it might as well be an old pal,' added the Edge, wryly.

Yeah! Yeah! gigged frequently, taking any support slots we could get, developing our stagecraft, defining and refining our sound and image and continually adding new songs to the set. Indeed, it became something of a matter of pride to debut a new song every time we played. A torrent of material was pouring out as Ivan and I got to grips with our chosen medium of expression, continually experimenting with form and content but absolutely adhering to the primacy of the chorus. Ivan was displaying a real flair for melody, finding a balance between the emotional satisfaction offered by traditional chord sequences and the flights of inspiration that could come with more obscure shifts and twists. As for me, lyrics were proving to be the easiest and most satisfying things I could write. I laboured over my journalism but songs arrived unbidden, in intense bursts of inspiration, with little of the gradual shaping and improvisation that Bono described. A title, a theme and a rhyming scheme was all it took to unlock my subconscious, and out would pop songs about superstition ('So It's in the Stars'), masturbation ('Got Your Picture'), sexual frustration ('Breaking the Lights'), global starvation ('Skin and Bone') and even, much to my own surprise, the eternal quest for an absent God ('Say the Word').

What do you do when the winds of the world lose their howl?
And you can hear the sighs in the silence that whispers around?
There are voices in the shade, there are hands in the air,
They are reaching for you, must they reach out forever?
When the last laugh chokes, the last fire smokes
And wheels of stone roll on cobbled hearts
And beauty sleeps and lovers leap
Armies meet and reason parts
And hope breaks in your hand like glass
Say the word . . .

If the lyrics tended towards the high-minded and poetic, the image of the band itself was anything but. Wearing clothes that referenced the swinging sixties (colourful shirts, lean-cut jackets), we adopted an increasingly wacky, comically self-deprecating, party-band attitude. The emphasis was on encouraging audiences to have fun. Leo certainly brought his influence to bear in this regard, debunking any tendencies to take ourselves too seriously.

He was a fierce opponent of pomposity and egotism in all its forms. How we ever became such good friends I will never understand.

There was a miniature local scene developing, involving a number of bands who were alternatively allies and rivals, sharing resources while vying with one another for local prominence. We would play shows at the Summit Inn with the Dark (who modelled themselves on the Doors) and the improbably named Deaf Actor (the latest incarnation of our old friends Sounds Unreel). As different as we all were, we began to influence one another, particularly in our search for wilder and trippier sounds. Bill Graham began to speak of a brand of Howth psychedelia. His mother lived in the village and, as Bill's heavy drinking slipped towards alcoholism and he found it increasingly hard to sustain an independent existence, he could frequently be found in the local bars, where young musicians would gather around for the privilege of buying him drinks and listening to his words of wisdom. Bill was an absolutely brilliant man, a genuine music-lover whose mind raced to make inspired connections between disparate musical sources, but he thought so quickly and spoke so fast it was hard to keep up with him at the best of times. After a few pints he verged on incoherence but we would just sit and nod, never quite sure if he was advising us to listen to Miles Davis and Cuban salsa or just asking for a pint of Guinness and another sausage. Noel Redding, former bassist with the Jimi Hendrix Experience, was another who sometimes frequented the village taverns and found himself plagued for advice by starstruck local wannabes. When Phil Lynott bought a large house in Howth, it confirmed in our fevered minds that this rather quaint fishing village was about to become a crucial landmark on the rock'n'roll map.

Hot Press was due to be launched in the UK in January 1981, a project that was consuming a great deal of my time. The pool of potential readers in a country as small and as musically conservative as Ireland was inevitably tiny and Niall became convinced that *Hot Press* needed to expand or would wither on the vine.

The magazine had a lot of goodwill within the British music industry, partly because the journalism was conscientious and rarely as wilfully mean as the UK music weeklies, and Niall felt that we could compete in that market. Besides, since the population of Ireland was effectively reduced every year by the mass exodus of any young person with the slightest ambition, he figured that even by appealing to this Irish diaspora we would be massively expanding our potential readership.

I was charged with coming up with a poster campaign to launch the British edition. My concept was simple: a photo of an Irish rock star reading a copy of the *Hot Press*, with flames leaping from the pages of the magazine. Naturally, I had only one person in mind for the part of the star. Niall talked Bono and Paul McGuinness into lending their support by persuading them that the campaign could work for U2 also. The shoot took place in the house of my favourite *Hot Press* photographer, Colm Henry. He was a gentle, soft-spoken, slightly spaced-out guy whose stark black-and-white prints had an indefinable quality of otherness and a professional sheen that put him leagues ahead of any other photographer then working in Ireland. I made up a mock copy of *Hot Press* featuring a full-page advertisement for U2's *Boy* on the back. I met Bono and Ali in the centre of town and drove out to Colm's house in some beat-up jalopy Bono had acquired. He chatted enthusiastically the whole time about U2's recent mini-tour of America while Ali pointedly reminded him to keep his eyes on the road and his hands (which would fly into the air to make a point) on the wheel.

In the photo studio (actually just a white-painted spare room) I produced, from a plastic bag, the tools I had brought along to create the desired effect: a wire coat-hanger, a box of paraffin-soaked firelighters and some matches. 'Very high-tech,' joked Bono. 'I can see we're working with professionals here.'

While Bono stood holding the *Hot Press* open in front of him, his mouth open and eyes popping in an expression of mock alarm, I lurked out of camera shot with a lit firelighter stuck on the end of the bent-out coat-hanger, so the flames appeared to be shooting from the pages. It took a while to achieve the required result, with a moment of panic when my only copy of *Hot Press* caught ablaze. 'Don't set fire to his hair!' screeched Ali, as I endeavoured to rescue the precious issue.

There was much laughter after that, with Bono reminding us, in a thick Dublin accent, to 'Moind the hair, roight? Can't be a rock star wid no hair!'

Afterwards, at Bono's behest, he posed for some photos with his girlfriend, Bono with his white shirt buttoned up to the neck, Ali in a flowery print dress. You don't see them often photographed together and perhaps these rare pictures illustrate why. Bono is at ease with the camera, alternately playing to it and ignoring it completely, while Ali, as beautiful as she is, looks distinctly uncomfortable, either watching the camera with wary distrust or watching Bono perform with an air of suspicious curiosity. Ali was never a seeker of the limelight. She loved Bono (of that there could be no doubt). Everybody loved Bono. He was such a charismatic force and he always seemed to have so much love to give, enveloping everyone in the room around him, whether it was a small photo studio or a huge rock venue. But Ali loved something different about him than the rest of us did, something vulnerable and unshowy, lurking deep within the extrovert exterior.

The three of us went out to dinner in a Dublin restaurant. And there the conversation turned once more to God, with Bono earnestly trying to explain the roots of faith.

'You have to trust your instincts,' he said. 'You're a writer, Neil. It's like working on a hunch, using your imagination to try and see the real story underneath the surface. D'you know the story of Elijah going up to a cave where he has been told he will hear the voice of God? It's in the Bible. Elijah gets to the cave and goes in but there's nothing there, so he waits and eventually he hears a roll of thunder. He thinks, "Ah, yes, the voice of God!" and goes to the entrance of the cave . . . But the thunder rolls again and he doesn't hear God. So he goes back in the cave and waits. Then he sees a bolt of lightning flash across the sky and he thinks, "Ah, of course, the voice of God." Goes back to the entrance of the cave and waits . . . But God says nothing. And he starts to think maybe he's been misled – maybe there is no God; whatever is going through his mind. Then a small puff of wind blows into the cave and he hears it, like a whisper, the voice of God . . .'

Bono paused for dramatic effect. 'I always liked the idea that God is in the small things. And when it gets too noisy and fuck ing crazy, and I'm running around like a madman, I have to quiet myself down to get in touch with God.'

I kept running into Bono around this time, in the audience at gigs, at various openings and parties and once in a while just aimlessly wandering the city streets. Every time our conversation would revolve around the same subject, rambling debates about the spirit that always ended with his 'God bless'. I suspect he thought there was purpose in the coincidence of our encounters and that I was ripe for conversion. And, in truth, he had succeeded in plunging me back into spiritual confusion. I found myself re-examining every aspect of the faith I had rejected, turning it all over in my mind during long, sleepless nights. I kept finding the same logical flaws that had first persuaded me of the fallacy of reli-gious belief but now I had a new problem, caused in large part by my huge respect for Bono: did I really think I was smarter than every believer, every mystic, every guru and every religious philoso-pher in history? It probably won't surprise you to learn that 'yes' was my answer to that particular question. But what if I was wrong? Was I really prepared to take the chance of damning my soul to hell? Besides, God was an appealing concept, representing the prom-ise of immortality – a condition of considerable attraction to me.

Bono invited me to a meeting of the Shalom Bible Group at Edge's parents' house in Malahide. He told me I'd get a chance to answer a lot of my questions. I took Ivan along for protec-tion, relying on my brother's studied spirit of irreverence to keep the forces of the spirit world at bay.

Shalom were Charismatic Christians, evangelical and fund-amentalist, committed to the surrender of the ego before the healing grace and fiery breath of the Holy Ghost. It was strange to find members of U2, who struck me as easy-going and liberal in their application of belief, keeping this kind of company but stranger still to learn that it was the provocative Virgin Prunes who had first been attracted to the Bible group; into the fold they'd brought Bono, who introduced the always inquisitive Edge, with Larry finding comfort there too following the death of his mother in a tragic road accident in 1978.

We gathered in the Evans' front room, where a sixteen-millimetre projector had been set up and a white screen erected. There were familiar faces, including members of Lypton Village and ex-pupils from Mount Temple, cups of tea and biscuits and everybody was being very nice and solicitous, as committed Christians almost invariably are, but it was hard to escape the feeling that this was some kind of recruitment drive and that they were more interested in my soul than in me. Someone got up and gave a talk, telling us about some films we were going to see, which had been sent by an associated Christian group in America. Allegedly these films graphically demonstrated scientific proof of biblical miracles and the power of the Holy Spirit. The lights were turned off. The screen flickered into life.

What followed was absolutely gobsmacking. Men in white laboratory coats chatted about the power of faith, while volunteers were subjected to powerful electrical currents, apparently relying on prayer to keep them healthy as lightning bolts passed through their bodies. There were a series of experiments which appeared to defy the laws of physics. Experts in the fields of geology, palaeontology and archaeology were trooped on to refute evidence of human evolution and to challenge conventional wisdom regarding the age of the earth, their own experiments conclusively demonstrating that the world was only a few thousand years old (correlating with figures laid out in the Bible) and had, in fact, been made in just seven days, complete with built-in fossilization.

The film flickered to a close. There was much excited chatter. Ivan and I stared at each other, wide-eyed and speechless.

'What d'you think, then, Neil?' one of the group leaders asked me. I could feel Bono's watchful eyes on me.

'I'm absolutely amazed,' I said, truthfully.

'God is amazing,' replied the evangelist, sincerely.

Ivan and I made our excuses and headed for the exit, thanking Edge for his hospitality. We were almost home free when Bono caught me by the front door. 'What did you really think?' he said.

'Oh, come on, man!' I sighed. 'That was the biggest load of shite I've ever seen. Blind, stupid, illogical hocus fuckin' pocus!'

He smiled ruefully and shook his head. I even heard him say 'God bless' as we headed off down the driveway. Always the God bless! Could nothing shake his conviction? At least the Shalom meeting had the effect of ending my crisis of faith. This lot, I was convinced, were several beads short of the full rosary.

With the (dis)honourable exception of Adam, U2's deep faith kept them from indulging in the traditional excesses of rock'n'roll, something which I think gave them extra reserves of strength to take on the world and helped them to avoid many of the obvious pitfalls that regularly derail the careers of young musicians. As Edge once said to me: 'It's such a sort of prostitute business that you would find it immensely difficult on your own steam to carry through a principle, single-mindedly.' Bill Graham, who knew the band as well as anyone and understood them better than most, speculated that, for Bono in particular, Christianity acted as a kind of shield. 'As the focus of the audience's apathy or acclaim, frontmen always have the most vulnerable and volatile egos,' Bill once wrote. 'But imbued with a missionary sense – however unfocussed – and believing his gift came from above, Bono may have been protected from those identity and ego problems that can upset those singers who find their fame has neither savour nor reason.' As far as I was concerned, if Bono, Edge and Larry wanted to surrender their egos to the mysteries of the Holy Spirit that was their own affair. I had another path to walk.

I was ready to embrace the hedonism promised by rock'n'roll. Hell, I was eager to be corrupted. The problem was, I was actually a rather sensible, clean-living fellow. I didn't drink, for one thing. Growing up in Ireland, where drinking is the national pastime, I had been put off the whole business by the regular carnage I witnessed around pubs at closing time, with grown men pissing on walls and spewing up in gutters and generally lurching about with all the gainliness and physical co-ordination of a herd of rhinos in zero gravity. My position on alcohol was considered quite controversial among my contemporaries, who were, for the most part, enthusiastic in their endeavours to prove themselves the equal of their pint-swilling forebears. Neither did I smoke, having witnessed my own parents' heroic efforts to forsake this particular vice, so my few attempts to share a spliff usually ended up with me coughing my guts up and then complaining it had had no effect whatsoever.

'You've got to inhale!' my friends would admonish me.

'My lungs won't let me!' I would protest.

As for the other much-noted rock'n'roll vice, Yeah! Yeah! were not exactly proving a magnet for the kind of pneumatic groupies I entertained in my rich fantasy life. We did have a small group of female fans who had begun to follow us around, and to whom Leo unkindly referred as the Alsatians. This was a reference to their attractiveness rather than qualities of dogged loyalty.

But while I did not drink or smoke and rarely got laid, I could secretly pride myself in having gone straight for the class-A narcotics in the form of Columbian Marching Powder (as it was known around the offices of *Hot Press*). We worked hard putting that magazine together. Indeed, such was the intensity of the work and the length of the hours, we used to mock bands who had the temerity to complain of the hardships of life on the road – a weekend spent with us would show them what it really took to keep Ireland safe for rock'n'roll. Operating on a fortnightly schedule, effectively there would be one week in which little was accomplished on the production side as we waited for the writers to produce their copy. Then it would be all hands on deck for the second week, with mounting pressure resulting in increasingly long nights, culminating in final production weekends that occasionally ran to forty hours or more of continual toil. Absolute deadlines were set by the schedule of the van departing from the depot of the *Irish Independent* newspaper, with whom we had an arrangement to deliver our pages to our printer in Kerry. We were supposed to rendezvous by one a.m. at the latest, but many was the time when I would still be frantically applying the final touches to the layout while the clock ticked and Liam or Mairin waited tensely beside me, snatching the page as soon as I was done and haring down the stairs to where Niall was already waiting, revving the engine of his beat-up mustard-yellow Austin Maxi. Then they would race through the streets in pursuit of the already departed van. One time they got all the way to Urlingford, Kilkenny, some seventy miles from Dublin, before they caught it.

However, it did not escape my attention that, on the longest nights, various exhausted members of staff would discreetly disappear into the editor's office, only to emerge minutes later with a spring in their step and a glint in their eye, merrily chattering away. One day I burst in and found them all poised around a table on which sat a small, square mirror with several fine lines of white powder arranged upon it.

'I knew it!' I declared, although in truth I only had the vaguest idea what was going on. I was an avid reader of Hunter S. Thompson but he was stronger on amusing euphemisms for illicit substances than on the techniques employed in their consumption. I insisted that I be included in this particular ritual and refused to be dissuaded by several parties apparently concerned with my youth and naïvety. So I was handed a rolled-up £5 note and instructed that the correct procedure was to put one end of it to my nostril and the other on the mirror then inhale deeply. I followed my instructions to the letter, resulting in gasps of either horror or admiration from my fellow members of staff.

'He's had the bloody lot!' shrieked one malcontent.

'You're only supposed to snort one line,' someone explained, a little too late.

'Bloody hell, Neil. We'll have to call you Hoover Factory!' said another (a reference to an obscure Elvis Costello B-side).

But hey, I wasn't complaining. I bounced out of the office with the spring of a kangaroo spoiling for a fight and threw myself into the creation of pages (not just pages! Works of art!) with renewed zest.

Actually, I am not sure how productive this period of cocaine consumption was. Certainly it would lift spirits but usually this would result in Liam and myself standing around blathering, making hats out of record sleeves, frisbeeing unwanted vinyl out the window, firing off jokes and pursuing surreal lines of thought that would have the office in stitches. Then Niall would inevitably emerge from his office to suggest that perhaps it might be in our best interests to get some work done, at which point the mood of euphoria would collapse and we would all sink back to our desks to contemplate the gruesome immensity of the task still in hand.

The worst was the launch of that first British issue. By then, my huge posters of Bono were pasted all over the London Underground, anticipating our arrival. I remember going in to *Hot Press'* offices on Friday and not getting home again till Tuesday morning, having snatched a few hours' rest over the weekend on the floor of Niall and Mairin's apartment. When we finally put the issue to bed we all stood out on the balcony, looking over sleepy Dublin in the washed-out colours of the early-morning sunrise. The exhaustion felt good, though. We felt as if we had really achieved something. We were wearily optimistic about the future.

By some process of bad planning, one particularly challenging production weekend was immediately followed by the first *Hot Press* awards ceremony, sponsored by Stag (a brand of cider) with a presentation in a hotel and a party in McGonagles. To my dismay, there was no marching powder left in the office to sustain our flagging spirits. Someone from what was optimistically known as the advertising department (despite the fact that staff numbers rarely exceeded two) volunteered to procure alternative stimulants and quickly returned with a large bag of speed. This was a new substance to me but what the hell, I considered myself an expert at narcotics consumption by now. I was handed an individual wrap, which I tossed out on the table and snorted in one go. My advertising colleague's mouth was agape. 'That was enough to last you a week,' he spluttered. Fuck that! The Hoover Factory was ready to party!

I don't remember a whole lot about the occasion, apart from the disaster with the statuettes. I had designed the award – a figure of Elvis in full hip-swivelling pose – and drafted in an art-college friend, Grainne, to manufacture the actual figurines in painted ceramics. They looked lovely but were extremely fragile; thus as the great and good of the Irish music business stepped up to collect their awards, the figures kept detaching from their bases and generally falling apart. U2 picked up two awards, for Best Band and Best Album. 'Are you trying to tell me something about my career prospects?' Bono joked, after I had helped him reassemble a broken statuette.

The night flashed by in an amphetamine blur. I recall hitching a ride back on Ivan's motorbike from a post-party celebration. Not being in possession of a helmet and not wishing to be stopped by the police in my present condition, I strapped a fruit bowl to my head with my trouser belt.

Just say no to drugs, kids.

I thought it was about time I got myself some transport. My dad (himself a former biker) had bought my brother a motorbike but I was discouraged from following suit. For some reason, it was taken as a family truth that, while Ivan was sensible (a damned lie! But he was good at pulling the wool over my parents' eyes) and physically graceful, I was impulsive and unco-ordinated, apparently not a good combination on two wheels with a couple of hundred horsepower. 'Anyone who rides a motorbike has to be prepared to face the fact that they will crash it,' according to my father, whose own biker days had come to an end with a write-off that grew more spectacular with each retelling. 'The trick is not to hurt yourself. The way you carry on, you could hurt yourself getting off a bus!' I couldn't really argue with that because, in fact, I had once hurt myself quite badly getting off a bus, my attempt to disembark while the bus was still moving having been interrupted by a car travelling behind.

Being a skilled mechanic and a compulsive DIY enthusiast, Dad offered not to buy me a car but to build me one instead. My mother had an old Mini Cooper which had broken down and was rusting in the driveway. Dad arrived home one day with another dilapidated Mini he had picked up for fifty quid and announced that out of these two Mini wrecks he was going to create one Super-Mini. Disregarding my ungrateful scepticism, he went to work in the garage, where he laboured for most of the summer.

Meanwhile, he financed a trip to Setanta studios in Dundalk for Yeah! Yeah! to make our first demo. Like most bands venturing into a studio for the first time, we had absolutely no idea what we were doing, but we took along a local sound engineer to guide us through – though I am not convinced he had much more studio experience than us. The band simply set up and played three songs live, to which we later added a smattering of overdubs. Timing was the most obvious problem. Leo was an inventive drummer who worked hard at his skills, but he was having difficulty playing to the relentlessly steady clicks of a metronome and in the end we had to abandon it, settling for backing tracks of wildly varying pace. But the bass was plump, the guitars were sparkly and the singing . . .

Fuck it! The voice I heard in my head was pure of tone, abounding with melodiousness, pulsating with energy and bursting with emotion. The voice coming back through the huge studio speakers was, well, 'adequate to the task' was about the best you could say.

'Ah, we'll just whack the reverb up on that; it'll be grand,' suggested our engineer.

Of course it would be!

We played our first headline gig at the Summit Inn in Howth, somehow selling a couple of hundred tickets in advance. Mind you, the tickets did promise an appearance by 'the tempting Bumpkin Betsy' who (rumour had it) would be performing an outrageous (and entirely illegal) striptease. Betsy was, in fact, a fellow called Anto, who even his closest friends would cheerfully describe as 'mad as a March hare'. Anto took to the stage in full drag, slowly divesting items of clothing to roars of encouragement until it became apparent that Betsy was not exactly as advertised. We thought this would be a merry jape but hadn't reckoned on a bunch of squaddies from the Irish army who had made a special trip all the way from their barracks in Dublin. They became so outraged at the absence of bona fide tits and ass that they attempted to storm the stage and assault the hapless Anto, who was quite willing to take on the lot of them. The ensuing mêlée was settled by the extraordinary diplomatic skills of Leo's friend Hughie O'Leary, who persuaded the squaddies that they should be satisfied with appropriating Anto's bra and stockings. 'I think you've got to learn to respect your audience,' Hughie cautioned us later — advice we took very seriously since Hughie's mother was Maureen Potter, Ireland's best-loved comedienne.

The evening might have been messy but it wasn't a disaster. We had pulled in a crowd, made some money and felt ready to step up a gear and start doing headline shows in Dublin. But before that there was a planned trip to the country. I had taken delivery of my hand-crafted Super-Mini, which, much to my surprise, was a thing of beauty — painted letterbox-red with a tasteful leopardskin interior. The plan was for Yeah! Yeah! to take the car on its maiden voyage to the West of Ireland, where we would attend a rock festival at which the Pretenders and Ian Dury were performing. Ivan could not make the trip, because he was due to take his motorbike licence test that weekend, so his spot in the Mini was appropriated by Hughie.

My dad had made it clear he did not approve of this trip. He appeared to be finding it hard to fully entrust his creation to me and repeatedly cautioned me about making long journeys before it was properly run in. But since my parents were currently enjoying a fortnight's vacation in France, I figured what they did not know could not hurt them. So off we went!

There was much carousing on the journey. The car had been loaded up with tins of beer, of which my passengers liberally availed themselves. Not to put too fine a point on it, Hughie, Leo and Deco were soon pissed as a trio of farts, singing, joking and hurling abuse at passing pedestrians. I was completely sober, of course, not because I was taking my duties as driver seriously (for I too was singing, joking and hurling abuse) but simply because I didn't drink. We raced down potholed country roads, rattling along at a fine old speed, with Dad's engine holding up much better than predicted. The sun was out. The roads were clear. Life was good.

We almost made it, too.

We were about fifteen miles from the festival, high with anticipation, picking up speed as we drove down a steep hill. And then something happened. The steering wheel jerked in my hands. We were slewing off the road, the car moving in a different direction than it should have been. I had lost control of the vehicle. I slammed on the brakes. We weren't stopping.

'We're going to crash!' I said. Cold inside.

'What d'you say?' asked Hughie, in the passenger seat.

'We're crashing,' I said, with the dead calm of utter hopelessness.

The Mini went off the road at the bottom of the hill, smashing head-on into a vertical grass bank.

10

I suffered concussion, so I have to rely on the reports of others to describe what happened next. Apparently, I got out of the car, which was savagely crumpled, and slowly walked around it, examining the damage, tutting and muttering, 'Hmm . . . I see,' while inside my passengers groaned. My spectacles had flown up during the collision, and I had smashed my face against the steering wheel, crushing my broken glasses into my forehead. Blood was pouring out, running down my pale face, getting in my eyes.

I vaguely remember the inside of an ambulance. I have an image of myself lying on a gurney in the corridor outside a busy emergency room, making a call from a public telephone. Apparently I spoke to Leo's father. I told him everything was fine.

I came to in a hospital ward, head heavily bandaged, the world a complete blur without my glasses. Deco was in the bed next to me, suffering only from a chipped tooth. Hughie was opposite, one broken leg in a cast. Leo was next to him and he was not in a good state. He had badly broken the ball joint of his right hip. He was moaning with pain. Hughie was calling out on behalf of his friend. 'Nurse, nurse, we need some fuckin' drugs here. We need them now!' In the distant background, bizarrely, we could hear an echoey wash of rock'n'roll from the festival.

'Well, at least we'll get to hear Ian Dury,' sighed Hughie. We all started to titter.

'Fuck it, Hughie, don't make me laugh,' complained Leo. 'It hurts.'

'Maybe youse should record that Liverpool anthem: "I'll Never Walk Again!"' suggested Hughie. 'You could all go onstage in motorized wheelchairs! Leo could play his bongos with a pair of customized walking sticks. It'll be fantastic. When you go onstage people'll be saying, "Break a leg . . . Oh, sorry, you're way ahead of me."'

'Stop it, Hughie, it hurts,' laughed Leo.

We listened to that distant music for two days, laughing with mounting hysteria as Hughie fired off lines of increasingly black patter about our situation, although every cry of pain from Leo would send a chill through the ward and an arrow deep into my heart. Was I responsible for that?

'The misfortunes of others are not a source for humour, Mr O'Leary,' a nurse complained after one of Hughie's comic outbursts.

'I think it was Shakespeare who said that life is a comedy of fuckin' errors, nurse,' countered Hughie. 'Though I may be misquoting.'

I'm sure the nurses were glad to see the back of us. Deco and I were informed we were free to go after two days, while Hughie and Leo would be dispatched back to Dublin by ambulance. My clothes were returned to me, unlaundered and caked with dried blood. I put them on and, looking like a refugee from a World War I battlefield, went to have my dressing removed. The young doctor who peeled off my bandages stared at me aghast. 'Uhm, it appears someone forgot to stitch you up,' he gulped, apologetically. I looked in a mirror. There were huge flaps of skin hanging off my bruised forehead.

So they stitched me up and released me and I went wandering off into some strange country town, sewn up like Frankenstein's monster, with a jagged, bulging, purple scar on my head, dressed in blood-stained clothes, unable to see more than a few inches in front of me, with only Deco and his chipped tooth for company. We found our way to the Garda station, where I had been asked to report. 'What the blazes happened to you, boy?' declared the shocked officer in charge.

'Nothing,' I said. 'I've come about my Mini.'

I was led into the yard, where the bent and broken remains had been towed. I peered in, through windows of shattered glass. Even with my bad eyesight, I could see that every surface of the car was littered with squashed, empty cans of lager, but the Garda made no mention of that in their report. 'The marks left on the road indicate that you suffered a spontaneous blow-out to the front-left tyre, son,' the officer told me. 'It was just an unfortunate accident. Have you got insurance?'

'Yes, sir,' I replied, feeling a weight of guilt lift off my shoulders.

'It'll be put down as an act of God,' he said.

I might have known that bastard would be behind it.

We had to take a train back to Dublin. The tickets were £15 each. I had only thirty quid on me and Deco was flat broke, so we weren't able to afford so much as a cup of tea during the journey of several hours. Nor could we find a seat, so we stood all the way back to Dublin, watching the Irish landscape pass in silence, the shock of the past few days finally sinking in.

This brush with mortality had the effect of quickening my resolve. Leo had metal plates inserted into his hip to hold it together. We visited him in hospital, pledging our loyalty and receiving his pledge in return. As soon as he was fit, we would be back on the road. It would take more than an act of God to stop this band.

U2 released their second album, *October*, in October 1981. I tend to think now that of all their albums this has weathered least well but back then I was an uncritical fan and I wrote a glowing, excitable review in *Hot Press*. I was utterly thrilled by the way they had expanded their sonic template, enriching the potential of their sound. Everything was bigger, brighter, shinier, with the addition of Edge's ringing piano chords to the mix. Even Bono's voice had started to fill out, strengthened by a year of relentless touring. The record's principal weakness, in hindsight, are the lyrics, or lack of them. Bono's notebook had been stolen backstage at a gig and so, while they had been recording over the summer in Dublin, he had to rely on his improvisational skills in the studio. The subject matter of *October* was spiritual faith, as indicated by the epic opening track, an all-cylinders-firing rock hymn, 'Gloria', in which Bono calls out, 'I try to stand up but I can't find my feet / I try to speak up but only in you I'm complete / Gloria in te Domine'. I wonder if my article had played a part in this, releasing Bono from fear of criticism about his Christianity? But if he was calling on the Holy Spirit to animate him in front of the microphone, the line to Heaven must have been faulty. This represented a curiously inarticulate speech of the heart, with Bono supplanting his former 'oo-ee-oo's with the oft-repeated phrase 'Rejoice!' After *Boy*, Bono had talked to me with typical ebulliance about making an epic album about the struggle between good and evil – their *Sgt. Pepper*, he'd called it in a moment of particularly extravagant enthusiasm. Well, this wasn't it. *October* ends with 'Is That All?' in which Bono repeats the question 'Is that all you want from me?' He may have been addressing God but a demanding listener's answer would surely have to be a resounding 'No!'

I now know there was a fierce debate going on within the band about their Christian commitment, with members of Shalom bringing pressure to bear about how they should behave. Gavin Friday had been the first to leave, reacting incredulously to suggestions that his band change their name to the Deuteronomy Prunes and desist from wearing eyeliner. Guggi and other Prunes had not been long in following. Larry was the first member of U2 to leave Shalom, fearing that he was in danger of turning into a bigot. Bono and Edge struggled somewhat longer, at times questioning whether God and rock'n'roll were compatible, but all eventually severed their links with the Bible group. 'I've never found a church I was comfortable in,' Bono admitted to me years later. 'Religion holds the church above the spirit of God. I think that religion is often the enemy of faith.'

That same month, Yeah! Yeah! started gigging again, playing a riotous set in the Asgard Hotel in Howth. It was such a relief to be back on stage, with Leo perched (a little gingerly, perhaps) behind the drums. A number of our more dedicated fans accompanied us back home, where a spontaneous party broke out. Deco and I ended up in my bed with a girl (who we shall name Viva for the sake of her dignity) sandwiched between us: now this was definitely the kind of behaviour I had signed up for! We were startled, however, by a knock on the door, which swung open to reveal my dad, who wanted to congratulate us on our performance (I should stress that he was referring to the gig). Viva hid under the covers while Declan and I sat bolt upright next to each other, naked, in my double bed, none of which seemed to bother my dad in the least. He chatted for a while then said, 'All right, time to hit the sack. Goodnight, Neil. Night, Declan. Night, Viva.'

She stuck her head out of the covers as the door closed. 'How did he know I was here?'

'I have no idea,' I confessed. 'How do parents know anything? They just do!'

When I slipped out of the room to go to the toilet, Dad caught me on the landing. 'Just try to keep it quiet in there, OK?' he said. 'I don't mind what you get up to but I don't want your mother being upset.'

On my return journey from the toilet, there was my mother! 'I know what's going on in there,' she said, coyly. 'Better not let Dad find out; I don't think he'd approve.'

What kind of fucked-up family values were they teaching me?

We gigged relentlessly throughout the following months, a headlining show at a packed community centre confirming that we had ascended to the same dizzy heights of local stardom occupied by the legendary Rocky De Valera.

In December, we landed the support for the Teardrop Explodes' tour of Ireland. The Teardrops were from Liverpool and were being hailed as one of the most exciting bands of the era, along with stablemates Echo & the Bunnymen. Their manager was a young, energetic, bespectacled Scotsman named Bill Drummond, whose sometimes eccentric enthusiasm for the possibilities of rock music was immensely engaging. 'It doesn't matter if you can play,' I heard him opine. 'Musicianship is very overrated. Belief should come first. Greatness will follow.' It was a philosophy I could identify with. Julian Cope, frontman of the Teardrop Explodes, was well-spoken, polite and friendly, with a kind of puppyish enthusiasm. ('All right, guys?' he said to us, thoughtfully popping into our dressing room before our set. 'Just go out and enjoy yourselves, because that's what it's all about.') Yet on stage at McGonagles he was an entirely different proposition, bouncing fearlessly around with little thought for personal safety, colliding with objects with a force that made the audience wince, berating his band for not giving enough and urging the crowd to give more. At one point, out of mounting frustration, Julian appeared to have an onstage nervous breakdown, collapsing with frustration at the proceedings, screaming at his bandmates to stop playing while he launched into a frantic monologue about how important it was to make this moment real, make this gig matter. I was mightily impressed. Then, at the Cork Opera House the following night, he suffered an identical breakdown at the exact same point in the show. Standing at the sound desk, I asked Bill, 'Does he do this every night?'

'How else do you get to become a legend?' replied Bill.

Learning such lessons as we went along, Yeah! Yeah! worked hard to make every gig an occasion, with new songs, new gags, new gimmicks. We drafted in comedians to support us and showed videos on TV sets at the back of the stage. In February 1982, we started a Thursday-night residency upstairs at a Dublin bar called the Magnet. We had finally unveiled our demo, wittily packaged as *The Tape of Things to Come*. The Magnet gigs slowly started to draw an audience. There were thirty people the first week. Seventy the second. More than a hundred on the third. We received our first review in *Hot Press*, from which we liberally quoted in a press release:

Yeah! Yeah! create 'the atmosphere of a youth club hop', receiving a reaction of 'uninhibited, all-enveloping enthusiasm', wrote Liam Mackey in *Hot Press* music paper. Liam went on to say, 'And certainly Yeah! Yeah!'s music inspires and deserves a suitably abandoned reaction . . . if the Yeah! Yeah! ethos baits such critical shorthand as "good-time dance pop", then that is neither to suggest they are one dimensional nor simplistic . . . they strive to inject originality, intelligence and modest adventure into an established methodology.'

Liam was none too happy when he saw what I had done, my judicious use of dots neatly excising the criticisms that had been at the heart of his review. 'That might be what I said but it is not what I meant,' he chided me. 'You should get a job writing press releases for the government.'

So, for the sake of historical probity and to allow readers a more objective analysis of this pilgrim's musical progress, let me restore some of the missing sections.

Creatively their ambition is always true but their aim is sometimes right off. As the group's sole lead instrumentalist, back-up vocalist/guitarist Ivan tries to shoulder more musical weight than he can, as yet, handle. When he allows a note to slip through his fingers or fails to nail down a chord with anything less than complete authority, Yeah! Yeah!'s whole sound suffers as a result.

And if the Yeah! Yeah! ethos baits such critical shorthand as 'good-time dance pop', then that is neither to suggest they are one dimensional nor simplistic. Indeed, it is entirely because they strive to inject originality, intelligence and modest adventure into an established methodology that their mistakes clang louder, their sloppiness is all the more disappointing.

Liam concluded that we needed to take more time and trouble perfecting our craft if Yeah! Yeah!

wanted to move beyond the admittedly enjoyable but ultimately self deceiving kind of gig, where the crowd is sympathetic to their mistakes.

My usual response to this would have been, 'Ah, what the fuck does he know?' But I was well aware that Liam knew his stuff. We were going to have to redouble our efforts in the rehearsal room.

We had to take a break in March anyway, when Leo went into hospital to have the plates removed from his hip. Ivan and I kept ourselves busy by looking up the addresses of every record company in Britain and Ireland and duly mailing off cassettes. After a few weeks we gave up checking the post for replies. The music industry had not apparently been gripped by a feverish conviction that the next big thing was lurking in an Irish fishing village. Perhaps the tapes had gone astray in the post.

On 31 March 1982, I turned twenty-one, an occasion chiefly notable for my first imbibement of alcohol. My parents threw a big party at the Summit Inn. Ivan, Deco and I performed a set of rock'n'roll standards with members of Deaf Actor and the Gravediggers. I was drunk. Pissed. Bladdered.

One lousy half-pint bottle of cider, that's all it took.

'Go on, Neil! Fuckin' get it down ya!' yelled my friends.

So I did.

And what a glorious time I had. I felt relaxed and free. Unshackled from any lingering chains of internal inhibition. What had I been so afraid of?

After that there was no stopping me. I fell in with a bad crowd, your honour. Principal among my corruptors were a pair of students, Ian and Clanger, much given to the demon weed, who made it their business to teach me how to inhale. They lived in a rented house with a shifting cast of other reprobates, with a pool table in the living room and a fish-tank full of piranhas in the kitchen, which they fed with live mice bought from a pet shop. I remember the first time I drank myself legless, at a midnight beach party at the bottom of Howth cliffs. Somebody had been handing me mugs of port, saying they would keep me warm, as we sat round a fire in the cold Irish air, singing and joking, the black sea lapping up around us. Watching the local drunks, I had always assumed some kind of mental fugue enveloped them, clouding their brains and slurring their thoughts. But I was fine, rabbiting away, not a bother on me. Until I tried to stand up and promptly fell over. Ian and Clanger propped me between them as they walked me around the stony beach, trying to sober me up for the journey home, which involved ascending a rope ladder up a sheer cliff face. Finally my custodians explained that I was just going to have to puke it all up. I assumed the position and disgorged the wine-red contents of my stomach. Oh what joy! I felt a cold shiver of relief spread through my body. And here was me, all these years, thinking the drunks throwing up in the gutters were sick and miserable. Vomiting was fantastic!

Leo came out of hospital. He had to use a walking stick to protect his hip but, with some adjustments to his drum stool, found his musical capabilities undiminished. Ivan and I proposed that we all take a year off regular employment. We wanted Yeah! Yeah! to turn professional, which would mean rehearsing every day and effectively treating the band as a full-time job.

Deco was easy to persuade but Leo was sceptical. He already had a full-time job, working in a junior position at OKB advertising agency, the facilities of which we frequently availed ourselves of to create our zany posters. And he wasn't sure if he wanted to give that up to spend all day in a rehearsal room with the monumental egos and intense ambitions of the McCormick brothers. It was not all fun and laughter, as anyone who has been in a band with siblings can probably attest. We could – and did – argue over everything, from whose name went first on the songwriting credits to what colour shirts we should wear in a photo session; from what tempo we should perform a song to who got to drive to and from the gig.

This is about average for the brotherhood of rock'n'roll. Around that time I met one of my heroes, Ray Davies, backstage after a Kinks concert in Dublin's RDS auditorium. 'I like your shirt,' declared the rock legend, admiring the purple, patterned, polo-neck, shoulder-buttoned psychedelic creation I had picked up on a trip to Carnaby Street (the very shirt I had fought with my brother about during a photo session). Ray was then married to Chrissie Hynde, and introduced me. 'I'm sure I used to have the exact same shirt when I was younger,' said Ray.

'The classics never go away,' said Chrissie, drolly.

Not about to let a networking opportunity like this slip through my fingers, I told the couple all about the group I had with my brother.

'It won't last,' was Ray's gloomy prognosis.

'Why?' I said, startled.

'Brothers shouldn't be in groups together,' said Ray, whose own brother, Dave, was lurking on the other side of the room. 'You both want what the other's got and you just wind up trying to outdo each other all the time. It's a recipe for great unhappiness.'

'Don't listen to him,' Chrissie reassured me. 'He's been fighting with Dave for twenty years and the Kinks are still together.'

'That doesn't mean I'm happy about it,' said Ray.

The sibling band is a more common phenomenon than you might think. Apart from the famous family bands (the Jacksons, the Osmonds, the Neville Brothers, the Allman Brothers Band, the Isley Brothers, the Beach Boys and the Bee Gees), there were brothers in AC/DC, the Black Crowes, INXS, Styx, Creedence Clearwater Revival, the Spencer Davis Group, Ten Years After, the Stooges, Crowded House, Dire Straits and Spandau Ballet. And then, of course, there were the Everly Brothers, whose relationship became so poisonous they actually broke up on stage in 1971, when Phil smashed his guitar and stormed off complaining about Don's performance. This tradition has been warmly revived by the squabbling siblings in Oasis, who have broken up on stage so often people think it's part of the act.

I have always thought that Cain and Abel represent a more realistic model of brotherly relations than television's all-for-one Waltons. As growing boys, you spend your childhood locked together in a love-hate battle for domination, competing for the attention of your parents, struggling to become individuals when the whole world behaves as if you are joined at the hip. And then, when you are old enough to forge a life for yourself, you elect to form a band with your closest rival and spend your adult life fighting over chord changes instead of toys.

There are, of course, certain advantages. Bands play together for years before achieving the kind of telepathy that comes naturally to siblings. A commonality of nature and nurture enables you to predict each other's next move and instinctively play to one another's strengths. Voices blend effortlessly through shared tone and timbre. And you don't have to take out an advert in a music paper to find your first group member.

But there is always another, darker side. I think Ray Davies was right when he said that you both want what the other's got. I remember how threatened I would feel when Ivan would, occasionally, write a song on his own. If he could write, play and sing lead vocals, what did he need me for? For my part, I could barely string four chords together on the guitar but I would insist on doing just that at every opportunity, composing at least a triple album's worth of material around those chords, arranged in every conceivable order. At our best, Ivan and I were more than the sum of our parts. But at our worst, we were in danger of cancelling each other out.

Leo took his concerns to Barry Devlin, the erstwhile leader of Irish folk rockers Horslips. The group had recently (and acrimoniously) split up and Devlin had taken a job as an art director at OKB. The former rock star came along to one of our Magnet gigs to judge our prospects for himself. Afterwards, Leo introduced us.

'You're not the same Neil McCormick who works for *Hot Press*?' inquired Devlin, suspiciously.

'No way,' I said, without blinking. 'It's a common name.'

'That bastard stuck the knife in Horslips and twisted it,' grumbled Devlin, with tangible bitterness. 'He slated our last album. Destroyed it. You'd think *Hot Press* would support a band like Horslips after everything we've done for the Irish music business, not let some pompous prat who doesn't know his arse from his elbow trample all over us with his facile drivel.'

'He sounds like a complete shit,' I agreed. 'I've always been a big fan of Horslips myself.'

We must have passed the Devlin test, because Leo decided to throw his lot in with us. My dad also offered his assistance. The motor industry was going through crippling problems and he had accepted voluntary redundancy, with a large pay-off. He was in no great hurry to find another job and in the meantime was taking a keen interest in our musical progress – turning up at gigs, where fans referred to him as Mr Mac. He felt we could achieve our goals if we kept focussed and suggested he might manage us.

To be honest, I was not happy about this development at all. On a purely selfish level, I worried that it would curb the potential for debauchery. How could you snort drugs off the naked bosoms of rampant bisexual groupies while your dad was in the dressing room? Not that this had ever happened, but I lived in hope. And besides, being managed by your father seemed to go against the entire rebellious spirit of rock'n'roll. Surely I was supposed to be offending my parents, not collaborating with them? We would be in danger of becoming a laughing stock, the Partridge Family of the Irish music scene. But Dad quickly demonstrated his potential by organizing the purchase of a Hi-Ace van and setting up a packed gigging schedule. Over two months in summer, we played sixteen shows, including dates as far afield as Wexford, Rosslare, Cork and Swords.

A small hardcore of friends and fans followed us wherever we played, the same faces turning up in the front row from one side of Ireland to the other. The gigs were rowdy, joyous affairs. Something clicked for me onstage. I would be consumed by the moment and the song. Time would expand and contract, as if moving in sync with my own consciousness. I could feel when attention was slipping away and it was as if I was able to reach out and draw the attention back in. I felt confident that I could cope with anything up there in the lights, that I had the ability to ensure a good time was had by all, whether there were ten or two hundred people in the room. We always got encores. Gigs regularly ended with a stage invasion, with our most ardent female fans joining in the backing vocals on 'Twist and Shout'.

One of these girls was Joan Cody, my new sweetheart. Joan was attending university with some of my friends and had been coming to Yeah! Yeah! gigs for a while. One friend thought we would be well suited, commenting that he had never met two people so utterly obstinate, controversially opinionated and wilfully contrary. I am not entirely sure if such characteristics were solid grounds for romantic compatibility but Joan was a pouting, beautiful blonde, much sought after by my contemporaries, and I enthusiastically joined the pursuit. Despite having legions of admirers, the object of our desires remained resolutely single, so naturally it was rumoured that Joan must be a lesbian. How else could she resist all those overtures from hot-blooded Irish males? In fact, she was fiercely proud and secretly insecure, not the most approachable combination. But I chipped away at her defences over the course of a long year until she finally surrendered, one moonlit night, in the romantic setting of a brown, second-hand, rusty, beaten-up and decidedly not very super Mini I had recently purchased for the princely sum of £100.

Did you know that, technically, you cannot commit rape in a Mini? This is a peculiar item of trivia I picked up from newspapers following the dramatic failure of a sexual-assault case in the Irish courts. Apparently, the interior of a Mini is too cramped for anything but consensual sex. And even that, I can testify from experience, tends to be of a complex and uncomfortable nature, requiring a great deal of physical flexibility and a willingness to overlook the potential dangers of the gear stick.

I remained art director at *Hot Press*, in a part-time capacity. Which actually did not change my working arrangements all that much; it just meant I wasn't hanging around the office when there was nothing to do. *Hot Press* was in a state of crisis, lurching eratically from issue to issue with mounting debts. The British launch had not gone well, having been poleaxed by industrial action from civil servants in the UK which commenced almost immediately afterwards. Lightning strikes seemed designed specifically to thwart the distribution of *Hot Press*. Entire issues ended up stranded in customs depots. Several early issues never made it on to the streets, money was being poured down a black hole, advertisers were refusing to pay their bills, *Hot Press*' credibility in the UK was fatally damaged and, after a year of trying to regain lost ground, it reached the point where even pulling out of Britain was not enough to save the magazine. Publication dates became increasingly unreliable, with matters hitting rock bottom when Niall had to borrow from his poorly paid staff to keep the magazine afloat. I put in my

£500 savings but there was no guarantee that bankruptcy could be staved off for long.

But Niall had made a lot of friends in the Irish music business and a few of these rallied round when it counted. A concert was organized at Punchestown Racecourse, outside Dublin, with performers donating their services free and proceeds going to the magazine. I designed a poster, featuring co-headliners Rory Gallagher and U2. It still seemed strange, putting schoolfriends in the elevated company of someone who had been a rock star as long as I could remember. I watched the show from the side of the stage with Ali and wondered how long would I be able to get up this close. Were U2 going to leave us all behind? As Bono perilously clambered the scaffolding and the audience roared their approval, I thought to myself, 'Well, at least I'll get my money back.'

Our new professional status meant that Ivan had to turn down an enticing job as recording engineer at Eamon Andrews, a tiny studio usually used for radio voiceovers. He recommended our roadie, Ivan O'Shea, for the position instead, who returned the favour by wangling us a day of free recording time. It was only an 8-track, yet still contained a desk covered with a quite bewildering array of knobs and switches. I could not begin to comprehend how recording a sound could have so many potential variables. Sadly I think our engineer felt the same way. And what were we supposed to do with all these tracks? We put drums on one track, bass on another, guitar on another, lead vocals on another, backing vocals on another . . . And found that we had three tracks left over with nothing to go on them. We recorded everything live and each musician had a hand in setting up the mix – which meant Deco called for more bass, Ivan for more guitar, Leo for more drums and me for more vocals, until all the faders were up full and there was no room left for negotiation. We blasted through something like eighteen songs and left mighty satisfied with our day's work. It was about the same amount of time The Beatles had taken to record their first album, we noted approvingly. What people were doing for three months in 24-track studios was a mystery to me. Lots of drugs, probably.

We packaged a demo of four songs and sent it out into the void where our previous demo had vanished without trace. Some of the songs had begun to get play on Dublin's pirate radio stations and we were convinced that this time the record industry could not ignore us.

When responses finally started arriving, the content of the letters was so standardized we weren't even sure which tape they were referring to. 'Dear Sir / Madam,' they began (though sometimes they had the group's name hastily scribbled in the required space), 'Many thanks for sending your material for our consideration . . .'; 'Thank you for sending your demonstration cassette, which we listened to with interest . . .'; 'Thank you for giving us the opportunity to hear your material . . .'

So far so good.

'Unfortunately . . .'

Things invariably took a turn for the worse at this particular juncture.

'At the present time . . .'; 'after careful consideration . . .'; 'having listened with great interest . . .'; 'we do not feel . . .'; 'we have decided to pass . . .'; 'not what we are looking for . . .'; 'not interested . . .'; 'not suitable . . .'

Still, there was hope near the end.

'If you would like to send any further material . . .'; 'in the future . . .'; 'we would be very pleased to consider . . .'; 'do not hesitate . . .'; 'please feel free . . .'

And finally . . .

'Thank you very much for your consideration.'

Oh, it was nothing, really.

The really disillusioning thing for us at the time was the fact that these were all form letters. Though couched in encouraging language, there was no comment on or criticism of the music other than to inform us of its unsuitability. At the present time.

Of course, I understand now why there was no attempt to address the actual content of our tapes. Because the chances are that no one in the A&R department had actually listened to them.

A&R stands for 'artists and repertoire'. A record company's A&R department's functions can include a great deal of involvement with its acts (booking them into studios, arranging producers and so on), but the principal responsibility of A&R is discovering and signing new acts. These people are the talent scouts charged with dealing with the unknown singers, songwriters and bands who fill the vast, uncharted depths of the bottom end of the music business. They deal with the hopefuls and are themselves the focus of an almost unimaginable amount of hope. It is not an enviable position to be in.

Record companies receive hundreds of demos every week, each containing three or more songs, recorded in wildly varying conditions by people with even more wildly varying degrees of talent, all screaming for attention. Senior A&R people are not interested in the time-consuming, tedious and largely unrewarding task of listening to these tapes so they are passed straight to the most junior members of staff for sifting. Any enthusiasm with which the junior initially approaches this job soon evaporates when faced with a constant influx of perhaps twenty-five or thirty demos a day, many of truly apalling standard and virtually none with the sound quality of an average record. So they flick through, listen to the music in short stabs and move on. And then they sign another rejection slip.

They may come across something interesting and put it aside for further appraisal but the very process severely restricts the likelihood of this. A junior A&R man (now managing director of a major label) once told me, 'Off the record, I listen to only about half the tapes. I'll eliminate them by presentation, name, song titles, anything. As far as I know we've never signed anyone based on a demo sent in on spec anyway. There's always been something else – press reviews, radio, independent success – to draw attention to them.'

This is what I have learned about A&R over the years: it is essentially a glorified system for keeping musicians out of record companies.

Yeah! Yeah!'s gigs were getting wilder and stranger. There was an edge to the band's performances, perhaps from a sense of growing desperation. Some of this was coming from Leo, whose hip joint was gradually disintegrating. Doctors were intimating that they would have to cement it into place, a process that would require extensive operations after which he could expect to walk with a limp for the rest of his life. Whether or not he would be able to continue playing drums was another big question. All of this was preying on him; he was drinking a lot, doing reckless things, bringing an element of hysteria to the band's wacky presentation.

At the Summit Inn before a show in September, one of the local trouble-makers muttered 'Cripple' as Leo passed on his way to the stage.

'I heard that!' said Leo, spinning suddenly and smashing the loud-mouth across the face with his wooden walking stick.

The howling miscreant's friends hurled themselves at Leo, who went down under a rain of kicks and blows. Huey piled in to the fray, battering all around him. Someone's shirt was ripped off. Huey somehow found himself at the bottom of a scrum of bodies, his hands and legs pinned. At which point there was a godawful scream of pain, then Huey's assailant leaped to his feet, clutching his chest, bellowing incredulously: 'He bit my fuckin' nipple off!'

The trouble-makers were hustled out of the venue. Huey was treated as a hero. 'It was nothing, really,' he said. 'I just saw this pink thing floating in front of my face and clamped my jaw around it!'

The gig was suitably intense. One of the best. And one of the last. We seemed to have reached a plateau. We had an audience but it wasn't growing; we didn't seem to be making a real impact on the local scene. Record companies clearly weren't interested. There was still a feeling that we needed to shift up a gear but in reality this group was already screaming along in fifth, with nothing more to screw out of the engine.

Leo decided to leave. Ivan and I did not try to dissuade him. Declan threw in the towel as soon as he heard the news. I think we were all, secretly, quite relieved. It was time to move on.

It was 1983. New wave was old hat. Pop was mutating, spawning new genres and subgenres with amazing rapidity, empowered by the increasing sophistication and adaptability of the synthesizer. No longer was it solely the preserve of sci-fi geeks (though there were plenty of them about, dreaming of electric sheep in the dreary sub-Bowie monotones of Gary Numan). Synths were at the flamboyant heart of the gaudy new-romantic movement; they provided the trashy settings for exponents of eccentric electropop such as the Human League and Soft Cell and the plastic extravaganzas of state-of-the-art bubblegum by *Eurovision* winners Bucks Fizz and blow-dried glamour duo Dollar. Synths could replicate banks of strings, percussion, horns, bass – entire orchestras of sound – with individual settings for pretty much every instrument you had ever heard of and some that had never even existed before (space bass? Ambient pads?). They had things with names like oscillators, arpeggiators and pitch-benders and functions like programmable patches, polyphonic voices and filter sweeps. It seemed to us that to make modern pop records in the eighties you no longer really needed a band. But you definitely needed a synth.

It was relatively easy to persuade Dad to invest in a Roland Juno 60, a high-performance analogue synthesizer. His faith in the unproven talent of his offspring was almost as blind as our own. I had a vision of a new kind of pop music. It would bring together apparently incompatible ingredients. It would take the glossy, sonic, ultra-manufactured, soulless perfectionism of Dollar (I really had a soft spot for this airbrushed couple, whose records dripped with hi-tech luxuriousness) and marry it to the lyrical complexity and emotional substance of Elvis Costello. It would take the driving propulsion of modern dance beats and fuse them to the melodic songwriting template of the Beatles. It would take the twisted rhythms, scintillating arrangements and hard-assed marketing force of Michael Jackson (whose *Thriller* was our turntable hit of the year, uniting the often divergent tastes of Ivan and I) and add a twist of Dylan to the mix. It would be designer pop: remorselessly, relentlessly, unabashedly commercial. But it would not be trite.

Actually it would not be all that original either. ABC had attempted something similar with *Lexicon of Love*, even down to using Dollar's producer Trevor Horn. But they went badly awry with the follow-up, the self-produced *Beauty Stab* (which was anything but beautiful and was roundly panned in the press). I was dispatched to interview their leader, the soft-spoken and usually rather mild-mannered Martin Fry, and ended up in a loud slagging match in a pub. His mistake was to ask me what I thought of his new album (a word to interview subjects: if the journalist does not volunteer his opinion of your latest masterpiece, don't ask; he's probably just trying to be polite) and he was evidently somewhat offended by my candid response. 'I say bollocks to all that,' he snapped. 'You must think we're fucking stupid!'

Things went from bad to worse. After ten minutes of increasingly heated debate he snarled, 'I suppose you think you could do better!'

You don't need a degree in behavioural psychology to anticipate my answer. I stood up in the bar to deliver an a cappella rendition of one of my songs, drawing amused applause from some of the boozy regulars.

'Well, it was in time and in tune and that's the best that can be said about it,' sulked Fry.

If I were him, I would have punched me.

But I was convinced we could do better than ABC, who to my mind were condescending in their self-consciously ironic appropriation of pop. We had learned from our previous stints in the studio, however, that we needed a producer at the helm with the technical expertise to realize our grandiose but somewhat vague ambitions. Trevor Horn's services were somewhat beyond our meagre budget but we were introduced to Peter Eades, who had recently opened Ireland's first 24-track mobile studio and was touting for business.

We liked Peter immediately. He was a naturally effervescent musical enthusiast, who had honed his multi-instrumental skills on the show-band circuit with a band called the Memories, playing note-perfect cover versions of other people's songs. He told us about the time he had seen Queen perform live. 'They walked off stage halfway through "Bohemian Rhapsody" and left a reel-to-reel tape recorder playing all the harmonies,' he said. 'I nearly choked! The Memories had been doing the whole feckin' arrangement. Do you know how long it took to get that right? And here's the feckin' originals and they can't even play their own song!' But what really tipped it was when Peter showed us a pair of wire-rimmed National Health spectacles he had stolen from John Lennon's effigy in Madame Tussaud's Wax Museum when he was fifteen. 'Sometimes I put 'em on when I'm recording harmonies,' he said. 'Sure, none of us is ever going to improve on the Beatles – but there's no harm in trying!'

Peter parked his huge mobile recording truck outside the front of our house. Inside was a desk that looked to us like something you would use to control a space mission, but for once we were confident that the man in charge actually knew how to send us into orbit. Lines were run into the basement room we used for rehearsals. As a rhythm section we drafted in Jack Dublin and Paul Byrne, easily the most gifted musicians in Howth. We played Peter our Dollar and Michael Jackson records and he showed us how to achieve our impossible musical dreams. He restructured and rearranged our songs. He identified and underscored the hook-lines. He added walls of harmonies to our simple two parts. He expanded melodies with fabulously inventive counterpoints. He made me record and re-record my vocals, tackling the songs line by line until they were perfect. I could hardly believe the sound of my voice as it came sailing out of the huge speakers: it had tone and timbre and character and emotion. This was the voice I had been hearing in my head all those years! I knew it was in there somewhere!

Watching Peter work, I learned more about music than I did in all my years as a fan and critic. I learned how to make it. And I also learned to show some much-overdue respect to the craft of the professional musician. I was dismissive of the show-bands. They were throwbacks to another era, human jukeboxes touring the country playing anodyne cover versions in matching suits, their mafia-like managers operating a monopoly on Ireland's best venues. Show-bands were seen by us as the enemy, first to be hated and then (as groups like the Boomtown Rats and U2 finally started to break this vice-like grip on Irish musical culture) to be pitied. All of which may have been true. Show-bands certainly were responsible for the stagnant state of the pre-punk Irish music scene. But Peter was a product of the show-band world and he was the most accomplished musician I had ever met.

'I've got to make a living,' Peter said to me one night, over a pint in the Abbey Tavern (recording always had to stop in time for last orders). 'My first priority has to be to my home and my wife and my kids. But at least I've been making my living from music. I'm not on the dole. I'm not a civil servant. I'm a musician and I'm playing for my bread and butter. There are people sneering at that and they're living in a run-down flat in Berkley Street, eating a tin of baked beans for their main course. But they'll tell you they believe in their songs! Imagine me arriving home to my wife and her asking, "How did the gig go?" and me saying, "Ah, it was brutal, the audience split, we didn't get paid . . . But we did 100 per cent of our own material!"'

Peter made a curious revelation that evening: he was related to Larry Mullen. 'I see Larry at family gatherings, you know, and I wish him well. I don't know how he feels about it, but I think we're both doing the same thing, we're both doing what we love. It's just a matter of scale.'

Peter spent a week producing two songs for us, even though we had enough funds to pay him for only two days. At the end we had a tape comprising 'The Kiss', a frantic, jumpy, dance track, and 'Amnesia', a moodily atmospheric, sonically epic ballad about the loss of innocence. Both had been live favourites for Yeah! Yeah! but were utterly transformed by Peter's input, resulting in what was probably the most polished, big-production, contemporary-sounding pop to have been produced in Ireland at that point in time.

The Gravediggers and Deaf Actor had also recently split up in the face of music industry disinterest. We talked to Jack and Paul about forming a new group but they opted instead to join forces with Ivan O'Shea, who was assembling a band that would combine folk and rock instrumentation in a contemporary setting. He called it In Tua Nua. I went down to the cliff-side cottage they used as a rehearsal room to check out the competition. Paul had spotted a young girl with an ethereal, crystal, tremulously soft voice singing at his sister's wedding and persuaded her to try out for the band. She seemed impossibly shy, singing with eyes closed and retreating into a corner between songs, but I had to admit she was something special. Her name was Sinead O'Connor. As for the rest of them, they were having problems getting the uillean pipes to tune with the keyboards. I thought that if Jack and Paul wanted to take a chance with this unholy cacophony then that was their problem. They were clearly never going to get anywhere.

I went to see Bono. I ran into him less and less these days as U2's touring and recording became all-consuming. And he was a married man now. Bono and Ali had tied the knot at the end of the previous year. But the truth is that I felt our paths had drifted apart since the evening at Edge's house. The whole Shalom scene was too weird for me. I could hardly even be bothered arguing about it any more. Their tenets of belief were so utterly out of line with my own perception of reality they might as well have existed in an alternative dimension, where the rules of logic and science did not apply. For his part, I could hardly blame Bono if he had concluded that I was a Godless pagan whose soul was unredeemable.

But I managed to get hold of him and, for some reason, we arranged to meet at Ali's parents' house in Raheny. We sat outside in his car and he slid my cassette into the stereo. I couldn't help grinning as he became increasingly excited. 'It's pop music, all right,' he said, 'but there's something nasty in there, a bit of acid in the mix.' The synth sent a dramatic rumble pulsing through the car. 'How did you get that sound? This is so far ahead of anything coming out of this country.' He played the tape a second time, banging along to the rhythm on the steering wheel. 'You know, I'd love to put this out,' he said.

'Are you serious?' I asked, amazed.

'I'm totally serious,' he said. He revealed that U2 were thinking of starting their own record label. He planned to call it Mother. 'It'll bring out my nurturing side,' he joked. It was primarily intended to release one-off singles, to help get bands started, although he had plans for a few offbeat projects of his own. 'I'd love to do a single with Ali,' he confided. 'It would be great to go into a studio with someone who doesn't know anything about music but has got so much natural spirit and just try to see if we can capture that on record!'

'How does Ali feel about that?' I asked.

'Oh, she doesn't know,' he laughed. 'She won't even sing in front of me. I'd have to sneak in and record her in the bath.'

Bono proposed that Yeah! Yeah! could be the debut release for Mother. 'Wow,' I said, contemplating my first offer of a record deal. 'That'd be fantastic!'

But there was a catch. It would have to wait until U2 had finished promoting their third album, *War*, which had just been released in March.

'How long is that gonna take?' I asked.

'Could be a year,' Bono admitted.

A year? He might as well have asked me to wait a lifetime. I took a deep breath and told Bono I would have to pass.

In Tua Nua eventually became first band to be released on the label, in 1984. Our former roadie's band went on to pick up an international deal from Virgin (which was galling news for us, much as we congratulated Ivan O'Shea through gritted teeth). Sinead O'Connor left In Tua Nua and landed her own deal (with

Ensign). Cactus World News also benefited from Mother's support (signing to MCA). And a group called the Hothouse Flowers went from Mother to London Records and had a massive worldwide-hit album. For a while there, Mother seemed to be spawning a whole new generation of Irish musical stars. We were its orphans.

But our tape was out there, working its own magic. Without any fancy packaging, witty press releases or pleading letters. It was just being passed around. After years of vain attempts to stir interest, we discovered that when you are in demand word spreads quickly. Several Irish record-company representatives approached us, some talking of local deals, others of taking it to their London offices. I was struck by how out of touch most of them were. We had a meeting in the office of a well-known Irish music-business figure who wanted to sign the publishing on 'Amnesia'. 'It could be a big hit in the right hands,' he said. 'I'd like to get it to Elvis Costello. I think it's a song he might be interested in recording.'

'Elvis Costello writes his own songs,' I pointed out.

'Does he now?' said the publisher. 'Well, he's a talented fellow, isn't he? Still, everyone's looking for a hit and I think this is right up his alley.'

'That's ridiculous,' I said. 'He's one of the world's leading singer-songwriters. It would be like asking Bob Dylan to record your song.'

'Oh, I don't see this as a Dylan song, at all,' said the publisher. 'But Elvis, now, that's another matter.'

'Forget Elvis,' I said. 'He wouldn't touch it with a barge-pole.'

'Well who would you have in mind to record your songs?' he asked, warily.

'Actually, we plan to record them ourselves,' said Ivan.

'Ah now, lads, lads,' said the publisher, in the patronizing tones of someone addressing a couple of naïve children. 'Forget about all of that. The money's in the writing. Trust me on this. If you want a hit record you need an established star. The bigger the star, the bigger the hit.'

'So who do you suggest?' said Ivan.

'And not Elvis Costello,' I insisted.

'Cliff Richard?' he said, hopefully.

Were these the kind of morons to whom we were supposed to entrust our careers?

Then, swimming like eager minnows into the lair of the shark, we were summoned to the offices of Ossie Kilkenny.

Ossie was an immensely charming, flamboyant and gregarious music-business accountant who had his fingers in every Irish pie. He represented U2, Bob Geldof, Chris De Burgh, Paul Brady and even *Hot Press*. I think Ossie was growing a little dissatisfied with his role. There was a lot of money flying about in the music business, and he was looking for a bigger slice of the action.

'You may think you have the best songs God ever wrote,' Ossie told us in a typically colourful turn of phrase, 'but there is more to this business than talent. A lot more. I could show you great songwriters who are working in Burger King now. You need to get the business side right.' And Ossie, of course, was just the man to do it for us. Under his guidance, Ossie promised us, we wouldn't just be talking about getting a record deal. We would be talking about getting a quarter of a million pounds. Maybe more. The theory was that the more record companies paid out in advance the harder they would work to recoup – a win–win situation for us. Ossie urged us to make some more demos while he sorted out our tax-exemption status.

The trouble was, we had spent everything we had and couldn't keep tapping up our dad for money. So Ivan made the ultimate sacrifice, selling his Honda 250 Superdream motorbike for £1000. The recording mobile was once again parked outside our house. Kids from the neighbourhood would gather outside, listening to the drums reverberate through the trailer, climbing the steps to peak into the dark interior of this sci-fi lair of sound.

'Are youse famous?' they'd ask, wide-eyed.

We would just smile mysteriously. It would not be long now. We recorded two more tracks. 'Say Yeah!' was another fran-tic, uptempo dance tune but 'Some Kind of Loving' was in a different league, as close to our new pop ideal as I felt we had come. We appropriated the propulsive beat to Michael Jackson's 'Billie Jean', underpinned with a deep, sinister keyboard motif and completed by an epic chorus with harmonies that put the Beach Boys to the sword. But if you listened close enough, the song itself was a very dark tale of rape and unwanted pregnancy, written in an angry burst when a girl I had briefly dated tearfully told me her own story.

> She staggers into the garden, throwing up amongst the
>   flowers
> Drunk on passion's poison after closing hours
> She didn't know his name, she didn't know his address
> Never took a second look till he was tearing off her
>   dress . . .

Ossie did a double take when he played it back in his office. 'Did I just hear you sing "throwing up"?' he asked. 'I've never heard of somebody throwing up in a hit record. But we can worry about that later.'

Ossie had a partner in London, a high-powered music business solicitor called David Landsman, who represented Shakin' Stevens, the biggest star of the moment. While we busied ourselves in the studio with Peter, we would hear a flow of encouraging reports from the music capital. An A&R man from MCA flew over to meet us. We had recently received a stock rejection letter from MCA for one of our previous demos but acceptance is apparently quicker than rejection. Ossie and David, however, were not interested in MCA. Not enough money and not a very encouraging rate of success, apparently. Neither were they interested in Stiff, the next company to show their hand.

Stiff were the home of Elvis Costello and Ian Dury, both of whom were among our favourite artists. But our advisors remained unimpressed. 'You could have a deal with Stiff tomorrow, be in the charts by the end of the year, but you'll never make any money,' they told us.

Money. That's what it was all about. I guess we had the fever now. Fuck art, put the cash up front.

(To be fair to Ossie and Dave, MCA signed fourteen acts that year and dropped thirteen of them after the failures of their first albums. Only Nik Kershaw enjoyed any success. And Stiff records went into terminal decline around the same time, with label boss Dave Robinson forced to relinquish control to ZTT records in 1987, a label set up by Trevor Horn.)

Big deals, we were assured, were imminent. Meetings were taking place every day. It was only a matter of time.

Ivan and I were getting itchy. We wanted to be where the action was. We decided to head to London. Three months, that was how long Ossie and Dave reckoned it could take to put the right deal together. I remember standing with Ivan on the deck of a ferry as it sailed out of Dublin bay, watching the coastline slowly dwindle in the distance, thinking, 'We'll be back in triumph very soon.' Flying back to a tickertape parade.

Then Dublin was gone. And there was just the sea.

12

London. The city drew us to it like a magnet. This was the metropolis of our dreams, the pulsing capital of pop, where the Beatles recorded at Abbey Road and the Sex Pistols started a riot in the 100 Club, where *NME*'s critics pounded on typewriters above the swinging stalls of Carnaby Street, making and breaking careers in poison prose, and scheming A&R men peered through the windows of luxurious offices in gleaming high-rise record companies, wondering who among the teeming hordes below would facilitate their rise to the corporate boardroom. London, where the Bow Bells rang with jingles and the streets were paved with gold records. Dizzy with possibility, we stepped off the train to meet our destiny.

Ivan had an English girlfriend, Cassandra Duncan, with whom he had hooked up at Trinity College. We wound up bunking in her sister Athena's living room in a flat in Finsbury Park. On our first day, we decided to head into the city to see the sights. It was the summer of 1983, Britain was in the midst of a heatwave and London was ripe and succulent. We left the flat in T-shirts and shorts but when we arrived at the Tube station we were astonished to see a man emerge from the lift wearing a thick black overcoat, with a Homburg on his head, his long hair tied in tassels and sporting a long, stringy beard. I realize now that he was a Hasidic Jew but I had never seen such a thing before. Then another Hasidic Jew emerged. Then another, this one holding a big bass drum.

'That is the weirdest image for a band I have ever seen,' I said to Ivan.

This was going to be one freaky, funky city!

We went to meet Ossie's partner, David Landsman. He was a smooth, besuited Englishman who operated from a large house on Camden Road. Famous names were dropped casually into the conversation. We were buoyed with stories about how impressed the great and good were with our tapes. We wanted to meet them but were told that negotiations were delicate and best left to professionals.

Suddenly we just seemed to be in London with nothing to do. Ivan had his girlfriend with whom he could while away the hours. I felt cut off, a long way from home, swinging between overstimulation and ennui and suffering that suffocating isolation you can feel in a city of millions where everyone fights for their own little square of space and no one really cares who you are. I had been at the centre of something in Ireland, a frantic social whirl that revolved around my band and my job and me, me, me. Now I was disconnected. There were gigs to go to, films to watch, art galleries to check out, but often, during those first weeks, I just walked the streets, tramping miles, all over London, looking at the endless parade of faces passing by, and cars full of strangers hurtling on journeys to other places, and all the lights in all the flats full of all the people to whom I meant less than zero, people with lives of their own, who would never know me or be known by me. I travelled on the Tube, scribbling in my notebooks, pondering the notion of insignificance. And it welled up like a fear inside me, an existential nausea. But (deep breath) I was going to be OK. Because I was going to be famous. It was just a matter of time before everyone would know my name.

Things began to improve when I was put in touch with Ross Fitzsimons, an alumni of *Hot Press* who had recently landed a job in the marketing department of MCA. Ross was some years older than me and moved in very different circles. At *Hot Press*, he had belonged to the mysterious advertising department, keeping nine-to-five hours, practically unseen by the hardcore staff knocking out pages by night. We would occasionally pass these other employees on the stairs, usually while they were arriving for work and we were leaving for home. We tended to think of them as part-timers. They thought of us as a bunch of incompetent amateurs who were forced to work the nightshift because we just couldn't get our act together, which was probably fair enough. Ross, however, would sometimes climb the stairs after hours to help us out when the going got really tough, putting in stints at the rock'n'roll frontline with the Letraset and cow gum. He had a taste for reggae and all its vices, dabbled in journalism, managed the odd band and harboured vague ambitions as a music-business entrepreneur. I think he must have taken pity on me when he offered me the spare room in his rented flat in Belsize Crescent. He clearly had no idea what he was letting himself in for.

Belsize Park is a rather posh area adjacent to Hampstead but it could just as well have been Brixton to me, as I still didn't actually know one end of London from another. Twiggy, the sixties supermodel, owned a flat opposite. Later on, Richard Thompson, the cult guitarist and songwriter, moved in next door. And in the penthouse flat above lived Jeff Banks, one of Britain's leading clothes designers, founder of the fashion retail chain Warehouse. Jeff was a squat, bearded, very dapper man with a forcefully friendly air about him. He took Ivan and me under his wing, and thankfully plugged me into a new social network.

Jeff had been married to British pop queen Sandy Shaw in the sixties, which was to us immensely impressive. For his part, Jeff declared himself an unabashed fan of our recordings. He would introduce us to people with the deadpan recommendation that they get to know us before we became famous and wouldn't talk to them any more. Soon we were out on the town with Jeff and his retinue of models, long-legged girls with perfect skin who seemed to have stepped directly from the pages of glossy magazines. Which, of course, they had. Sometimes you would catch them from a certain angle or in a certain light and an image of a perfume ad or a *Vogue* fashion shoot would flash into your mind.

For all their impossible beauty, I was quietly appalled by how dim they seemed to be. They were great fun on the dancefloor, where they would smile and giggle and strike catwalk poses; but try to engage them in conversation about anything other than their beauty regime and they became pouting and vacuous, which had a terrible effect on my libido. I was intimidated enough by their appearance without having to make all the effort to sustain conversations while they blinked at me like goldfish. I began to wonder if there was some kind of universal law balancing physical attractiveness against mental development.

One night we had all been out painting the town various shades of red and ended up in Jeff's apartment, snorting cocaine off the balcony and watching the twinkling lights of London. A willowy blonde was telling me she had been named Face of the Year or somesuch honour I had never before contemplated the existence of. She was currently featured in a cinematic advertisement for deodorant which had made a big impression on me. Every time I saw it, I wanted to nudge the stranger in the cinema seat next to me and say, 'I know her.' Such was her beauty, I was willing to overlook the fact that she believed Ireland to be overrun by terrorists and that I had fled to London to escape the ravages of war.

'Was there, like, a watchtower at your school?' she asked.

'A what?'

'A watchtower, like, for the army to watch over the playground and make sure the kids didn't get shot?'

'Sadly, no,' I said. 'We just had to defend ourselves.' And then, because I was desperate to keep her talking, I asked her the same thing. 'Was there a watchtower where you went to school?'

'Don't be silly,' she said. 'Not in England! We don't need things like that at school.'

And the penny finally dropped. 'Are you still at school?' I asked.

'Yeah, course,' she said. 'Mum and Dad want me to stay on for uni but I think I'm going to leave when I'm seventeen, give the modelling a chance.'

I had to make a swift readjustment in my damning IQ appraisal. With her poise, physical self-assurance and air of cosmopolitan sophistication, I had assumed she was older than me. It had never crossed my mind that all those impossibly slim, leggy ideals of femininity placed before us on the supermarket shelf of culture for our admiration and aspiration might have just been gamine kids fresh out of braces. I felt strangely cheated.

Did this realization bring an end to my dishonourable intentions? Did it fuck! Rather, it emboldened me, lending me a sense of advantage in the delicate area of amorous negotiation, until I finally succeeded in smarming my way into the bed of one of the teen catwalk queens, although I can't recall if it was Face of the Year or Rear of the Year or just Hand Model of the Week. What I do remember is walking into a bedroom to be confronted by a large colour poster of Bono taped to the wall.

'How do you know Bono?' I asked, rather stupidly.

'U2 are great, aren't they?' she said.

It took me a moment to adjust to the notion that my schoolfriends had moved into this realm of iconography, where complete strangers might display their pictures as if they were part of the family. The whole experience was strangely offputting. Every time I glanced up from the perfect form of the naked beauty writhing beneath me, I would catch sight of Bono looking down at us. Was that a faint hint of disapproval in his eyes? Did he know that I was only with this girl because she was a model and I could brag about it later?

'Do you mind if we turn the lights off?' I asked. My breathless little beauty seemed surprised by my bashfulness but nonetheless complied. Even in the dark, though, I could feel Bono's reproving gaze burning into my back.

U2 were out there now, dwelling in that hyperreality whose inhabitants have an existence quite separate to their real lives. They were off touring the world, waving white flags on stages erected from one corner of the earth to the other, but they were simultaneously here in this girl's bedroom and scaling scaffolding on *Top of the Pops* and singing their songs on a million hi-fis. *War* had done that. It was the album in which Bono had begun to fulfil all his latent promise, stamping his passionate personality on music that was rougher, funkier, grittier and more vibrantly contemporary. It was as if the Edge had stepped back, stripping down his wall of sound to allow his songwriting partner some sonic space. Bono's voice was filling out and the words were pouring forth. For the first time in his career as a lyricist, Bono risked being called verbose as he gave us his thoughts on love in a time of danger and spiritual survival in an era when the forces of chaos and disorder seemed to rule the world.

I listened to *War* with admiration, not envy. I was honestly amazed that they were progressing in such creative leaps and bounds, producing songs of the transcendent quality of 'Sunday Bloody Sunday'. 'You don't write songs,' I had once admonished Bono. 'You make these fantastic records but if you took away all the layers of sound what's underneath? There's nothing you could just sing in the shower.'

'I don't have a shower,' he jokingly replied. 'I have a bath. Maybe that's the problem!'

Now U2 had somehow reached the sacred ground of the singles hit parade with 'Two Hearts Beat As One' and 'New Year's Day'. We had some catching up to do. But Ossie and Dave were still whispering their million-dollar supplications in my ear. Be patient. It would only be a matter of time.

Hanging out with this model crowd, we were dining in places where we could barely afford a starter and being led into VIP rooms in exclusive nightclubs where you could take out a mortgage on a cocktail. Funds were running dangerously low. At the end of a night partying, when everyone was air-kissing their goodbyes and jumping into taxis, Ivan and I would hang back, making sure we were the last to leave, then we would walk back to Belsize Park from central London, traipsing miles under the lamplights, cutting across Regent's Park, all the while talking about songs and albums and hatching fanciful plans for what we were going to do in the future. The very near future. When we got the deal. Everything would be all right if we could just hang on a little bit longer.

Meanwhile, we were advised to sign on the dole. I was incredulous that I could come over from Ireland and receive money in England for not working but I was assured that this was the case. So I duly went along to an unpleasant building down the back streets of Camden, reeking of despair and hopelessness, and cheerfully filled in the requisite forms. I was summoned into a tiny, airless office, where a rather severe woman read my paperwork and, without once looking up to see who she was addressing, asked me what steps I was taking to find gainful employment.

'I'm sorting out a record deal,' I told her.

She sighed loudly and finally raised her eyes to meet mine. 'You can't depend on that,' she said. 'We need to see evidence that you are actively seeking work.'

I patiently explained that I really didn't need a job as a major record contract would be in my hands any day now.

'You don't know how many times I have heard that,' she said, with a disturbing mix of pity and condescension.

'Yeah, well, maybe,' I said. 'But I'm different.'

Her long-suffering look suggested she may have heard that line before, too.

At last we were summoned to meet one of the movers and shakers apparently so enamoured of our talent. Lucien Grainge ran a publishing company and was considered a real up-and-comer in the music business. Ossie and Dave were certainly most impressed with him. After all the build-up, Ivan and I were a bit nonplussed to find Lucien occupying a cramped and not particularly well-maintained suite of offices up a narrow staircase off Oxford Street. He was a small, stocky man whose chubby features were mostly hidden behind an enormous pair of bright-red, plastic-framed spectacles. He had the habit of interrupting our conversations to apparently take calls from major rock stars. 'David . . . David,' he'd say, 'love the new tracks,' then he'd cover the mouthpiece and whisper to us, conspiratorially, 'Bowie'. Then the line from his secretary would buzz again. 'Gotta take this call,' he'd say. 'Mick, Mick . . .'

But Lucien had ideas about how to progress. He thought we needed more recordings, to keep bombarding the record companies while they were hot. 'Ossie tells me you've got songs coming out of your ears, so let's get 'em down.' He had a producer he thought we should work with, a fellow called Phil Thornalley. 'Very contemporary sound,' said Lucien. 'He'd be perfect for you.

Might be a bit hard to get, could be expensive, but I think we could work something out.'

Ivan and I were nervous about working with someone we did not know, scared our lack of studio nous might be exposed. 'What's wrong with the production on our demos?' we asked.

'Nothing wrong with them at all,' said Lucien. 'But who is this guy, Peter Eades? No one's ever heard of him.'

'They've heard of him in Ireland,' said Ivan. 'He's a bit of a genius, actually. Everybody wants to work with him.'

'I hear he's talking to U2,' I improvised. 'They're thinking of a bit of a change in direction for the next album.'

'Really?' said Lucien. 'And you can get this guy?'

'We've got a relationship,' said Ivan.

So we persuaded Lucien to fund a trip to Ireland to record with Peter again. We knew we had to pull out all the stops. We recorded 'Say the Word' as a banner-waving epic, replete with layers of harmonies. And we recorded a dreamy new ballad, 'Sleepwalking', with an epic production built around a sparse, decaying drumbeat. The lyric was an attempt to evoke the sense of dislocation I felt in London.

> The spirit of electricity
> Flickers like a torch through the bones of my hand
> Dreams are making a mess of me
> They say I'm looking like a ghost, but they don't
>   understand
> I'm the haunted not the haunting
> I need to get some peace,
> I'm walking in my sleep . . .

I surprised myself by hitting a sweet falsetto at the song's dramatic peak. My singing was dramatically improving under Peter's tutelage. The recording was gorgeous. The best thing we had ever done.

While in Ireland, we also had a session with a fashion photographer, complete with hair and make-up (we had learned something hanging around with models after all). My glasses had been replaced by contact lenses and with that change came a growing sense of confidence in my physical appearance. I was losing some of that skinny, boyish, gawkiness that I felt might have impeded my attractiveness to the opposite sex. My face was decently proportioned, my teeth nice and even and, once in a while, one of the models I was chasing about would even describe me as handsome. That was praise indeed, given that physical appearance was about the only thing to which they gave any serious thought.

Ivan had longish hair and I kept mine short but otherwise we tended to co-ordinate our appearance. Our image at the time might best be described as colourful. For the photoshoot, we wore luridly bright-orange and red shirts, matching green army fatigue waistcoats and oily blue Levi 501 jeans. Who could resist us?

Well, Lucien for one, apparently. We returned to London in high spirits but our meeting did not go well. Lucien glanced over our photo sets and declared, in his Jack-the-laddy fashion: 'I thought you guys were meant to be pretty. You look like a couple of rent boys from the sticks.'

'Look who's talking,' sneared Ivan. 'Do you wear those specs just to distract people from your ugly mug?'

Lucien recoiled as if wounded. 'What's wrong with my glasses?' he asked, all bonhomie suddenly absent.

'Maybe you need a new prescription,' I said, joining in the abuse. 'Could be you're too shortsighted to see how ridiculous you actually look.'

Ivan and I thought our cheeky irreverence was part of our appeal but I don't suppose many others felt the same. Lucien made us an offer nonetheless. He said he could set up a singles deal with a major label. 'We want to make albums,' I pointed out.

'Look, boys, what can I tell you?' he said. I got the impression he was enjoying our disappointment. 'You're a pop act. It's a very expensive market to operate in. And it's all about hits. You've got good songs, you'd have a shot. We'd have to do something about the way you look, obviously. We want you to make the little girls scream but not 'cause they're having nightmares.'

We told him to stuff it. And not in so many words. It went against everything Ossie and Dave had been advising. It did not escape my attention that our offers seemed to be getting worse rather than improving, but I wasn't impressed with Lucien Grainge. I thought he was full of shit. He evidently thought the same about us and sent us on our way, telling us we were too big for our cowboy boots.

These days, Lucien is one of the major players in the British music business (just as Ossie and Dave predicted), chairman and chief executive of Universal Music UK.

This episode, remarkably, did nothing to dent our confidence. Ossie and Dave informed us they were having talks with London Records and CBS and proposed that the time had come to sign a management contract. A thick document duly arrived through the post. Being unable to afford the services of a lawyer, I sat down and read it all very carefully, working my way slowly through huge tracts of almost impenetrable legalese. The word gross (which kept recurring) is a fair description of what I found in there.

Essentially the contract stipulated that we delegate all decisive power to them (they apparently preferred sole discretion to mutual agreement) while they charged us for all expenses incurred (including their own fees for accountancy and legal services) on top of which they would take their substantial management commission from the gross receipts of all our earnings from the entertainment industry (and a few subsidiary industries besides, including the literary industry). Since many activities in the music business (notably touring) are often conducted at a loss, it would mean that our managers would profit from things that actually cost us money. Indeed, there would be very little incentive to maximize profit as opposed to simply maximizing turnover. But what really struck me, reading the contract, was that there was no sense that we were in this together. Ossie and Dave had been so friendly and supportive, I really thought they believed in us and wanted to be a part of what we were trying to achieve. I thought our interests and their interests were the same. But the true nature of our relationship was spelled out in this document, if you only took the trouble to read between the lines of legal jargon. They saw us as a source of revenue. Nothing more, nothing less. I felt crushingly betrayed but at the same time I knew it was ridiculous to be upset. I experienced another little life shock as I mentally readjusted to encompass this new information, seeing myself as a naïve wannabe who had sailed gaily into the clutches of professional hustlers.

I confronted Ossie at our next meeting. He just laughed. 'Lads, lads,' he said, waving his arms dismissively. 'These are starting points, a basis for negotiations.'

'The thing is, Ossie,' I said, sadly, 'if you'd just given us a fair contract we'd have signed it right away.'

'Look,' he said, 'we'll draw up another contract. We'll address your concerns. Don't take it so seriously. It's a game, boys!'

Ossie cheerfully buoyed our spirits and sent us back out convinced that record companies would soon be battering down our door, begging us to sign to them. He was good at that, a real cheerleader. But something had changed in our relationship. It was not just the trust I had placed in him that had been damaged; it was an entire framework of trust that had been shaken – that somewhat childish, possibly very middle-class faith in the benign motives of the adult world. I certainly resolved to keep a closer eye on Ossie. It may have been a game to him, but this was my life.

It was not like people weren't telling me. I guess I just hadn't been listening. Forced by growing financial desperation to contemplate gainful employment, I occasionally wrote an article for *Hot Press* (with the stipulation that, for a change, they actually pay me for my services). I was dispatched to interview Paul Weller, ex-leader of the Jam, who had recently formed the Style Council, attempting to shed his angry young man image by remodelling himself as the frothy Cappuccino Kid. Weller had been a real idol to me and proved to be impressively down-to-earth. When the interview was officially over, we wandered out to an Italian café in Hanover Square and indulged his new European aspirations by sitting in the cold at a pavement table, beneath dreary London skies, drinking cappuccinos. He listened sympathetically while I told him of the problems I was having.

'The whole music business is shit, it's run on a dirty basis,' he said. 'But what business fuckin' ain't? Can you name a noble business? There must be a few, I suppose, but I don't think there's very fuckin' many. You always got to bear in mind that the record business works this way: if you're successful you can do what you want. If you're not . . .'

He let that thought drift. That was the unthinkable.

In March 1984, Ossie and David came up with a new angle. They told us that Rod Stewart's former manager was interested in taking us on. Billy Gaff was the owner of Riva records and currently manager of John Cougar Mellencamp, who had been the biggest-selling white act in America during the previous year (topping even Bruce Springsteen, to whom he was often unfavourably compared). Ossie set up a meeting and told us to be on our best behaviour.

We met this rock'n'roll kingpin in a house in Knightsbridge that looked like it shared an interior designer with Buckingham Palace. The reception room was bigger than our entire flat. Gaff was a portly, balding, extremely well-spoken Englishman with very camp mannerisms. Spread out on a vast mahogany table he had our photographs, images of us boisterously clambering all over one another. He picked up a shot of me kissing Ivan on the cheek. 'I like this,' he said. 'Very striking. Very seductive. Maybe you should tell me how you two got together?'

'Uhm, we've been together since childhood,' I said, uncertainly.

'Really?' said Billy. 'How interesting!'

'Well, we are brothers,' I pointed out.

Billy seemed oddly put out by this information. But he sat with us for half an hour, telling us of all the songs he had picked for bands that had reached number one in America. 'I've got ears,' he kept saying. 'Very important in this business.'

He did indeed have ears, sticking out either side of his head. But then so did Ivan and I. What was he getting at? Finally he spelled it out: he had a song he was looking for the right act to record.

'You want us to do a cover version?' I gulped.

It was a guaranteed mega-hit, according to Billy. A sure-fire American number one.

'But we're songwriters!' I spluttered.

'Oh, really?' he said. I began to get the impression he hadn't actually paid much attention to our demos. But at least he liked our publicity shots.

'Look,' he said, 'you can record what you want once you've had a hit. It's getting that hit that's all important. And I can pick hits. I've got ears. Have you got an American number one up your sleeve? Because if you have, I haven't heard it.'

A second meeting was scheduled for the following week, when he would play us the song he wanted us to record. Meanwhile, we were to get together with Billy's producer, Jon Astley.

We went away in a quandary. The idea of launching ourselves with a cover version was the absolute antithesis of everything we believed in. On the other hand, if we made this compromise now, everything we ever wanted would be within our grasp. Everything except artistic credibility. And musical satisfaction. And self-respect.

'Look, if he wants an American hit, we'll write him one,' I said to Ivan.

For the next few days we were ensconced in the flat, putting our hearts and souls into creating the ultimate pop thriller. Wasn't this what Lennon and McCartney had done, after all, writing 'I Wanna Hold Your Hand' to conquer the US market? We studied the American top ten, which was full of punchy, ultra-rhythmic, pop rock and dance songs like 'Jump' by Van Halen, 'Thriller' by Michael Jackson and 'Automatic' by the Pointer Sisters. We decided we needed something with a melodramatic edge, a driving beat and a big chorus. We came up with an out-and-out rocker, 'Love Is Stranger than Fiction', and a strange, rhythmically jagged track called 'Faithless', a song naked in its expression of desire and ambition, on which I shamelessly pleaded 'All I want is my share / All I want is all'.

Jon Astley turned out to be a tall, fresh-faced, amiable fellow, who had cut his studio teeth assisting the Who's legendary producer Glyn Johns. He was making a step up from engineering to production, so this Billy Gaff project was as important to him as it was to us. We played our new songs on the acoustic guitar and he was delighted. 'They're superb,' he declared. 'We could do fantastic things with them.'

'What about this song Billy wants us to record?' I asked. 'Is it really good?'

'I haven't heard it,' Jon admitted. 'He's been keeping it under wraps.'

'Must be really good,' I said, glumly.

We were all present at the next meeting for the unveiling of Billy's hit, a track called 'Photograph' by Phil Thornalley. Not him again! I settled down uneasily at the far end of the massive table, steeling myself to hear something so amazing it would put all our songwriting efforts to shame. I was ready for my resistance to melt. I was contemplating how it would actually feel to sacrifice all my artistic ambitions on the altar of fame.

The sound of a monotone bass came thud-thud-thudding out of the speakers as a voice intoned 'All I wanted was a photograph . . .' ('duh-duh-duh-duh' went the synths) 'A small reminder of things gone past . . .' ('duh-duh-duh-duh') 'The way you looked and the way you laughed . . .' ('duh-duh-duh-duh') 'All I wanted was a photograph . . .'

And so on.

I was aghast. It was like Bucks Fizz without the fizz. Still, I hedged my bets and asked to hear it again. It was even worse second time around. I looked for confirmation from Ivan. He rolled his eyes and shrugged.

Ossie had told us to nod and agree to anything. Oh, but I tried. I really tried.

'So what do you think?' asked Billy.

'It's . . . awful,' I said.

'What?' said Billy, apparently flabbergasted by my impertinence.

'It's drivel. It's got drippy lyrics and a two-note melody.'

'Who listens to lyrics?' said Billy, petulantly. 'You could add some lyrics of your own, if that's what bothering you.'

'I think our songs are much better than that,' I insisted.

Jon Astley, to his credit, piped up in our support. 'They've got some good songs, Billy, you really should give them a listen.'

I asked why Phil Thornalley didn't release it himself and Billy glumly admitted that Phil thought it 'a little bit twee'.

The meeting did not end well. 'What did you say to him?' asked Ossie, in an exasperated phone call. 'He was quite upset. He described you as nasty.'

Nasty! Me?

Jon Astley went on to sign a solo deal with Atlantic, releasing two albums and scoring a minor hit in the States in the late eighties. The opening song on his second album, *The Compleat Angler*, was a sardonic take on the music business entitled 'But Is It Commercial?' He never really graduated to the frontline of production but became well-respected for his remastering work with the Who's back catalogue.

Phil Thornalley had a strange, disjointed career, producing and then briefly joining art-Goth rockers the Cure, departing for an equally brief stint producing and later singing with Johnny Hates Jazz (whose popularity crashed when he took over lead vocals), before settling for a successful role as a backroom writer/producer. He composed 'Torn', which became a worldwide hit for Natalie Imbruglia in 1998.

Billy Gaff signed the Roaring Boys instead of us and landed them a £300,000 advance from CBS records. They flopped completely and were dropped after their first album.

To the best of my knowledge, no one ever did record 'Photograph'.

13

In July 1984, I was back in Ireland laying out *Hot Press*. My replacement as art director, Jaqui Doyle, had quit suddenly to take up the same position at *Smash Hits* in London. I agreed to temporarily step into the breach although I was so paranoid about losing my Unemployment and Housing Benefit (or Government Arts Grant, as Ivan and I referred to it) that I insisted the magazine fly me back to London on a Monday morning so that I could get a train from Heathrow to Camden, sign on the dole, then head straight back to the airport to fly to Dublin, returning to work at *Hot Press* by mid-afternoon after a round trip of 600 miles.

Bob Dylan was playing a huge open-air concert at Slane Castle and the entire staff of *Hot Press* headed up to cover the great event. It was Dylan's first visit to Ireland since the sixties, an occasion treated with due reverence by the nation's large tribe of unreconstructed hippies. More than 100,000 gathered on the hillside to pay homage but, being a professional freeloader, I managed to wangle my way into Lord Henry Mountcharles' castle. U2 had recently been recording sessions for a new album in the castle's ballroom so I was not surprised to encounter Bono and Ali among the liggers. 'The very man!' said Bono, mysteriously, grabbing my arm.

I hadn't seen my old schoolfriend for over a year and a lot had happened in all our lives (or hadn't happened, in my case) but he didn't want to talk about it. Bono revealed that he was being taken to meet Dylan, who had expressed an interest in this young pretender. 'Why don't you come along?' Bono casually said to me. And, seeing as I had nothing better to do right then, I said I would love to, right after they picked me up off the floor where I had collapsed in a gibbering heap.

It quickly transpired that Bono had his own agenda in inviting me along. Niall Stokes had got wind of Bono's meeting and had persuaded him to take a tape recorder and interview the great man. This was quite a coup for *Hot Press* but not so great for Bono, who was beginning to worry that he might be out of his depth. The truth was, he didn't actually know much about Dylan, beyond the obvious (world's greatest lyricist, voice like sand and glue, changed popular music for ever, Amen). It might be hard to believe given Bono's latter-day status as keeper of the flame, regularly called upon to induct legends of yesteryear into the rock hall of fame, but there was a time when he did not express much interest in rock's past. Bono was all about the future. When I originally interviewed U2 in London, questions about the origins of their style had been met with vociferous denials of any and all influences. 'The way it is, there's not much music I do like,' said Bono, emphatically. (Oh, he would probably try to deny it now . . . but I have it on tape!)

So there he was, being summoned for an audience with the master but afraid he might betray his ignorance. But Bono is both a natural-born bluffer and a quick learner, and I think he figured with me there to back him up he couldn't go wrong. While Bono, Ali and I were escorted to the sprawling backstage enclosure where performers were ensconced in gleaming Winnebagos, I gave Bono a crash course on the subject of Bob Almighty.

I had a lot of information to impart. Now that Lennon was gone, Dylan had ascended to primary position in my personal pantheon of living rock gods. His dazzling wordplay, connecting the emotional with the philosophical, was something I returned to again and again. Dylan was my idol and my inspiration. And now I had the chance to meet him.

Or not, as it so happened. I got as far as his Winnebago, where Ali and I were stopped by a mountain of muscle in a security jacket and Bono alone was ushered into the inner sanctum where Dylan and Van Morrisson were sitting playing chess. I watched that door shut in front of me and felt a keen, sharp stab of exclusion. It was a reminder that I was in this VIP world as a guest, not an inhabitant.

Ali and I wandered about backstage, observing the calm but concentrated activities of musicians, roadies and support crew preparing for the show. We were approached by an MTV airhead in micro-skirt and matching breasts who was in Ireland to film a segment for her programme, which, she assured us, was, like, totally cool, especially since she was, like, one sixteenth part Irish herself, though she didn't reveal what the other fifteen parts were constituted from. Silicone by the look of it. Standing with her were two young Americans, Sam and Jake, both adorned in MTV passes, with whom Ali and I chatted while Airhead practised pouting. It transpired that they were avid fans of U2 and wanted to talk about Bono and the Irish rock scene but I found it hard to concentrate. While they rattled on, I kept thinking, 'Bob Dylan is sitting in that caravan!' It seemed wonderful and absurd, like discovering that God had put up a tent in your garden.

After a while Bono returned. I immediately seized upon him, demanding to know what had transpired, but he seemed uncharacteristically withdrawn. 'He was . . . you know,' he said, which did little to assuage my curiosity. 'I'll tell you later.' By now, a crowd was milling around and there was a buzz of excitement in the atmosphere. I noticed this weird-looking fellow sidle up alongside us, his jowly face caked in orange make-up and baggy eyes ringed with thick black liner. I didn't actually recognize him at first, perhaps because he bore so little resemblance to the skinny beatnik with the tangled psychedelic curls whose poster adorned my bedroom wall. 'Hey, let's get a picture taken here,' he said in a stoned drawl, throwing one arm around Bono's shoulder and the other around the MTV airhead, who squealed with delight. It finally dawned on me that this paunchy, wrinkled old peach was Bob Dylan. I gaped at the strange vision, simultaneously amazed and disappointed. 'He looks so old,' I whispered to my new American buddies. Then, gripping his electric guitar, Dylan waved imperiously with one hand and declared, in that strangely flexible drawl of his, 'Let's go,' whereupon he began to head towards the stage, while a whole crowd trooped in his wake, until the only people left behind were Ali, Bono, the young Americans and me.

'Is he stoned?' I said, unable to contain the anticlimactic sense of disenchantment welling up in my chest. 'He sounds so out of it, I can't believe he's going to go onstage like that. He looks like shit.'

Ali fixed me with a fierce glare, but I was never one to shut up just because people didn't like what I had to say. 'It's true what they say,' I glumly declared. 'You shouldn't meet your heroes.'

Ali kicked me fiercely but discreetly in one ankle.

'What's your problem?' I said.

Sam and Jake made their excuses and departed. As they wandered towards the stage, Ali started laughing. 'Do you know who you were talking to?' she asked between fits of giggles.

I got a familiar sinking feeling.

'They're Dylan's sons,' she said.

Oops.

After everyone had followed Dylan towards the stage, Bono asked if I knew the words to 'Blowin' in the Wind'. It seemed Dylan had asked if Bono would like to join him for an encore. Naturally, Bono said it would be an honour. 'Do you know "It Takes a Lot to Laugh, It Takes a Train to Cry"?' inquired Dylan.

'Uhm, no, I don't think I know that one,' admitted Bono.

'How about "Stuck Inside of Mobile with the Memphis Blues Again"?' suggested Dylan. But Bono once again had to confess ignorance.

'Well, you must know "Blowin' in the Wind",' said Dylan, beginning to show the faintest signs of exasperation.

Bono could feel his chance slipping away, so, recognizing the familiar title, he boldly seized the opportunity and announced that, yes, of course he knew 'Blowin' in the Wind'. And so it was settled. The problem was that Bono did not have the faintest idea what the lyrics were and, for that matter, had only the vaguest notion of the melody.

So, while Dylan and his band were kicking off behind us, I

tried to recall the words to 'Blowin' in the Wind' for him. This earnest folk ballad was not one of my personal favourites but I had a notion of what the first verse was from being made to sing it by the Christian Brothers in school assembly. Something about roads, white doves and cannon-balls flying. I wrote down what I could remember and Bono wandered off to find someone who might have a better idea, while I went to watch the show from the side of the stage. Dylan was playing a blinder and I got sucked right in to the maelstrom. Even the orange make-up and black eyeliner didn't look so ridiculous on stage. After a short while, Bono arrived stageside, entranced, eagerly watching the gig. His makeshift lyric sheet was nowhere to be seen.

When it came to the encores, Dylan and his band launched into an epic, electrified 'Blowin' in the Wind'. 'How many roads must a man walk down / Before you can call him a man?' he demanded to know, with a righteousness bordering on anger. 'Yes, n' how many times must a white dove sail / Before she sleeps in the sand? / Yes, n' how many times must the cannon-balls fly / Before they're forever banned?' And the whole crowd hurled back the pay-off line: 'The answer, my friend, is blowin' in the wind / The answer is blowin' in the wind'. Whereupon Dylan nodded to the wings and declared, 'Ladeez and gentlemen . . . Bo-No!' A roar went up as the local hero took the stage, grabbed a microphone and began to sing . . .

. . . the first things to enter his head.

Dylan looked rather startled as Bono improvised lines about the Northern Irish conflict. 'How many times must the news-papers bleed / With the lives of innocent men?' Clearly Bono wasn't about to let a little thing like not knowing the words stop him performing the song. 'And how much longer must the barbed wire stretch / Across this divided land?' Bono was always a confi-dent extemporizer so, as the guest of a superstar, in front of the largest crowd of his fellow countrymen he had ever performed for, he decided to wing it. 'How many times must people die / For a cause they don't understand?'

It was all going so well. And then the band launched as one

unit into the famous chorus while Bono, oblivious to the chord change, continued making up lyrics to the verse. 'How many times . . .?' he sang as the crowd bellowed, 'The answer, my friend . . .' Dylan's head swivelled as he turned to look at his guest with an expression of complete eye-popping, jaw-dropping disbelief. For one terrible moment, Bono's ignorance of Dylan's oeuvre was horribly exposed. Was he the only person among the 100,000 present who didn't know 'Blowin' in the Wind'? I watched transfixed as Bono hovered above this abyss, on the verge of a spectacular crash, when, realizing his mistake, he started howling, 'How many times? How many times?' like a blues mantra while the band brought the chorus home.

Wisely, Bono let Dylan sing the final verse.

Later, I caught up with Bono and Ali among the backstage revellers. He was still flushed and ecstatic after performing to the biggest audience of his life. 'Nice lyrics,' I said.

'D'you think anyone noticed?' said Bono, grinning.

Oh, I was sure they had noticed. Wasn't that the whole point? Being heard. Bono had stood up there naked, with nothing to rely upon but his own self-belief and somehow he had made it work for him, carrying all before him, plucking another personal triumph from the jaws of disaster.

As for me . . .

Let me bring you up to speed with life back in London. A room came free in Belsize Crescent and Ivan moved in. We bought a Tascam 4-track cassette recorder and spent a great deal of time making primitive home demos. Things had gone very quiet with Ossie and Dave after the débâcle with Billy Gaff. Still, there seemed no reason to panic. On the infrequent occasions when we did speak to them they insisted they were still actively supporting our cause. They encouraged us to keep writing songs and we assured them that was exactly what we were doing. When other things weren't getting in the way. Like life.

One day Joan, my ex-girlfriend from Ireland, arrived with all her belongings in a bulging yellow suitcase. She had effectively run away from home. Hers was a loving but somewhat complicated family, where everything seemed to be conducted in an atmosphere of high melodrama. I think Joan's parents liked me well enough but they had difficulty in adjusting to the notion that their daughter might be dating such an obvious reprobate with dangerous libertarian tendencies. Her father once interrogated me, quite out of the blue, on my views regarding that great Catholic *bête noir*, abortion. 'I suppose you approve of abortion?' had been his rather leading question.

Joan was shooting me warning glances across the kitchen table but her concern was misplaced. I wasn't stupid enough to be sucked into that one! So I neatly sidestepped by saying: 'A girlfriend of mine would never have to have an abortion, because she wouldn't get pregnant in the first place . . .'

Joan's father looked at me suspiciously. 'I'm glad to hear that, Neil.'

'Because I use condoms,' I said. Oh, it was worth it just to see his face!

'That's it!' he roared, looking like he was going to have a heart attack. 'You! Out of this house!'

Our romance had been conducted guerilla fashion, with Joan often climbing out of her bedroom and across the roof of the garage to rendezvous with me. Even in my absence the soap opera continued and Joan had had enough, dropping out of college, against her parents' wishes, to flee to London.

Joan was madly in love with me, I had never been in doubt about that. She was broken-hearted when I left but we kept in touch with a constant stream of letters and our romance was reanimated with each trip home to Ireland. I was happy to see her in London but a little worried about the implications. I was not ready for the commitment of cohabitation. It was agreed the flat would just be a resting point while she got herself together but somehow things became more complicated, as things are wont to do. We were lovers, our lives inexorably and increasingly intertwined, and it was gradually accepted that we were living together until . . . Well, until I got my record deal. And then things would have to change. Joan lived with the insecurity of threatened abandonment while I worried about being tied down. It was very brittle, fragile terrain for a relationship that veered wildly between passion and antagonism. We were constantly breaking up and making up in the cramped environment of a three-room flat.

None of this was helped by the fact that Ivan did not approve of Joan in the least. I don't know whether Ivan felt threatened by her connection to me, or whether it was just some particular incompatibility of personalities. Joan was not the easiest person to get along with, striving to hide her insecurities behind a proud exterior, but Ivan always managed to make situations worse, seeking out weakness with cruel humour.

And somehow we fell out, rather dramatically, with Jeff Banks. I was never entirely clear on the sequence of events leading up to this, though he had every right to be fed up with us. He had a televison (which we did not) and so we always trooped up to watch *Top of the Pops*. When he went away on a business trip to Japan, Jeff gave us the keys to his flat and invited us to make use of it. A bit of a party broke out there one night, as parties were liable to do at the time. Now, Jeff was a Buddhist and extolled the virtues of daily meditation, which he used to practise in front of a ceramic dish full of ashes and burning incense. During the evening's revelry someone knocked the dish over, spilling the ashes on the floor. We guiltily cleaned up the next day, restoring the flat to a state of spotless order, but the ashes provided a bit of a conundrum. Quite apart from the question of whether they might be the remains of someone dear to him (in fact, they were just the remnants of incense sticks), I had noticed that the surface of the ash seemed to be arranged in a pattern, which may have been random or may have held spiritual significance. I had no idea. If it was the former, I figured the various replacement lines and squiggles I etched might go unremarked. But if it was the latter, I imagined Jeff's next meditation session was going to be somewhat puzzling. I comforted myself with the thought that Buddhists were known to be very forgiving and put the whole matter out of my mind.

Then there was the incident with the clothes. Ivan and I

returned to the flat one day to find a whole lot of suits and jackets perched on top of the dustbins. This was a goldmine for a couple of impoverished scavengers used to shopping for clothes in charity stores. We scooped them up and took them into the flat, trying them on for size. There were some pretty sharp and stylish garments in there. Some we kept, some we liberally doled out to friends who popped by.

A few days later, I ran into Jeff on the stairwell. He proceeded to tell me he had fought with his girlfriend who had thrown out all his clothes in a rage.

'That's awful!' I said, thanking my lucky stars I wasn't wearing one of his jackets. It was too late now to even begin to try and explain. I just told Ivan that the rest of the stuff had to go to Oxfam. And we'd better make sure Jeff didn't see us dumping it there.

Joan got a job as a photographer's assistant. She often worked with model Annabel Giles, a former fiancée of Jeff's, who mysteriously warned her that our neighbour was a more volatile character than he might appear. We got a rather dramatic demonstration of that when we returned to the flat one day to find that the door had been knocked down. We rushed in, looking to see if we had been robbed, but nothing appeared to be out of place. Apart from the door, that is, which had been violently removed from its hinges. Our flatmate Ross went up to speak to Jeff, to find out if he had suffered a similar attack.

'That was me,' Jeff revealed unrepentantly. 'I wanted my roasting tray back.'

Apparently he had been planning to cook a chicken but had been unable to locate his roasting tray. Convinced we must have borrowed it without asking, he had angrily knocked on our door. Finding no one in, he ran the length of the corridor and karate-kicked the door down. As you would.

The thing is, we were entirely innocent on this count. The tray he removed was ours, which we never used anyway because our cooking skills were pretty much limited to heating up tins.

Jeff moved out not long after, which was a relief given the

poisonous atmosphere that had descended. Nowadays, when I see him on TV in his guise as one of Britain's best-loved fashion gurus, I wonder if his co-presenters appreciate his martial-arts skills. But I wish Jeff well. He was nice to me when it really mattered. When I was just a young immigrant, adrift in London, in need of a friend.

Given the increasingly boisterous nature of the household, it was hardly surprising when Ross also moved out. After that, the flat became a staging post for an Irish invasion. Tens of thousands of young Irish people emigrated every year and, for a while at least, it seemed that most of them passed through our flat, pausing briefly on their migrant journey to stay in the smallest bedroom or, if that was occupied, to sleep in the bath. Or, if the bath was taken, to put their sleeping-bag down on any bit of spare floor they could find. For a whole month my sister Stella camped in the middle of the bedroom I shared with Joan, which played havoc with our love life. One time I counted fourteen Irish people sleeping in different parts of our three-room apartment. Things started to get a little crazy. The flat became party central, aided by the arrival of two girls, Lynn and Alison, in the flat below. The neighbours sometimes complained about the noise but our landlord did not seem to care. We lived in the most rundown house on the street and as long as he got his rent on time he left us to our own devices.

One of the itinerants who wandered into my life around that time was Gerry Moore, singer with an Irish band called Street Talk. Gerry was twenty-seven but looked ten years older, a grizzled, working-class, hard-drinking, dope-smoking Dubliner with a big hooter of a nose that looked like it might have been hit a few times and a voice, well . . .

It was a voice you could set up home in, a big, expansive, oak-timbred voice, with enough room to raise a family in love and laughter, with a musty cellar reeking of whiskey and cigarettes and some quiet recesses for moments of solitary contemplation. Gerry was quite a singer and a whole lot more besides. Music poured out of him. He could snatch songs out of thin air, making them up as he went along. And he was a gifted mimic, capable of impersonating vocalists as varied as Frank Sinatra and Tina Turner. But there was more. There was something truly special about him. He was an incredibly dynamic individual, observant, clever, compassionate, outrageous, sometimes a little scary (Gerry had sharp edges), but more often than not hilariously funny.

When he paid a visit, guitars would come out and the cheap wine and the cider and the beer and the vodka and the spliff and we'd be singing and laughing all night. Gerry's philosophy for life was simple: 'Legalize hashish, listen to Nat King Cole and make music!' I remember Ivan strumming away one night while Gerry improvised a melodramatic country-and-western song about star-crossed love and unwanted pregnancy, entitled (for reasons I was not entirely clear about) 'The Big O'. He ended with a perfectly pitched radio-style voiceover for an abortion clinic. 'At thirty quid a shot, just remember: when in doubt, have it out!' 'Jaysus, if me mother heard that she'd kill me,' he giggled as the song came to its natural conclusion.

'I think you've got a hit there, Gerry,' I said. 'But where on earth does the expression the "Big O" come from?'

He looked amazed at my stupidity. 'Obortion!' he exclaimed.

Gerry couldn't spell too well but he was the most talented man I'd ever met who wasn't a household name. And that was the thing that really fascinated me about him. He was a born star who wasn't famous.

'What's "making it"?' Gerry said to me one time, when we were discussing our elusive dreams. 'Making lots of money? Having musical fulfilment? Having a wife and kids? There was a girl called Rosie used to go to Sloopy's Nite Club and I had a mate and his idea of makin' it was gettin' Rosie. Straight up. That's all he wanted. And he worked really hard on it! I mean, when I was a kid, makin' it was gettin' a chance to sing. I've made it, man!'

But I don't think he really believed that. There was more than a touch of desperation creeping in by the time we met. Street Talk were a funky, gritty rock band who had been working the

Irish circuit for a few years. They released a couple of singles but didn't seem to be able to make the next step up. I was persuaded to accompany them on an overnight trip to play a gig in Rotterdam and got a glimpse of life on the bottom rung. We travelled by train and boat to a dirty venue for a fee that barely covered the drinks bill (mind you, there was a lot of drinking going on). There was no accommodation arranged so after the show (a blast of a gig, a rock'n'roll stonker) the band just opted to stay up all night with the aid of cocaine pilfered from the briefcase of a promoter known as Dik Heavy. The party was wild but it eventually reached the point of collapse, with musicians and a few hardcore fans crashing out in various corners of the venue. Gerry, almost the last to give up the ghost, passed out in mid-conversation, falling unconscious on the floor of a toilet. He started to vomit in his sleep. When his manager, Al Richardson, failed to wake him we turned him on his side so that he wouldn't choke. 'A rock'n'roll death. That'd be a fine thing,' said Al, wearily.

Nobody could wake Gerry the next day. We shouted at him. Slapped him. Kicked him. Nothing. We were just starting to talk about calling an ambulance when his bloodshot eyes popped open. He sniffed the air and looked down at his yellow-stained clothes. 'Who puked all over me shirt?' he yelled.

I got to see the other side of the rock'n'roll coin the next time U2 came to town, to play two sold-out nights at Wembley Arena in November 1984. *War* had established U2 as a major attraction, with relentless touring and a mini live album (*Under a Blood Red Sky*) swelling their fan base, and they reaped the benefits when *The Unforgettable Fire*, in many ways their strangest, most free-flowing and impressionistic recording, swiftly gave them their first million-seller. A million! It was the magic number, six zeros representing global awareness. Could all those people around the planet really know and care about the band from Mount Temple school? Yet, on the night, the transition from gymnasium to arena seemed seamless. Bono was the same dynamo, stalking the stage, relentless in his need to reach out and embrace the audience, not 100 screeching schoolkids now but 12,000 baying, singing, arm-waving fans. And the music, well, it was bigger now, of course, wilder, more emotional, more daring but its core was the same: thunderous, electric three-piece rock that hauled you to your feet and dared you not to be involved. During a tumultous, epic version of 'Bad', Bono wrapped himself up in the song, encircled by Edge's shimmering spectrum of guitar sounds, then kicked and scratched and punched his way back out, roaring his defiance. It was an astonishing performance in which one man's spirit seemed more than the match for the thousands in front of him. The essence of this gig was everything I remembered and everything I had ever loved about U2; it just seemed the group had expanded somehow, swelling up to fill the available space.

Oh, and, just to confirm that some things would never change, Adam made a couple of clunking mistakes.

Afterwards, Ivan and I made our way backstage. There were guest-lists to be negotiated and coloured VIP stickers to be collected. In keeping with the band's rise up the ladder of success, access was starting to be restricted, yet we were ushered into a hospitality area where the band were greeting friends and admirers.

'How's the music?' asked Bono, after we had offered our congratulations on his performance.

'I don't know,' I admitted. 'It's a bit frustrating at the moment and we can't seem to get hold of Ossie . . .'

'Well, your prayers have been answered,' said Bono. 'He's here.'

And indeed he was. U2's gregarious accountant was in one corner of the room, beer in one hand and triangular sandwich in the other, engaged in animated conversation with Paul McGuinness. Ivan and I made a beeline for him, ready to give him a piece of our minds. He must have seen us coming out of the corner of his eye because he turned towards us, opening his arms in greeting as if we were the very people he had been waiting for all evening.

'Lads, lads,' grinned Ossie. 'I was just talking to Paul about you. Two of the finest songwriters to have come out of our little island. We've just got to find a way to persuade the music industry to share our opinion of your talents.'

Oh, the devious shit. He could always out-manoeuvre us with his wiley charm. Ossie assured us our career was uppermost on his mind and told us to give him a call in a couple of days, when he was back in Dublin.

'But you never take our calls,' I complained.

'My priorities are probably slightly different to yours. Some people actually pay for my consul, you know,' chuckled Ossie, nodding towards U2's manager. 'Give me a call on Monday and we'll discuss how to proceed.'

It was difficult to talk to Bono backstage. There were so many people around, all demanding his attention, and I didn't like to join that throng, pressing in on the hero of the hour. There was an element of vampiric bloodsucking about the whole experience. It seemed to be the boldest and pushiest interlopers who surrounded the band members in a noisy swarm of chatter. Ivan and I hung back, chatting with old acquaintances, drinking free beer. I wound up sitting alone on one side of the room, watching the action unfold, when Bono came and settled down next to me.

'I'm glad you could make it,' he said. 'What did you think? Really.'

'You looked like you belonged up there, all of you,' I said. 'But, you know, I was in the front row. I was probably closer than when I saw you in the school gym.'

'I don't think it's about physical proximity,' said Bono. 'You can be in some clubs and you can be right up a yard from the lead singer and it seems like you're a million miles away. It's something to do with generosity that makes for a great live event. It's nothing to do with scale.'

And then, before we could really get into a conversation, a young, attractive woman, vaguely familiar to me from television, squeezed into the non-existent space between us and, behaving as if I wasn't there at all, started enthusiastically telling Bono how excited she was to meet him. I got up to leave but Bono grabbed my arm. 'We're in the studio tomorrow – Good Earth, in the West End,' he told me. 'Why don't you come around and we'll have a chat.' Then he slipped out of the clutches of the TV starlet, leaving her with me. She looked me up and down, trying to work out whether I was of any interest. 'So,' she said, by way of an opening gambit, 'how do you know Bono?'

Is that the measure of my significance, I wondered? Not who I am but who I know. The next day in the studio, where U2 were working on some B-sides, we talked about that incident. 'I'm starting to realize what it must be like to be a beautiful woman,' said Bono, who was adjusting to a whole new level of fame. 'That's what fame does to you. Everybody wants a piece of you. It's hard on Ali. Because she is a beautiful woman, and she is used to getting that kind of attention in a way that she almost wouldn't notice it. A year ago, if I walked into a restaurant with Ali, all eyes would have been on her. It'd be like, "Who's the lucky gobshite with the babe?" you know? But now, if she's with me, people look right through her. They don't see her at all. They push her out of the way to get to me. It's as if she's invisible.'

We talked about fame and I became belligerent when Bono linked the concepts of talent and destiny. 'I don't believe in destiny any more,' I rebuffed him. 'The reason you believe in destiny is because everything is working out the way you always thought it would.' I told him about Gerry Moore, so copiously talented and yet struggling to be heard.

'Maybe talent on its own isn't enough,' said Bono. 'It comes back to faith. And that's a hard thing to explain to another person. It hasn't happened to you, so why should you believe it?'

This wasn't what I wanted to hear. I wanted to hear that talent would conquer all. Fuck faith.

I called Ossie at the appointed time. Lines to Ireland back then were notorious, buzzing and crackling, cutting off with no warning or invading your conversation with the ghostly traces of other people's calls. Often, even if you got through, people on the other end would tell you they couldn't make out a word and just hang up. If you really wanted to avoid somebody, it provided a built-in excuse: blame it on a bad line. But this time I was fortified and ready for anything. There was no way Ossie was going to get rid of me. Through the usual crackle, I made out the buzz-buzz of a dialing tone. I had a connection!

'Kilkenny and Co.,' said the secretary's voice, faint but audible.

'Is Ossie there?' I inquired.

'Who's calling?' she replied. As if she didn't know. She must have been well used to my miserable voice by now.

'Neil McCormick,' I said.

'Hold on a moment . . .'

Long pause. I could feel my heart beating. So much was riding on this phone call for me. I had made up my mind, I was not going to be fobbed off with some pathetic excuse this time. I wanted to know where Ossie stood.

'I'm afraid he's on another call at the moment, Mr McCormick, and he has two calls waiting . . .'

That wasn't going to get rid of me. I was ready to give her a piece of my mind. I'd keep calling back all day if necessary. Hell, I would get on the next plane to Dublin, head straight for his office and kick the fucking door down if it was the only way to get his attention.

'But he does want to talk to you . . .' she continued.

Eh? This wasn't the way these calls usually went.

'So can he call you back?'

'Uh . . . Yes, of course,' I mumbled.

'It may be after five thirty. Are you at your usual number?'

'Uh . . . Yes.'

'Thanks for calling.'

The line went dead.

The sly bugger had turned the tables on me again. Taking the initiative like that was about the only thing he could have said that would have got me off his case, temporarily at least.

I sat by the phone all day. He didn't call back, of course.

As someone with a keen interest in pop history, I wonder why it took me so long to recognize that we had made a classic botch-up? Ossie and David were music businessmen who wanted to score a big, juicy deal and couldn't get fired up over a small one. When it boiled down to it, we were more interested in making music than making money. But I don't think we ever discussed that. I don't think we ever sat down and talked with them about our motivations, our creativity, our love of pop, all the things that made us tick. So it was hardly surprising that, in the end, nobody got what they wanted. Ossie and Dave didn't make any money. And we didn't make any music.

I walked Hampstead Heath, churning things over. My frustration was physically palpable. I felt as if electricity was coursing through my body, about to erupt from my fingers in crackling bursts of static. I felt like a racehorse trapped behind a faulty starting gate, snorting, kicking and stamping the ground in frustration, straining to be set loose. I found myself at the top of Parliament Hill, looking down over the enormous vista of this foreign city that seemed to hold nothing for me but frustration. I stood up there and yelled out at the top of my voice: 'Give me a fucking chance!' I just wanted someone out there to hear me. I imagined my words floating out into the city and being carried on a magical breeze into the offices of a record company, where they would take up residence in the mind of an executive looking for the next big thing. But all that happened was a couple of people flying kites shot me nervous glances and shifted a few paces down the hill.

Back at the flat, I had a long chat with Ivan about what we were going to do. It was pretty clear to both of us. We had to form another band. And we couldn't afford to mess about. We would only accept the most brilliant musicians. We would create something that was undeniable. That was the key word. This band had to be so good that no one could turn their back on us.

14

With a keen sense of our priorities, we immediately set about the task of coming up with a new band name. We loved Yeah! Yeah! and wanted something that maintained a sense of continuity, eventually settling (after the usual rounds of surreal word games) on another phrase from rock history: we would be Shook Up! (fondly retaining an exclamation mark).

We placed a small ad in the back of *Melody Maker*, the established forum for contacting musicians. The phone did not stop ringing for five days. It began to dawn on me that we weren't alone in our ambitions. Like a musical Hollywood, London draws in every dreamer in the land. Entire industries are apparently staffed by people in a state of occupational denial. Shop assistants are getting a band together; waiters are working on demos; builders are talking to publishers. We met and auditioned hundreds of our fellow wannabes, musicians of wildly varying degrees of ability, putting them through rigorous tests in our pursuit of greatness.

Our method of whittling down the numbers of bassists was rather cheeky. We would ask what they thought of Adam Clayton. If they expressed admiration for U2's bassist we immediately struck their name off the list. If, on the other hand, they said something like, 'Forget it, man. The guy still uses a plectrum!' then they got invited to audition.

Looking back, it's hard to avoid seeing this as a first sign of resentment at U2's success. I did not think of it in that way at the time because I loved U2, admired Adam as an individual – he was always very courteous and friendly to me – and knew that his idiosyncratic but inventive approach to his instrument was an integral part of the group's distinctive sound. Still, he was probably the only bassist in a band of that world-beating stature who could be counted on to make mistakes in every gig he played. I suppose that identifying this as a weakness, a chink in U2's incredible armour, imbued Ivan and I with hope that we could still, against all odds, somehow equal and even (dream on) better our old associates.

Our first new recruit was a bassist called Vlad Naslas, who passed our test with flying colours. 'You must be joking!' he said, when Adam's name was mentioned. In his very first phone call, Vlad told us it was fated that we work together so there was no point in auditioning anyone else. He had learned this information from his girlfriend, who was psychic. She also told him we were going to be one of the most successful groups in the world, so of course we took her predictions seriously.

Vlad immediately struck us as a rather strange bloke. He was extremely tall and gangly, utterly deadpan in expression, with no discernible sense of humour and imbued with a quality of inner confidence that was almost preternatural. Meeting us for the first time, he shook our hands and said, 'We're going to go a long way together.' It was almost embarrassing pointing out to him that he still had to audition, but somehow not in the least surprising when he turned out to be the most fluid, modern and stylish bassist we had ever heard.

The rest of the crew were not so easy to come by. In that synth-dominated era, keyboard players were much in demand. Anyone who could combine serious musical skills with the knowledge of electronics, computing and sequencing required to operate the kind of multilevel keyboard set-up we envisaged was in a position to charge a small fortune for their services – money we did not have. Drummers posed another problem. It occurred to us as we listened to around 150 of them play that very few can actually keep time. Perhaps that was why most studio work was being delegated to machines.

There was a kind of musical tyranny at work in the eighties, an impossible and in many ways self-defeating quest for mechanical perfection. Up until the end of the seventies, records related to what musicians could actually play. Technological advances in studio recording equipment, synthesizers, samplers, sequencers and drum machines, along with the advent of digital recording (allowing sounds to be moved around with no loss of quality), meant that rhythm tracks could now be laid down with metronomic precision and musical arrangements constructed with mathematical exactitude. You could have plotted out many of the era's recordings on graph paper. Add to this an obsession with sonic crunch, so that every individual sound was tailored for maximum dynamic impact (drums, in particular, began to take on the qualities of percussive battering rams), and the effect was musical overload. The apotheosis of this trend were Trevor Horn's astonishing, everything-and-the-kitchen-sink productions for Frankie Goes to Hollywood (actually not a very technically proficient live band), but the same devices were employed for every two-bit pop, rock and dance record, turning the charts into a kind of sonic assault course.

Standing somewhat forlornly against this trend was the rise of what was known in Britain as 'indie' (for independent), a dogmatically non-conformist movement who retained a human dimension to their recordings even if it meant sometimes being out of time and out of tune. Indie's spiritual godfathers may have been the dark, dirge-like Echo & the Bunnymen, its prime exponents the jangly, lyrical Smiths. The peculiar thing is that, if one was to count the survivors of new wave among these non-conformist ranks (such as the Pretenders, Elvis Costello, Talking Heads, Dexys Midnight Runners, Squeeze and, indeed, U2), then this is the music that I preferred, even as I enthusiastically embraced Shook Up!'s participation in the fashionable quest for the perfect beat. In the first indication of a divergence of our tastes, Ivan was a fan of the good-time, cocktail pop of Wham! and pretentious posturing of Duran Duran (both of whom I detested). We found common ground, however, in Prince, the Minneapolis wonder whose remarkable musical skills brought a human dimension to the hi-tech. *Purple Rain* replaced *Thriller* on the household turntable as the very model of a modern pop record.

It was against this background that we started making demos with Vlad. He had a decent 8-track home-recording set-up in his house in Walthamstow and he quickly assumed the role of producer, although Ivan and I had learned enough to pull our weight. Recording on this limited facility was a painfully slow process, but, through the intense work involved in building up an entire set's worth of material, the three of us forged a strong bond.

After much painful auditioning, we found a further recruit, a charming Welsh psychology graduate, Steve Alexander, who was the most technically accomplished drummer we had ever heard. He had a double bass drum and a huge, sprawling kit mixing synth drums with real drums. Steve could play the kind of complex jazz-funk arrangements that get musos stroking their beards with excitement and he could rock out like John Bonham on speed. And he had something else going for him, a quality I've rarely come across before or since, certainly not in someone who wasn't rich or famous or even particularly handsome (although he did have a big, twinkly smile). Steve had an utterly magnetic appeal for the opposite sex. Perhaps it was pheromonal. Girls buzzed around him, wherever we went. Indeed, all our girlfriends lobbied us to take him on, which was mildly disturbing.

We still did not have a keyboard player but (guess what?) we had a plan. We would entice all the record companies with our new demo and then invite them to a showcase, hiring extra musicians for the event as necessary. The fact that, once again, everything depended upon our sheer talent was not seen as a possible flaw. We were back on the beat and our confidence was riding high.

One thing we had learned was that there was absolutely no point sending tapes into A&R departments. We knew we had to do this eyeball to eyeball, which meant getting into their offices and being physically present when our tape was played. Record companies don't particularly like this but I soon discovered that if you absolutely insist they will let you. Especially if you tell them who else you are seeing. For as much as they really don't want to be bothered by pesky musicians they are also afraid of being left out. Nobody wants to be Dick Rowe, the A&R man at Decca who notoriously told the Beatles that guitar groups were on the way out.

'He's probably kicking himself now,' Paul McCartney later remarked.

'I hope he kicks himself to death,' John Lennon snapped back, neatly summarizing most musicians' attitude towards the company men who hold our fate in their hands.

Using every contact I had, I wangled my way into the offices of all the major (and many minor) record companies in London. Well, all of them except MCA, where Lucien Grainge had become head of A&R and refused to see me. I had some new photos of Ivan and I (the band, for the moment, would remain in the background) taken by Joan, and very handsome we looked too. And I had a nicely packaged demo featuring the songs we wrote for Billy Gaff and a new track about a bitter one-night stand, called 'Sweets from a Stranger', which Bono had phoned up raving about, describing it as a 'pop classic'. Bono suggested we see his A&R man, Nick Stewart, which seemed a good place to start.

At Island Records, I found myself in the most enormous office I had ever seen, floor space being an indication of status. A tall English gentleman politely ushered me into a seat opposite his desk and asked if I wouldn't mind terribly if he had a quick listen to something that had just come in before we got down to business. 'Of course,' I said, graciously. He then stuck on a test-pressing of a new Grace Jones track produced by Trevor Horn. At full volume. I sat there pinned to my chair by the sonic blast, listening to something that had probably taken six weeks to record in a £1000-a-day studio. It was utterly mindblowing. When the opus was finished (some twenty stupefying minutes later), Nick turned the volume down halfway, muttered, 'That was rather good', and put on my cassette.

Minds were not blown. Hair was not even ruffled.

On my travels around the A&R departments of London I learned something truly extraordinary. A&R people don't understand what a demo is. They know what it looks like, all right.

And they know it features the songs and performances of an unsigned act. But they don't know what it *is*.

'That's a good song but I'm not sure about the production,' is a fairly standard A&R comment. What production? No one seems to be interested on how on earth you managed to squeeze that much life out of a cheap, out-of-date and probably faulty 8-track machine. Instead they want to know why you didn't go for a tougher drum sound and more backing vocals. They don't approach demo tapes the way an art teacher might look over his pupils' sketches. They don't listen out for the shape of things to come. They want to hear something that can compete with the records that are blasting out of office stereos all day. They sit in their chairs waiting to be knocked out.

Only, in most cases they don't sit in their chairs at all. While your demo is playing away, they wander round the office talking. Or they read a newspaper. Or make phone calls. Or watch cricket on TV with the sound turned down. It is all too rare (and hugely heartening) for someone to listen conscientiously. Most often they barely pay attention and then have the presumptuousness to comment as if they were the world's greatest authority. Play half a song, talk throughout and then say, 'I don't think much of the lyrics.'

The first few times that happened, I just sat on my hands and tried to be polite, because no matter what rubbish they spouted almost everyone was promising to come to our next gig. But by the time I got to WEA records my edges were beginning to show. I sat in the cramped cubicle that passed for an office of the company's most junior A&R person, who read the *NME* while playing our demo at low volume on a cheap, muffled hi-fi, reaching up to hit the fast-forward button halfway through each song. 'Frankly, I don't think it sounds particularly interesting,' this oik sniffed at the end.

I snapped. 'Not interesting?!' I yelped. 'It sounded completely crap!'

'Well, I wouldn't go that far but . . .' he stuttered. I cut him off before he could come out with any more rubbish.

'I can't believe you actually listen to music on that shitty stereo,' I said. 'Your cassette player needs its heads cleaned, which is something you might have noticed if you had actually been fucking listening!'

He gaped at me in shock. Perhaps he'd never had a musician do anything but kiss his spotty behind before. 'Give me back my tape,' I demanded.

'What?' he gulped, evidently having difficulty adjusting to this dynamic shift in the nature of our relationship.

'Just give it back,' I said. 'I'm going to find someone else around here to play it to. Someone who's got more than wax between his ears.'

'Look, I didn't like it,' he snapped defensively. 'And if I don't like it nobody else here's gonna like it either.'

'Just give me the tape, shithead,' I snarled.

He nervously handed my package back. I stormed out of his office, cheeks burning with outrage and humiliation.

And then my luck finally changed. Walking down the corridor came the familiar figure of Bill Drummond. 'Hi, Neil,' said the Teardrop Explodes' former manager cheerfully. 'What brings you to WEA?'

It transpired that Bill had a label called Korova, to which his bands (including Echo & the Bunnymen) were initially signed. Bill had sold a controlling interest to WEA, where he now operated as an independent A&R man. He would be paid a percentage of the company's earnings for any new bands that he picked up. He took me into his office (a much more impressive affair than the A&R hack's cubicle) and, out of politeness, listened to the tape that had just been rejected. He listened carefully, at high volume, with growing enthusiasm. He stopped the tape after each track and asked questions before continuing. He played some parts twice. By the end he was grinning widely, declaring that he was eager to see us perform.

We needed money to affect this next step so we did what we always did under such straightened circumstances: went running back to our daddy. Thankfully, he remained convinced, against all evidence, that the McCormick genes were abundant with talent. We hired the Clarendon Ballroom in Hammersmith for the night of Friday 14 June 1985. We hired a PA and lights and a dry-ice machine. We printed posters and tickets. We engaged the services of a professional keyboard player and booked a rehearsal studio. We could afford only a week but it was all the time we needed. After all, we had been getting ready for this our whole lives. This was an ensemble of high-calibre musicians and, fired by our enthusiasm, they pulled out all the stops. After years of vainly trying to flog demo tapes to a disinterested music business, I had almost forgotten the pure joy of performance. Because something amazing takes place every time musicians play together, from the rehearsal room to the stage: melodies and rhythms emerge as if from nowhere – complex patterns of sound spontaneously created by the intermingling of even the most simple ingredients. By the end of that week we were really cooking. Other bands would stop by to watch our set. We had three-part harmonies, choreographed moves and one highly drilled monster of a modern, funky, hard-rocking multifaceted pop group firing on all cylinders.

We inveigled all our friends, and friends of friends, to come to the gig. We invited everyone we knew in the music business, from the post room to the boardroom. And then we waited, nervous enough to puke, to see if anyone would actually turn up.

Slowly, the venue began to fill. By nine o'clock there were at least 250 people in the ballroom. At nine thirty the lights went down and, under a cold blue spot, dry ice started to pour off the stage. The sound of a Gothic church organ spiralled up to the rafters as we filed out in the darkness. I hadn't been on a stage in two and a half years. But, as I looked out into the faces before me, I knew this was where I belonged.

What a gig that was. We went out all guns blazing, performing as if we were playing for our very lives. And the audience reacted in kind. We brought the house down, ending with two loudly requested encores – and, while the audience may have been sympathetic, I have been at enough other showcases to know that this is not always the case. Afterwards, I walked out into the crowd, accepting the congratulations of our friends. Dad had made it over for the gig and was grinning from ear to ear. 'I always knew you had it in you,' he said. 'That was fantastic, boys.' But there was one thing uppermost on my mind. I had to check the guest-list. When I got to the entrance, Ivan had already beaten me to it, eagerly scouring the pages for the crucial ticks that would show us who had attended. There were almost a hundred names on the list. But something was definitely wrong. He handed the sheets of paper to me without a word. All of two people from the music business had shown up. And one of them was a secretary from Virgin who had taken pity on us. Of all the A&R people we had seen, only Bill Drummond had been there. But he had not hung around after the show.

Let me pass on another piece of wisdom to any aspiring musicians reading this sorry saga. Once you actually get into an A&R man's office he will say almost anything to get you out. Promising to come to your gig is one of the easiest ways.

A spontaneous party broke out in the flat that night, a kind of wake mixing celebration and despair. The gig had been a triumph, no doubt about it, but we had put all our eggs in one basket . . . and dropped it. I crashed out, drunk out of my mind, about five in the morning. Somebody had videoed the gig and it was still playing on the TV set in my bedroom, with the sound turned down.

I woke to static on the TV screen and a phone ringing. Sunlight poured in through the windows. My head was spinning and when I lurched to my feet I thought I might throw up. I staggered into the kitchen. There were bodies all over the place. What the hell had been going on here? It looked like a massacre.

I picked up the phone. Waves crashed against the side of my skull. I held on to the door jamb as I croaked my hello.

'Neil,' said a familiar Scottish voice. 'Bill Drummond here. I just had to call and say last night was out of this world.'

'Wow, thanks, Bill,' I replied.

'I don't know who else you're talking to,' said Bill, 'but I want to sign you.'

15

U2 played Milton Keynes Bowl on 22 June 1985. It was their biggest UK gig to date, a huge open-air event for 50,000. Ivan, Vlad, Joan and I travelled up by train to the concert, buzzing with anticipation. Hell, we were just buzzing in general. We were floating about in a bubble of happiness, heads spinning from a whirlwind week in which the Good Fairy of Fame & Fortune had waved her magic wand over our heads.

I spoke to Bono on the phone shortly after Bill gave me the good news. 'What do we do now?' I wanted to know. Because our every effort had been focussed on getting this far and no further. I well remembered our conversation on the 31 bus when Bono warned me that the work starts after you land the deal. 'You cannot possibly understand how frustrating the last few years have been,' I told him. 'It's like we've been denied access. We've just been hammering on locked doors. Sometimes they open, just a crack, and we start to go through and *bang*! They slam shut in our faces. And suddenly the door is wide open and I'm standing here thinking, What am I supposed to do now?'

'Get yourself a solicitor,' said Bono. Such practical advice. I was glad I knew a rock star who had been through all of this before. Unfortunately the first name Bono suggested was David Landsman.

'I don't think he's talking to us,' I said.

Bono came up with an alternative, a solicitor named Nicholas Pedgriffe, who had apparently negotiated their deal with David Landsman.

'You've got lawyers negotiating deals with other lawyers?' I said.

'That's rock'n'roll,' said Bono.

Bill Drummond and Max Hole, head of A&R at WEA, took

Ivan and I to lunch in a chichi Chinese restaurant in London's West End. 'I could get used to this,' I declared, tucking into a strange twist of something unidentifiable with a bit of something else I didn't recognize elegantly arranged along the side of the plate.

'Whatever it is,' added Ivan.

Oh, we were on good form. Bill and Max were effusive in their praise of Shook Up! They got it. They knew exactly where we were coming from. Nothing needed to be explained.

'We see you as a big pop band with crossover appeal,' said Bill. 'You've got the whole deal. You're young enough for a teenybop audience, you've got the showmanship to build a live following and enough substance in the songwriting to attract older listeners.'

'Wow,' said Ivan. 'We sound great.'

'It's a very unusual balance of elements,' said Max. 'We think you have the potential to be as popular as Duran Duran or – dare I say it? – the Police.'

Yes, dare to say it, I thought, smiling contentedly as I watched something that looked like a scale model of a volcano arrive for my main course. Was I supposed to climb it or eat it?

'I think you could be one of the biggest groups on the planet,' said Bill.

It was as if he could read my mind! Bill explained that we would be signing directly to WEA (not his label, Korova). We were a mainstream act and would require a lot of investment. The deal on offer was not the kind of megabucks arrangement Ossie had been gunning for (indeed, I have a sneaking suspicion that he had turned down more on our behalf in the past), but a £30,000 advance was not to be sniffed at – especially with a record company who were so enthusiastic about our potential. We met with Bono's solicitor the next day to look over the draft contract. A few of the clauses would have to be negotiated but, since this was our only offer and we were eager to sign, he suggested we act with all haste and we agreed.

Oh, happy days. Bill arranged for us to go into a studio to

demo tracks he had identified as possible singles. Oddly enough, they included 'Some Kind of Loving' and 'Sleepwalking', songs Yeah! Yeah! had been touting around to no avail, but we opted to keep quiet about that. The musicians were fantastic and we knew exactly what we wanted, laying down fresh arrangements with a funky, punchy edge. We were on a high. Bill came to see us in the studio and nodded enthusiastically to the play-back of 'Sleepwalking'. 'That could be your first number one, right there,' he said. We liked the sound of that. The first of many!

At Milton Keynes it rained all day but nothing was going to dampen our spirits. We wandered round the huge backstage encampment, greeting familiar faces from the U2 camp. Frank Kearns was there and Ivan and I wrapped our former bandmate in a bear hug. His new group, Cactus World News, had just finished recording an EP for Mother Records, with Bono producing. We were delighted to hear his news and he was delighted to hear ours. We were one big bundle of mutual delight. We stood in the drizzle at the side of the stage, with plastic bags fashioned into makeshift hats, and watched our old heroes, the Ramones, support our old schoolfriends. 'It's a great day to be here at Woodstock,' said Joey, one foot in a puddle of rain and a sly grin on his face. Count it, Dee Dee: 'Wan–tu–tree–faw!'

The sunshine punks from Rockaway Beach cut through the miserable weather, Joey singing like a newspaper vendor, making aural shorthand of all his hook lines ('Blitzkrieg Bop' became 'Bliree Bip') and tossing in 'Yeah! Yeah! Oh Yeah!' whenever he forgot the lyrics (which was often). After their set we took shelter in a hospitality marquee and in wandered Joey himself, a spidery, string-bean geek, moving with the stilted grace of a puppet. Frank looked like he was going to pass out. 'It's . . . It's . . . It's *him*!' he gulped.

'Let's go and say hello,' I suggested.

'We can't do that,' said Frank.

'Of course we can,' I insisted.

'What would we say?' asked Frank.

'We can say whatever we want, Frank. We're all recording artists now! Let's go and tell him about our record deals.'

So we did. And Joey was gracious, bending towards us and chuckling as we told him how we started out by learning his songs. 'Well, you just remember that when you get to number one,' said Joey. 'We might be looking for some support dates.'

'Oh no,' said Frank, aghast at this sacrilege. 'But maybe we could support you one day.'

Joey laughed. 'Maybe!'

Could life get any better than this? Bono came in and slapped me on the back, but he was uncharacteristically anxious and untalkative. 'If the sun doesn't shine for us today, I'll be really disappointed,' he admitted.

'Who needs the sun?' I said.

'What are you so happy about?' said the Edge, who had joined our merry little corner.

'Life,' I said. Life was great. It was beyond great. Life was fanfuck-ingtabulous. And here was our solicitor, Nicholas. 'Hey, Nicholas,' I said. 'Come and join us! How are the negotiations going?'

Nicholas looked at me like a rabbit caught in the headlights. 'Haven't you heard?' he said, nervously.

'Heard what?' I said.

'Has nobody from WEA spoken to you?'

Was that the earth moving under my feet? 'Spoken to me about what?' I demanded.

'Well, it shouldn't be down to me to tell you,' said Nicholas, unhappily.

'Tell me what?' I demanded.

'They withdrew their offer. The deal's off.'

I stared at him, empty, unable to even react, thoughts draining like blood from my head.

'I'm sorry to be the one to break the news, guys,' said Nicholas.

People were patting me on the shoulders. I could hear murmurs of sympathy but I couldn't really distinguish what anyone was saying. I felt stoned, in the literal sense. I was numb and utterly bewildered.

The dream had lasted a week.

I went out front during the U2 show. I wanted to get away from my sympathetic friends, my solicitous girlfriend and my equally bewildered brother. I wanted to get drenched by the rain and covered in mud. Out there among the paying customers it looked like a lost scene from *Apocalypse Now*: 50,000 bedraggled refugees from real life, caked with dirt, standing hopefully on a hillside, waiting to be transported to another realm. The rain stopped but everything had turned to mud. People were sliding down the hill, caked in brown sludge.

And I lost myself in the music and the beer, the swimming lights, couples swaying under umbrellas, people dancing in the mire, brown and soaking and grinning despite it all and punching the air and raising our voices to the heavens, 'How long to sing this song?' all together, an immense crowd, singing as one while Bono swayed and Larry beat a lonely drum, 'How long to sing this song? How long? How long? How long? How long?'

How fucking long?

I had a big choking feeling inside, moved once again by the sheer, elemental power of music that seemed to ripple right through me, to speak for me, to know my very being.

There were fireworks at the close, deafening and dazzling.

'We thought we'd play one gig and we played a different gig altogether,' said Bono after the show, as drenched in sweat as I had been by the rain. 'But there's nothing wrong with that, nothing at all!' He was smiling happily. Words of congratulation were flying around. Champagne was being popped. I wanted to rip the fucking marquee down. I wanted to kick over the caravans. I wanted to light a bonfire under the stage and burn a living sacrifice to whatever dark gods had control of my fate. But my problems were not U2's problems, I knew that. So I just drank the champagne and kept myself to myself.

Joan got food poisoning and was throwing up all the way home.

A meeting was convened with Bill, to discuss what had gone wrong. 'It has to be off the record,' he said, 'but I think you boys are due an explanation.' In the quiet of his lair, he launched into a detailed description of office politics and internecine warfare within WEA. What it boiled down to was that Rob Dickens, head of WEA UK, had returned from a conference with his international superiors in the US, where he had been reprimanded for the performance of the UK division. He was accused of spending too much money, not selling enough records and, in particular, failing to break certain major signings (notably Simply Red, whose highly commercial white soul was falling on deaf ears). Dickens had come back in a foul mood and promptly stomped on our deal.

'Didn't he like the new demos?' I said, 'Because we've got other demos.'

'He hasn't listened to the demos,' said Bill, embarrassedly. 'He looked at your photo, though. He said the singer's hair was too short.'

'I can grow my hair!' I wailed.

'It's not about your hair,' said Bill. 'Look, no one here doubts that Shook Up! could be really huge, but you're a pop band and pop bands require the biggest investment. Duran Duran are probably the most popular group in the world right now but they could just as easily have been dropped after two singles if they hadn't had a hit. And making a single a hit is an expensive business. You don't just need the right song, you need the right producer, the right marketing. Videos. Image. It's an enormous outlay and if it goes wrong the company has lost a fortune. Whereas if we sign a rock band that's played the circuit, built up its own audience and got good reviews, they don't cost as much to market and they are guaranteed to sell a steady amount of records. Or at least that's the theory. And those are the kind of band we'll be signing in the immediate future.'

Bill let this sink in. 'It really has got nothing to do with you or your talent,' he assured us.

Was that supposed to make us feel better?

It was beginning to seem as if it never had anything to do with us or our talent. It was as if we were caught in the middle of some complex game and nobody was telling us the rules. What we needed was the same thing every unsigned band needs: a good manager. But where do you find one? It's a catch-22 situation: managers with a track record get their pick of all the acts who already have deals. Otherwise, you take your chances on an unknown who probably has no more idea of the rules than you do but, if you're very lucky, at least has some idea of what kind of game you're playing.

Bill left the business side of music not long after and became a recording artist in his own right. He wrote a book entitled *The Manual (How to Have a Number One the Easy Way)* then demonstrated the efficacy of his theories by scoring a number-one hit with the Timelords' 'Doctorin' the Tardis'. In 1987, he formed KLF, the revolutionary sound guerillas who became a chart-topping, multimillion-selling success before publicly disbanding with a violently antagonistic performance before a stunned music business audience at the 1992 Brit Awards ceremony. Afterwards, they left a freshly slaughtered sheep at the entrance to the post-awards party, with a tag reading 'I died for ewe. Bon appetit.'

I run into Bill occasionally, when he emerges from a quiet life of semi-retirement with his young family to promote his all too rare and rather brilliant books (I recommend his collection of essays, *45*, to anyone who cares about music and art). 'I don't think anybody wins in rock and roll,' he told me once, when I asked about his disenchantment with the music business. 'I think on the whole most people come through it damaged. Most people get to their forties and either they haven't had success and they're full of "if onlys" and "I-was-as-good-as", or they had success when they were young and they don't know why it went away or how to get it back. And the ones who are still successful, it doesn't matter how many records they sell, you look at them and think: "Oh, dear me, doesn't he realize he's making a complete prat of himself?"'

It's all to easy to see what category of forty-something rocker Bill would put me into.

So there we were, bereft, abandoned, well and truly fucked.

And then an extraordinary thing happened. The new issue of *Record Mirror* hit the stands. It was the poor relation of the music weeklies (*NME*, *Sounds* and *Melody Maker*) and had recently become a glossy A4 mag to try to survive. But, while the bigger papers had ignored our show, *Record Mirror* attended and were clearly impressed with what they saw. They featured a huge photo on page two of the next issue, over a declamatory piece heralding us as the future of pop:

You've had the Kemp brothers, the Jacksons, even the Osmonds. Now meet the McCormick brothers – the latest in a long line of musical siblings. Neil and Ivan McCormick form the nucleus of Shook Up! – a new band from Dublin, ready, willing and able to thrill you with their sharp pop sounds. With Neil on vocals and Ivan on guitar, they have now been joined by regular bass, drums and keyboards to produce a tight, dance-orientated rock sound that bursts with NRG . . . Mega success approacheth. Definitely NOT to be missed.

Record companies started to call us. All the A&R men who had failed to turn up to our showcase wanted to know where they could see us play. And who were we talking to? Word of the WEA débâcle was getting around, which was a bit of a double-edged sword. Other companies were interested to find out what got WEA worked up but were also seeking out the flaws that had made them dump us so quickly. But at least A&R departments were talking to us now. Of course, 'talking' in A&R terms is a euphemism for extended bouts of procrastination. When a record company wants you, they act. When they're not sure if they want you but they're afraid somebody else might, they talk.

We had to get another gig together. The problem being that we were broke. Shattered. Beyond penniless. In debt. Heading for bankruptcy. Living off our girlfriends and far too embarrassed to ask our dad to bail us out again. We explained this situation (well, perhaps not in detail) to an A&R man at London Records who was especially eager to see us perform.

'They don't hand out grants for showcases at the Unemployment Office,' I pointed out.

'I thought you worked as chefs,' said the A&R man.

'What are you talking about?' I said.

'Well, what's with the outfits, then?' he asked.

It dawned on me that he was referring to a pair of matching, white, side-button shirts that Ivan and I had blown our dole money on. 'This is high fashion, I'll have you know!' I protested.

'I didn't mean any offence,' he apologized. 'Some chefs look very cool.'

Anyway, he agreed to contribute £100 and we managed to scrape together enough money to put on a gig in an out-of-the-way pub venue, the Half Moon in Putney. This time the music business came out to see us, a row of watchful men conspicuously lining up along the bar at the back of the room. The place was rammed, with most of the audience returning from our first show. The atmosphere was charged with excitement. I went to the toilet before we were due on stage and an extremely pretty girl followed me in. 'I want to suck your cock,' she announced.

This is not the kind of thing that usually happened to me. My would-be groupie's timing was terrible, however. 'I've got to get on stage,' I apologized.

'After the show,' she said, invitingly.

I could tell you we were great that night. But I don't want to keep blowing my own trumpet so maybe I should let someone else blow it for me (and I'm not referring to my new female admirer, who, as far as I know, wound up blowing our drummer's trumpet, having succumbed during the show to his peculiar pheromonal charm). Damien Corless from *Hot Press* was in London on an interview assignment and came along to review the gig. Damien was part of a new generation at *Hot Press*, a writer I did not know and who owed me neither friendship nor favour, but he subsequently became a big champion of the band.

Shook Up! have catchy tunes to offer – and a great deal more. Principally there's frontman Neil McCormick, whose wit keeps the party bubbling from first to last. Brother Ivan plays a mean guitar without ever descending into axe-hero cliché while bassist Vlad completes the front row admirably. The threesome's carefully choreographed and highly eccentric stage antics proved a real crowd pleaser . . . Shook Up! are fun, they're Irish and they're going to be big.

I couldn't have put it better myself.

After two encores, we descended into the crowd like a conquering army. Some of the A&R people had even hung around and they were full of praise, offering such over the top flattery that I felt it had to climax with the declaration 'We want to sign you'. But the magic words never came.

We went to see the man from London Records, who was umming and awwing, apparently having come down with a terminal case of vacillation. 'Very entertaining, very good songs, great presentation,' he said, as if to himself.

After a long silence, Ivan exploded. 'What else do you want?!' he demanded.

I don't think he really knew what else he wanted. 'There's no doubt that it would sell,' he said after some thought. 'But I'm interested in something with a little more substance as well.'

He was sitting in front of a poster of Bananarama, London Records' biggest act.

But still, he didn't say no. He did not throw us out and tell us never to darken his doorway again. He just asked to be kept informed of developments. This was one of the phrases we were beginning to hear with depressing regularity.

'Don't sign anything without talking to us first,' was another. 'Has anyone actually made you an offer?' That's a good one.

As we settled into a gigging routine, our shows became regular meeting places for London's A&R community. Even journalists noticed. 'Their opening gambit's a good one, a commercial *tour de force* which grabs the attention before the watching A&R men can even think of turning down their deaf aids,' reported a *Melody Maker* review of a Shook Up! gig at the Embassy Rooms. "Love Is Stranger than Fiction" states the band's case to perfection, building from a solid bassline purpose-built for the 12-inch remix and erupting into a beautifully crafted melody.' The reviewer went on to say, 'Forty minutes with Shook Up! is like listening to an embryonic *Greatest Hits* album.' For some reason, this did not seem to be enough to impress the watchful A&R community, although others benefited from their attendance. We were supported at that show by a band from Liverpool called Black, who played dirgey post-Bunnymen rock and trashed the dressing room while we were on stage, defacing our posters with witty slogans like 'London wankers' and nicking anything that wasn't pinned down. They were offered a deal by one of the A&R men who had come to see us, although I am happy to report that lead singer Colin Vearncombe immediately split from his backing band of thieving bastards and essentially went solo. I spoke to the A&R man in question afterwards and he proudly told me that among the blizzard of noise he had spotted 'an enormous hit'. And he was right. Ish. Black reached number nine with a song called 'Wonderful Life' which had been transformed from its rocky origins into a kind of mournful, easy-listening ballad. Mind you, that was pretty much the last anybody ever heard of him, so there would be no *Greatest Hits* album for Black. But sucking on sour grapes never made anyone feel any better about their own misfortunes. Colin had his hit and, in the immortal words of Loudon Wainright III, it is 'better to have been a hasbeen than a never was.'

We dispensed with the services of our mercenary and expensive keyboard player and recruited a young maestro called Damien Le Gassic, who acted as if he might have been prepared to pay us to be in our wonderful group. Damien was a skinny, pale, wide-eyed whiz-kid fresh from music college whose naïve enthusiasm made us feel like grizzled veterans but whose musical skills put us all to shame. We had to keep an eye on Damien, however. He was so small and frail, he once passed out while loading his equipment into a hired van on a freezing-cold morning and developed frostbite lying unconscious in the snow. He proved immensely popular with a particular section of our growing army of fans. Every gig, we noticed increasing numbers of Oriental girls in attendance. They turned out to be foreign students of English and they loved Shook Up! – though presumably, given their still rather basic grasp of the language, it was not my lyrics that got them going. One of the girls, a very cute, teenage, self-proclaimed virgin, offered herself to Steve for deflowerment. It was an experience which he later described as so stressful he was unable to perform – until he convinced her it would be better if her concerned friends waited outside the room, rather than sitting in attendance offering helpful tips. A couple of the girls succumbed to the charms of Ivan, who did not set much store by the concept of loyalty to his long-suffering girlfriend, Cassandra. But the Oriental favourite, by some distance, was shy Damien. In an apartment shared by several of the girls I saw a shrine to Damien, with flowers and memorabilia arranged around an artfully assembled montage of photographs, with candles and incense burning beneath. It was explained to me that in the East pale skin was considered very attractive; Damien was the palest white boy they had ever seen.

By now I had entered into what was simultaneously the most rewarding and most frustrating phase of my twisted relationship with the music business. This was the best band line-up I had ever played in. Superb musicians, intelligent people, all getting off on the music and fired by a common cause. Even rehearsals were thrilling as we assembled intricate arrangements of new songs. And as for playing live, well, it was positively euphoric. There were moments when every element of the musical puzzle would fall perfectly into place. It was like an alignment of the planets. We would achieve lift-off, rocketing into space on a groove, the aftershock sending a musical vibration through the room that would drag the whole crowd into orbit in our wake, everybody communicating on the same wavelength, floating in zero musical gravity. This band was everything a musician could dream about. It was, surely, undeniable. Why then, did the music business continue to deny us?

Reviews were glowing and audiences growing. Every

performance ended in multiple encores. We stole the thunder of any act we supported and got invited back to every venue we appeared at. Soon we were regularly filling London nightspots like the Rock Garden, the Embassy Rooms and Fulham Greyhound in our own right. U2 played Live Aid at Wembley Stadium and, for once, I paid for my ticket and went to see them. I was moved and impressed by Bob Geldof's extravaganza; it seemed incredible that an Irishman could bring the world together like this. And I was enthralled by U2's part in it, a strangely manic performance in which Bono, desperate as ever to make a connection, disappeared for huge periods of time into the flag-waving crowd while the band, shorn of their lead singer, improvised sections of 'Ruby Tuesday', 'Sympathy for the Devil' and 'Walk on the Wildside'. But I did not feel in any way belittled to see my old friends on such a stage, for Shook Up! contributed in their own small way to Live Aid, headlining a bill of fifteen up-and-coming bands at a charity event hosted by Radio One DJ Bruno Brookes at Le Beat Route, raising a few hundred pounds for our efforts. The music industry might not be impressed but fuck them, we were creating our own momentum.

We did not have to pay for demos any more, as studios started to invite us to work with them. We recorded a live favourite, 'Stop the World', with talented producer Terry Thomas, who went on to work with Bad Company, Foreigner, Richard Marx and Three Colours Red. It was a punchy little Motown-influenced rock song about global anxiety, a typical Shook Up! subject.

We got ourselves an agent, a dour Northern Irishman called Barry Campbell who specialized in reggae and indie rock, a roster from which we protruded like the proverbial sore thumb. But he could get us into colleges, where you could actually make some money. We toured Ireland twice, with the help of In Tua Nua's manager, Mark Clinton, where we were greeted like returning heroes. We appeared on a primetime RTE TV show performing 'Stop the World'. We were written up in every newspaper in the country. 'Shaking Their Way to Fame and Fortune' trumpeted the *Sunday Press*, who quaintly noted that 'Shook Up! received tumultuous applause from raving teenagers and well-known stars such as Bono'.

Bono and Ali had joined an appreciative audience at Trinity College. Bono declared himself suitably impressed. 'I don't know much about pop,' he joked, 'but I know what I like!' He told us that what we were doing reminded him of Queen, which we took as a compliment, even though they were probably one of least hip bands in the universe. 'The showmanship is great, the songs are classic. I don't see how record companies can fail to go for it.'

Oh, but they could. Our reviews were astonishing. I am convinced that we had more enthusiastic reviews than any other unsigned band in history. I put together a ten-page booklet featuring the best of them and circulated it among record companies. The front page of the booklet read:

'A REALLY EXCITING NEW BAND' – Capital Radio
'SHAKING THEIR WAY TO FAME AND FORTUNE' – *Sunday Press*
'DANCE-ORIENTED ROCK SOUND THAT BURSTS WITH ENERGY'
  – *Record Mirror*
'CATCHY CHORUSES AND WELL-STRUCTURED SONGS' – *In Dublin*
'A SET FULL OF GUSTO, NIFTY LITTLE DANCE ROUTINES AND
LOUD, DISTINCTLY POPPY DANCE MUSIC' – *Evening Press*
'SHOOK UP! REALLY GET STUCK IN' – *Sounds*
'MEGA SUCCESS APPROACHETH. DEFINITELY NOT TO BE MISSED'
  – *Record Mirror*

I spoke to one of our regular contacts in A&R (or 'Uhm & Ahh' as we had started to refer to it). 'The quotes are a bit over the top,' he said. 'I suppose you made them up yourself?'

What was the fucking use?

There were so many great gigs, such fantastic reactions, so much confidence – we were convinced record companies could not see this and walk away from it. But they did. Again and again. I visited Ross Fitzsimons in MCA, where Lucien Grainge was no longer employed. I was playing Ross our 'Stop the World' demo when the door of his office flew open and in stormed Gordon Charlton, the new head of A&R.

'What are you listening to?' he demanded to know. 'It's bloody fantastic!' He wanted to know where he could hear more and I told him we would be appearing that very night at the Rock Garden. 'I'll be there!' he said. And he was true to his word. I saw him walk in halfway through the set, stand at the back and watch two numbers before walking out again, which (as you can imagine) was extremely disconcerting. The next day I rang for his reaction. 'It's too commercial for my taste,' he said.

'Too commercial?' I spluttered. 'How can something be too commercial? You mean it might be too popular? We might sell too many records?'

'It was all a bit well played,' he said. How did this man get his job?

'Maybe we should fucking rehearse a bit less,' I muttered.

He told me he liked things rougher around the edges. He signed Cactus World News.

I was beginning to faintly comprehend that the very area we had chosen to operate in was working against us. We were upbeat, danceable, unashamedly commercial but we had songs about rape, greed, fear, religion, love, pain and the whole damn thing. We were a square peg and no matter what angle the music business looked at us from (and, to be fair, they did keep coming back and taking another look), nobody could figure out how to fit us into the round hole labelled 'pop'.

And then the inevitable happened. At the end of the summer of 1986, after a year of gigging, Vlad announced he was leaving.

'I thought you believed in fate,' I said.

'I do,' said Vlad.

'Well, didn't your girlfriend tell you we were going to be the biggest band in the world?' I pleaded.

'She spoke to her father about that last night,' said Vlad. As we knew, his girlfriend's father was dead but made occasional appearances to bring her up to date with developments in the spirit world. His verdict was that 'Destiny is not set in stone, there are different paths we can all choose', Vlad reported. Apparently we had taken a wrong turning at a spiritual T-junction. 'Cosmically speaking, you're fucked,' said Vlad. I hoped he was joking. You could never really tell.

Vlad hung up his bass and decided to concentrate on production. He signed a record deal with 10 (a subsidiary of Virgin) and, in January 1988, reached number six with 'The Jack that House Built' by Jack'n'Chill (he was Jack), Britain's first home-grown house record.

Damien was the next to depart, going back to music college, disillusioned with the music business. We did not hear from him for years but, in the late nineties, started seeing his credit appear on major records. He co-wrote material on Madonna's *Music* album and produced an album for K. D. Lang. Ivan ran into him at a London club. Damien was reportedly very happy, living in LA, his skills much sought-after by A-list stars. Our former pale Oriental sex symbol was, according to Ivan, looking very tanned indeed.

Steve was getting session work for busty female pop stars such as Taylor Dayne, Tiffany and Samantha Fox (must have been those pheromones). Brother Beyond, a quartet of handsome lads signed to Parlophone, started to employ him and I went to see them play a showcase. I wondered what the difference was between them and us. They had two talented songwriters, Eg White and Carl Fysh, and a handsome lead vocalist, Nathan Moore, and crafted funky, modern, dance pop. It was all very smooth, lacking Shook Up!'s live extravagance and spiky edges. But the crucial difference emerged when their recording career began with material written for them by top Europop producers Stock, Aitken and Waterman. Eg quit the band in disgust. Steve, meanwhile, proved so popular with their fans (those pheromones again) that they asked him to become a full-time member. We were close friends and Steve was reluctant to leave us in the lurch but he was being presented with pop stardom on a plate. In the event, Brother Beyond enjoyed short-lived careers as pin-ups (they reached number two in 1988 but lost their grip on the top ten a year later and were bankrupt by 1991) before Steve returned to session work, playing with everyone from Duran Duran to Jeff Beck. He remains one of the leading session drummers in the recording industry.

As for Ivan and I, well, we briefly contemplated tracing our steps back down the cosmic highway to try to work out where we had gone wrong. But fuck it. We didn't believe in that shit anyway. We'd just have to press on and hope we were still travelling in roughly the right direction.

16

I was summoned to interview-room number 4 in the Department of Health and Social Security. Mysteriously, the door had 'No. 58' stuck on it and was consequently quite hard to find, resulting in my arriving some five minutes after my name had crackled over the tannoy.

It was my third visit to the DHSS offices in as many weeks. Each time, I had made the journey to Euston, waited around for hours, only to be informed that (because of backlogs of work or other such excuses) my appointment would have to be postponed. I had a feeling they were testing me.

'So, we meet at last!' I joked to the sombre, matronly, fifty-ish woman sitting at the other side of a thick file, presumably mine. She did not respond, other than to pointedly look at her watch. I wasn't sure what was in store. I had always been confident that if I kept my wits about me I could spin this whole dole racket out indefinitely. My previous interviewer was a skinny, nervous pushover who seemed to expect to get pushed. But I had the distinct feeling my new case officer was a step up and a stage heavier.

'Do you know you have signed on late every fortnight for the last three years?' my interrogator commented, perusing my notes.

'Really?' I said. 'You know, it's not easy getting to the dole office at that time of the morning when you've got no money for transport.' I had mentally debated what attitude to adopt (indignant? Stupid? Penitent?) and decided the safest best was to smile and be as pleasant as possible while I worked out what she was after. She launched into a stern lecture about my responsibilities to the state. 'You haven't held a job since you left college five years ago,' she noted.

'Is it that long?' I asked, innocently. Well, what was I supposed to say? 'I'm sorry, officer, I'll give up all my foolish ambitions and take the first paid work that comes my way'? This occasional hour of boredom was the price I paid to follow my rock'n'roll dream. But then she made a tactical mistake.

'You've got to play by the rules of the game,' she said. I couldn't believe my ears. Her and Ossie and the music business and all these fucking games! I considered boldly declaring 'This is no game, this is my life!' but decided it would be too corny. So I let her ramble on until she bullishly announced: 'These are the rules of the game . . .'

That was quite enough. 'This is no game,' I declared passionately. 'This is my life!' She actually bought it. She became flustered and apologized for her comments while I pressed home my advantage with a sincere, slightly desperate: 'Do you know what it's like to live on £24 a week?'

No, of course she didn't. But then neither did I.

I was still doing bits and pieces for *Hot Press*. I drew a regular cartoon strip, the subject matter of which is rather revealing. It was called 'Situations Vacant', and it featured a couple of unemployed scoundrels sitting at a bar discussing matters of the world. For example:

'Did you hear Mad Mick got done for joyriding?' says one scoundrel.

'No, what happened?' says the other.

'He went to a nightclub, got really drunk and couldn't get a taxi, so he stole a BMW and crashed into a police car on the way home!' reports the scoundrel.

'That's becoming a serious problem in the city today!' says his gloomy friend.

'Yeah,' agrees the scoundrel, 'you can never find a taxi when you need one.'

Boom! Boom!

The interview ended with another stay of execution. In order to satisfy my unemployment officer, however, I needed evidence that I was actively seeking work. So I sat down to apply for several creative jobs gleaned from the Media section of the

Guardian newspaper. The problem was I wanted replies but I didn't want interviews, which would be too time-consuming by far and might result in my accidentally finding myself employed.

I initially found it quite upsetting applying for jobs for which I was eminently qualified while deliberately selling myself short. My ego had taken quite a battering of late, and the idea that someone might take me for an idiot (despite the fact that I would, hopefully, never meet them) made me squirm. But, resigning myself to the task, I started to draw perverse pleasure from the subtle constructions of my letters, handwriting them on paper that was far too thin, folding them too many times and, to top it off, liberally spraying them with a pungent, butch deodorant. I could only hope they would not be kept on file and pulled out to embarrass me after I became famous.

You see, I was still convinced that I would make it. It was just taking a bit longer than planned, that's all.

I had a chilling moment while sitting with Yeah! Yeah!'s old drummer, Leo Regan, in a pub in Kilburn (an area of London known by locals as the twenty-eighth county of Ireland). Leo still walked with a limp from our accident, a physical disability that (following a stint playing stand-up drums with a hugely popular rockabilly trio named Those Handsome Devils) had eventually curtailed his musical career. Leo received a substantial insurance payout and had done some travelling around the world, during which he developed an interest in photography. He surfaced in England to do a course at the London College of Printing, and became the latest emigrant to move into our flat.

Anyway, Leo had come up with the idea of doing a photo feature for *Hot Press* on London's Irish community, which was a good excuse to trawl around drinking pints of Guinness in every watering hole in Kilburn. I was interviewing a publican, when our attention was drawn to a wrinkled old fat man sitting at the bar, chuckling away to himself.

'Are you Irish, yourself?' asked Leo.

'Oh, I am, yes, indeed,' chuckled the old fella in a thick Galway accent.

'When did you leave Ireland?' asked Leo.

'I came over to London in 1952 for a game of soccer and I never went back,' said the old man. He began to tell us how he played for Galway Rovers and emigrated on the promise of a professional football career that never materialized. He was twenty-six then. He was sixty-three now. And he had never returned home. But he was adamant that he would be going back some day. 'I never signed anything!' he insisted.

'What do you mean, you never signed anything?' I asked.

'Oh, I signed the dole, all right, but I never pledged allegiance to the Queen!' declared the old man. He supped from his pint of bitter. The Guinness was too expensive for him these days. 'I'll go back someday, I will,' he said. 'Oh yeah, I'll go back.'

'That's you in another forty years,' said Leo as we left the pub. I didn't laugh. The thought had already occurred to me. I was in danger of turning into the character from the beautiful old Irish ballad 'The Mountains of Mourne':

Oh Mary, this London's a wonderful sight
With people here working by day and by night
They don't sow potatoes, nor barley, nor wheat
But there's gangs of them digging for gold in the street
At least when I asked them that's what I was told
So I just took a hand at this digging for gold
But for all that I found there I might as well be
Where the mountains of Mourne sweep down to the sea

Joan left, travelling to Australia. I had driven her away and I was sick with myself. Joan was beautiful and she was funny and she loved me totally, unreservedly, hopelessly. And I . . . didn't know what I wanted. Just something else, something different. I worried that I would never feel anything more than I felt for her but I was afraid of going through life without finding out for sure. Our relationship was all push and pull but those last few months together had been weirdly harmonious. Once Joan posed a solution to my commitment dilemma by telling me she was leaving, all problems between us evaporated. We spent the summer of 1986 like a young couple tenderly in love. Then, one day in October, I accompanied her to Heathrow airport. Joan was in tears. We kissed goodbye at the departure gate. Then she turned. And she was gone. Out of my life. And it was as if a huge wave of nausea came rolling down the airport concourse and blasted through my body. I found myself staggering from the shockwave of emotion, dazed and bewildered, a cold sweat prickling my skin. I lurched into the public toilets and just made it to a sink to throw my guts up. A toilet attendant stared at me with reproach as I wiped the vomit from my lips.

'I'm sorry,' I said. And I *was* sorry. Truly, truly sorry. But not for him.

That night I wrote a song, which was the way I always dealt with my emotions. It was called 'Fool for Pain'.

> Your disappearance moves through me like a tenant
> Touching all the things you left behind
> Whispering your name for my penance
> Leaving fingerprints on all I thought was mine
> So this is what it means to be free
> And all my independence was in vain
> How could you be a fool for me
> When I'm such a fool for pain?
> All alone, I know there's something missing
> I fill the space but the emptiness remains
> It tugs my mind, like the sound of gas escaping
> Fool for Pain
> On the phone, the sound of heavy breathing
> It's just mine, there's no way to explain
> I wanted you to go . . . till you were leaving
> Fool for Pain

Can there be any greater art form than the song for exorcizing a feeling? It's poetry with melody to fill in all those spaces that words can't touch. But surely songs need to be released into the world to work their magic? Mine were becoming congested inside the studio of my own mind, turning cancerous.

Bono phoned one day to tell me he had just written a song. He was full of the excitement of the creation, bubbling over with the need to share. 'You know how you are always saying U2 don't write real songs? Well, I think we've cracked it,' he said. 'I think we've written a real, classic song.'

'What's it called?' I asked.

'"I Still Haven't Found What I'm Looking For",' said Bono.

'Great title,' I admitted.

He proceeded to sing to me down the phone line. 'I have climbed highest mountains / I have run through the fields / Only to be with you . . . / I have run, I have crawled, I have scaled these city walls / These city walls / Only to be with you . . . / But I still haven't found what I'm looking for.'

It gave me a chill. How could Bono know what was going on in my head? After all, he was the man with everything. Fame, riches, love, faith, creative fulfilment. But as for me, I was still searching.

You might have thought that Ivan and I would have given up by now. Surely any sane person would know that it was over? We had shot our bolt. We had exhausted all avenues of inquiry. But we had each other to sustain our mutual madness, talking up the notion that what did not kill us could only make us stronger and that talent would win out in the end. We even took rejection as a kind of perverse encouragement, rationalizing that we had learned a great deal along the way, improving as musicians and growing as people. And we were still young and free and without responsibilities. The future was ours. And the prize would be all the sweeter when it came.

We had other encouragement, too, to keep us hanging on. We were told that Clive Davis, the legendary head of Arista in the US, had taken an interest in our demos. The problem he identified was the lack of that all-important first single, the unstoppable hit that seemed to us to be the Holy Grail of an A&R community too timid and unimaginative to trust the artists themselves. Have you ever wondered why so many manufactured bands are launched with cover versions? Because the songs have already been hits. They are tried and tested. Even George Martin wanted the Beatles to record a cover version as their second single, before John and Paul, stung at the implicit criticism of their songwriting, delivered 'Please Please Me' and unleashed Beatlemania.

Ivan and I decided to do something we should have done years before: record and release our own single. We had been too precious about our songs. Because we aspired to state-of-the-art pop, which is an expensive business, we had spurned the idea of releasing anything that was less than perfect. Now we wanted something that at least acknowledged our existence, some kind of testament to years spent making music. We wanted something we could actually hold in our hands and play on our record decks. As usual, there was one overriding problem. We had no money.

Our agent, Barry Campbell, stepped in. Barry was basically a small-time, hard-working hustler, who cheerfully admitted to being no more knowledgeable about the machinations of the big-time music business than we were. But, in exchange for a management contract, he was prepared to put his money where our mouths were and frankly we had no one else to turn to. He would pay for the recording and arrange its release on an independent label he was in the process of setting up. We shook hands on a budget figure of £4000 and while contracts were drawn up we booked three days at Terminal studios in Elephant and Castle.

Vlad came back on board as producer and bassist. Steve returned to play drums. We got hold of a new keyboard player through *Melody Maker*. Richard Ford was a young television repairman and a brilliant, highly technical musician. The only problem being that he lived hundreds of miles away in Yorkshire, which was costing us a fortune in petrol money. It was a round trip of 500 miles just to rehearse.

The song we chose was 'Invisible Girl'. It had been a live favourite but it was, for us, an unusually subtle track, with a lovely, gentle groove and a rich, melancholic melody. The lyrical topic (in typical Shook Up! fashion) was child abuse – inspired by a news story in which a victim of abuse had complained that no one ever listened to her – and it included the striking phrase 'We are the silent children / We speak but no one listens'. The sentiment seemed to draw audiences in. A young woman came up to me after one show, crying and desperate to talk about 'Invisible Girl'. 'I'm the girl in the song,' she kept saying.

Work at Terminal studios was laborious. Hours were spent just fine-tuning the drum sounds. Making records is like assembling a sonic puzzle, and we were still painstakingly slotting the first pieces into place when Barry called. He seemed oddly nervous as he related a long, involved saga about a promoter in Eastern Europe who had ripped him off for a considerable amount of money.

'That's terrible,' I said, wondering what any of this had to do with me.

'The thing is, Neil, I find myself stuck between a rock and a hard place,' he said.

I did not like the sound of where this was going. 'What exactly is the problem?' I said.

'I don't have the money to pay for the studio,' he admitted. 'I'm going to have to pull out.'

What is the deal here? You must surely be wondering the same thing as I was. Just what is the fucked-up deal with the mismanagement of this godless universe? I mean, did somebody really have it in for me up there?

'You can't pull out,' I said. 'It's too late to stop now.' What a joke. We should have stopped years before.

'I'm sorry,' said Barry. 'That's just the way it is.'

Of course it was. Why would I have expected anything else?

I whispered the news to Ivan. We had a hushed confab. It would have cost us at least half the amount to stop recording there and then, so we elected not to confess our sudden insolvency. While Vlad and the musicians worked on oblivious, Ivan rushed around behind the scenes, begging from various allies and associates. His close friend Martin Lupton, a trainee doctor from a well-to-do background, came up with £1000. Leo, who still had some money left from his insurance settlement, came up with another £1000. A phone call to our long-suffering dad in Ireland delivered the rest. By the time it came to mixing, a day or so later, we had the money to pay for everything, and a string of IOU notes hanging over our heads.

Ah, but when we listened to the playback, it was all worth it. 'Invisible Girl' did not sound like a demo. Plush and full and crystal clear, sweet and sad and dreamy, it sounded like the real thing, a proper record. But it was a record that did not have a home.

There was one call I could make, however. One favour I had always been reluctant to ask. I went back to Ireland, to see Bono.

U2 were ensconced in a studio off St Stephen's Green, working on mixes and B-sides for their new album. Everybody was there. Bono, Edge, Adam, Larry. Even Paul McGuinness. The playback snatches I heard were astonishing: tough and dark and muscular, burning with emotion. They had made another bold creative leap and at its forefront was Bono's voice, tearing his way through the band's wall of sound. The gap between U2 live and U2 on record had always been the gap between the Edge and Bono. Now they had come together with a vengeance.

'What do you think?' said Bono, his secret smile telling me that he already knew.

'I'm speechless,' I said.

'That makes a change,' said Edge.

Bono and I retired to the studio's recreation room where we sat together while I explained the situation to him. I pointed out that he had really gone to bat for Cactus World News and In Tua Nua, among other Dublin bands, making calls to record company bosses to press their cases. I had never asked him for anything like that. But I reminded him that he once offered to put a single out for us on Mother and I wanted to know if his offer still stood? 'I don't want to put you on the spot,' I said. 'But we really need a break.'

Bono explained that all decisions concerning Mother were made by five people: the members of U2 and their manager. Decisions had to be unanimous. Each person effectively had a veto. 'I don't want to fall out with you about this,' he said, 'so you have to understand the process.'

'We're not going to fall out,' I promised.

'Let's take a listen, then,' said Bono, slipping the tape into the rec-room stereo.

'Invisible Girl' came gliding out of the speakers, sweet and melodic. It was a million miles removed from the dark-hewn rock we had just been listening to.

'Pop music,' Bono noted with a warm smile.

'Everything is pop music,' I said.

'Leave it with me,' said Bono.

As I got up to go, Adam came into the room. 'Nice groove,' he observed.

'Well, thank you, Adam,' I said with genuine delight. I felt as if the weight of the world was lifting off my shoulders. Everything was going to work out fine.

My younger sister, Louise, had left school the previous year and got a job in a recording studio, apparently unperturbed by the fact that her brothers were pretty much a walking advertisement for everything that was wrong with the music business. She was following a much more practical course than we ever did, however. She studied musical engineering and now had the run of the Lab studio, a small 8-track in Dublin. With time on our hands, Ivan and I availed of this facility. In the absence of a band, we opted to record some of our less-poppy, acoustic-oriented material, offbeat songs that we always imagined would provide us with a future folky sideline. The titles might give you some idea about my general state of mind: 'King of the Dead', 'Buried Alive', 'Heaven Bent', 'Fool for Pain' and 'This House is Condemned'. My lyrical bent was becoming ever so slightly twisted.

A couple of days later, I got a call to meet up with Bono in a pub close to where U2 were rehearsing. We sat in a dark recess and ordered a couple of pints. Bono was tapping the table, thoughtfully.

'The answer's no,' he suddenly announced.

I was incredulous but I bit my tongue. I had made enough enemies with my outspoken reactions to criticism and rejection. I was determined not to fall out with Bono over this.

'You knew the deal,' he said. 'I don't want to say who voted against; it's not important, because if one says no then we all say no – that's the way it works. All I can tell you is it got vetoed.'

I didn't say anything. I supped from my pint and digested this latest rejection, perhaps the cruellest rejection of all because it was delivered by a friend.

'The thing about it is, Neil, it's pop music,' said Bono. 'I don't think we understand pop music. It's not what we've ever been about. So there it is. Are you gonna be OK with that?'

'Yeah, I'm OK,' I said.

Two American girls were hovering conspicuously at the corner of our table. They took the silence that had fallen as an invitation to speak.

'Are you the Bono?' asked one.

Bono laughed, relieved by this absurd distraction. 'Yes, I am the Bono!' he admitted.

'Can we have your autograph?'

'Of course,' he said, scrawling his moniker on the proffered piece of paper. The girls weren't quite done yet, though. They nervously pushed the piece of paper towards me. 'Are you the Edge?'

'Sign the girl's paper, Edge,' teased Bono.

So I signed. 'God bless – the Edge'. It was probably as close to the trappings of fame as I was ever going to come.

17

There was an opening gala for something or other, a big club-night launch. I was used to attending such occasions, blagging my way in to album launches and showcases as a representative of *Hot Press*. I would spend half my time filling my pockets with hors-d'oeuvres and tucking a couple of bottles of wine into my jacket to take home to our impoverished household. But this was a very big do and, for some reason, my name was not on the guest-list. 'There must be a mistake,' I insisted. 'Look again.' But the hatchet-faced bouncer was having none of it. He pushed me, protesting loudly, back into the huge crowd pressed up against the red ropes that separated the VIP guests from the gawking public. Spotlights arced through the cold night air. I really wanted to get inside, where the action was, and hopefully scanned the invitees for a familiar face. Which is when a white stretch-limo pulled up and, amid popping flashes, the four members of U2 climbed out, waving to the crowd. As luck would have it, they were going to walk right past where I was standing. I waved. But everyone was waving. Adam, Larry and Edge trooped down the red carpet, acknowledging the applause, with Bono taking up the rear.

'Bono!' I shouted, but everybody was shouting his name. This was pathetic. But he was just inches away. I reached out and touched his shoulder. 'Bono!' He turned my way. But he just looked right through me, a look of such blank detachment it cut me to the bone.

A bouncer grabbed my hand, twisting it painfully. 'Fuck off! He's a friend of mine,' I shouted. The bouncer looked to Bono for confirmation.

'I don't know him,' said Bono. And walked on by.

I woke up with a shudder. What the fuck was that about? I

lay in bed, staring at the ceiling, trying to shake off the emotions my dream had evoked. I felt humiliated. But, worse, I felt ashamed of myself. Ashamed of dreaming of my friend in that manner. Ashamed of so blatantly craving his recognition. Ashamed of dreaming about him at all. I didn't want Bono taking up residence in my sleep, as if he had the freedom of movement of my subconscious.

But Bono was everywhere, so why not inside my head? *The Joshua Tree* came out in March 1987 and went to number one all over the world, the fastest-selling album in British music history, occupying the top spot in the American charts for nine consecutive weeks and clocking up in excess of sixteen million sales. U2 were hailed as the torch-bearers for rock'n'roll, analysed in newspaper editorials, snapped by the paparazzi and featured on the cover of every conceivable magazine. They even made the front of *Time*, an exceedingly strange place to see the familiar faces of old schoolfriends. Bono was embraced as rock's latest mystic seer, a sort of holy cross between the Morissons, Jim and Van. There was a kind of mania in the air. They played two nights at Wembley Stadium, a venue with a 70,000 capacity. That was outrageous. There were only a handful of groups in the whole world who could fill Wembley Stadium and U2 sold it out twice over.

I saw U2 three times in June 1987, and I was never bored. The shows were awe-inspiring. After years in which, musically, they had made themselves up as they went along, priding themselves in their self-sufficiency and never looking back, U2 had finally begun to embrace rock's past, digging into a tradition that stemmed from folk and the blues and extended to heavy metal and art rock. Their set stretched from the intimate to the apocalyptic, encompassing a shambling, singalong rendition of Ben. E. King's classic 'Stand By Me', the aching sadness of 'Running to Stand Still', the all-encompassing emotional swell of '40', the brooding tenderness of 'With or Without You' warping into an uplifting version of Van Morrison's 'Gloria', a caustically rewired anti-Thatcher version of Bob Dylan's 'Maggie's Farm' and the show-stopping, heavy-rock apocalyptic epic 'Bullet the Blue Sky', with the band drenched in blood-red lighting, the Edge's psyched-out guitars howling like Led Zeppelin after the levee broke and Bono commandeering a hand-held spotlight and intoning rambling Beat poetry: 'I was walking through the streets of London, walking through the streets of Kilburn, Brixton and Harlesden, and I felt I was a long way from San Salvador, but still, the sky was ripped open, the rain pouring through the gaping wound, pelting the women and children, waiting in line to the hospitals, waiting in line to pick up money, pelting the women and children who run ... who run into the arms of ... Margaret Thatcher!'

The first gig I saw was actually at Birmingham National Exhibition Centre. It was a mark of how far U2 had come that the 12,000-seater Arena was now an intimate venue for them. My uncle Jim, who lived in the midlands, wanted to see the show and U2's office had duly furnished me with tickets and passes. Ivan and I travelled up by train, along with Ivan's girlfriend, Cassandra.

During a playful version of Curtis Mayfield's 'People Get Ready', Bono would regularly invite someone from the audience up on stage to play his guitar. It was an attempt to break down the divide between band and audience, to share the music. There was also a fair chance that, if the guest was even the least bit competent, they would make a better job of it than Bono, which was certainly the case at Birmingham's NEC. Bono asked his virtuous guest if he was in a band. The guy nodded eagerly. 'Is the whole band here?' asked Bono. They were 'Well, get 'em up,' said Bono. The band members excitedly made their way on to the stage where they were given instruments and joined U2 in a chaotic rendition of Dylan's 'Knockin' On Heaven's Door' before a roaring audience of 11,000.

I looked at Ivan and he smiled weakly back at me. The pangs of envy emanating from the pair of us were strong enough to be almost visible. 'Bet you wish that was you,' said Uncle Jim, which was rather ungracious, I thought. That would be the last time I sorted him out with tickets.

Afterwards, we showed our passes and were admitted back-stage. But it was all very strange. Our passes gained us access only to the huge, empty space immediately behind the stage, where roadies were pushing equipment around and a smattering of guests seemed to be hanging aimlessly about. I felt awkward, unsure what the protocol was. The band were nowhere to be seen. There was a further gated area, in front of which stood a couple of yellow-jacketed security men, but when I showed my pass they just shook their heads. 'Are the band coming out?' I asked. 'They might – can't really say,' is all I was told. We retreated, wondering whether there was any point in staying, just for the half chance of saying hello. The whole thing gave me a bad feeling. The U2 machine had become so big now, I didn't know where I fitted into it – or even if I did any more. Then Larry emerged to chat with a couple of people and spotted us lurking uncomfortably on the other side of this vast chamber. He waved us over. 'You should have asked someone to come and let us know you were here,' he reprimanded us amiably, instructing the security men to admit us.

It was a relief to be welcomed into the dressing room, where Bono and Edge greeted us warmly. Adam was nowhere to be seen. 'As soon as the show's over, he's always disappearing with the most beautiful women you've ever seen,' said Bono. 'A different woman every night. I don't know how he does it! The man is a complete charmer.' It struck me as a bizarrely naïve comment, a kind of wilful denial of the obvious truth: Adam was a rock star, indulging in rock'n'roll vices.

Bono was exhausted and hoarse, a towel wrapped around his neck absorbing the sweat, but he invited Ivan and me to visit his hotel the next day, where we could talk at leisure. But once again we ran into security problems. 'There is no one of that name registered here,' said the desk clerk, when I asked to be put through to Bono's room.

'Try Paul Hewson,' I said.

'I'm sorry, no one of that name either.' I have to say, the clerk did not look sorry at all. In fact, he looked rather smug.

'Look, I know he's here,' I said. 'There are people standing out the front with U2 banners. Bono invited us over so can you just let him know we've arrived?'

'I'm afraid I am going to have to ask you to leave,' said the clerk, beckoning for the attention of a doorman.

A rather bedraggled Adam wandered through the lobby in the nick of time, arm cast over the shoulder of some beauty who didn't look like she'd got much sleep. He smilingly reassured the clerk that we weren't deranged stalkers. Bono was apparently booked under a false name which he had neglected to supply. We went up to his room, where he was sitting alone, sipping red wine, half watching the swampy New Orleans thriller *No Mercy* on TV, a film he had evidently seen several times before. It struck me as a curious kind of velvet prison Bono found himself in – the fans outside restricting his movement, his days spent in an endless chain of hotel rooms lacking the personalized familiarity of home. He certainly seemed very happy to see us, insisting we join him in polishing off the bottle of wine while he regaled us with long anecdotes about his recent adventures. He was charming and attentive towards Cassandra. Bono can be very flirtatious around women. Obviously, if he wanted to, he could have followed the Adam Clayton route to satisfying his every desire with the pick of the world's most attractive women. But then, he already had one of the world's most attractive women waiting for him at home. Bono's strong faith may have served to keep temptation at bay but it did not stop him entertaining possibilities, flirting with his sexual power, playing with fire.

I once accused him of being a voyeur of the dark side of life. 'I am a voyeur of my own dark side,' he laughed. 'There's nothing seemier than your own plans, made in the dead of night!' But it struck me in Birmingham that Bono was lonely. Ali lived her own life in Dublin, refusing to become a satellite to Bono's star. She went to gigs when it suited her, rather than joining the entourage on the road. And Bono used to joke that she occasionally threw him out, just to keep him in line. I think the truth was that when he returned from tour, all hyped up after months of adulation, she would insist he stay in a hotel for a couple of weeks to reintegrate with the values of her more ordinary life before he could come back home. It was a kind of reality decompression chamber. 'Ali will not be worn like a brooch,' was Bono's admiring phrase. 'She's her own woman.' But I have also heard him complain, from time to time, that 'it's almost impossible to be married and be in a band on the road'.

'You know, this fame business can be quite tough,' he said in Birmingham. 'There's some strong stuff out there. And I'm not talking about drugs or drink. I'm talking about other ways of seeing the world just through the prism of being a star and being so privileged you can get bent out of shape. The whole business of people thinking you're important because you can write a song and sing it rather than being a nurse or a fireman, how absurd is that? This guy said to me a while ago, "My son's a doctor, he saves lives; how many lives have you saved?"'

'You can't complain about fame,' I said. 'You've got everything you ever wanted.'

'I've got everything *you* ever wanted,' countered Bono. 'How do you know what I want?'

'I've got a theory about fame,' I said.

'Why am I not surprised?' quipped Bono.

'You always hear famous people being described as larger than life,' I said. 'I think fame can actually make human beings bigger inside. Because you have the freedom to be whatever you want to be. Everything you do is accepted and encouraged so you can expand into the space that creates. You are free from the mundanity of everyday existence.'

'Yeah, that's a fact, I am,' he replied. 'But you make that sound like an accusation. The truth is, I was never very good at the mundane. Now I don't have to deal with it, don't have to worry about the mortgage and the bills. It's all taken care of. But I've got concerns of my own. You know, Neil, you're very talented but you're still wrestling with a lot of things. And I don't mean just wrestling with paying the rent. You're wrestling with things inside yourself. I don't want to tell you how to live your life –

although telling other people what to do happens to be one of the things I am very good at! – but surely you can't expect to beat the world while you're still busy beating yourself up?'

That sure shut me up. Bono took another sip of wine and lit a cigarette.

'You're smoking?' said Ivan, who detested the habit.

'How stupid is that?' said Bono. 'To take up smoking as an adult? You see, it's all the stress I have to deal with. Fame is hard, man. Believe me, you don't want it.' He was grinning widely. He knew he wasn't going to put us off that easily.

We left Bono with a tape of the songs we had recorded in Dublin.

The next time I saw him was backstage at Wembley Stadium. I went both nights. I have seen very few acts capable of holding the complete attention of a stadium but U2 carried it off as if this were their natural habitat, sucking us into their performance until we might as well have been in their rehearsal room. They share a complex mix of elements with Bruce Springsteen and the E Street Band (my other stadium favourites), combining showmanship with integrity (not an easy feat) and creating intimacy in even the largest spaces by sheer force of personality and musicality. They were stunning. Again.

After the show there were two distinct hospitality areas, the largest catering for hundreds of representatives of the music business with a separate, smaller gathering reserved for special guests. When you get that successful, even the VIP rooms have VIP sections. In the smaller section was Ali, along with other friends from Dublin. This was U2's big night so I was quite taken back when Bono approached me and immediately started talking about my music.

'That tape you gave me,' he said. 'It's extraordinary. The song "Fool for Pain", it's so raw it's painful to listen to. You're standing naked in that song, with your trousers down and your willy hangin' out for everyone to see. I was almost embarrassed to listen to it. That's the stuff you should be doing. Forget the pop music. You and Ivan are two of the best songwriters ever to come out of Ireland and nobody knows. Why? Because you're not letting anybody hear what you can really do.'

'We've played Wembley,' I said, defensively. Bono looked at me sceptically. 'Wembley Coach & Horses,' I added.

Bono laughed.

'I don't know what you think's so funny,' I said. 'It was a really good gig.'

The gap between us now was so large you could lose yourself in it. What were the chances of this happening? It wasn't enough that I had gone to school with some guys who became rock stars. No. They had to go and become the biggest-selling and most acclaimed rock stars of their generation in the whole wide world. All I wanted when I was a kid was to be famous. Now, even if I was to somehow miraculously achieve my dream, it would be dwarfed into insignificance by the sheer scale of the achievements of some kids who used to sit next to me in class. It was a twist of fate worthy of the vindictive God of Bono's Old Testament.

My life was taking some dark and twisted turns. Steve and I were picking up girls. He too had recently come out of a long-term relationship and we spent a lot of time together, hanging out in wine bars, talking about life and trying to get laid (not necessarily in that order of priority), preferably for one night only, no strings attached. Of course, the problem with trying to pick up women in the company of the Walking Pheromone was that he always got the best-looking ones, including a Playboy model whom he later claimed to have carefully inspected for signs of staples in her stomach. The thing is, neither of us seemed to be enjoying the whole experience very much. We were just doing it because it's what we had signed up for. The rock'n'roll had proven to be a bit of a disappointment. Steve wasn't into drugs and, frankly, I couldn't afford the drugs I wanted. So all that was left was the sex.

I was not a happy bunny. I fulfilled most of my sexual fantasies, checking them off a mental list in my head, and, let me tell you, compared to intimate sex with someone you care about, these assignations proved a sad disappointment. I even had a three-way tryst with two gorgeous bisexual girls, who were into each other, while snorting cocaine and drinking champagne, which is probably right up the top of most men's fantasy list. And you know what? After I had ejaculated a couple of times, I lost interest. The pair of them went at it all night. I got up and went into the other room and watched TV.

And I really don't want to think about the woman who introduced her dog into the proceedings.

You know the problem with a Godless universe? You're on your own. Responsible for no one but yourself. And every time you contemplate the future, you are forced to conclude that your ultimate fate is simply to cease to be. It makes it hard to care about things, even yourself. The distractions of vice are all too easy to surrender to. You tend to think, I know I shouldn't be doing this but . . . fuck it!

You could say I was experiencing an existential wobble.

Then Steve went and got famous with his boy band and I lost my partner in misdemeanour. That was a rather bruising lesson about the nature of fame. It wasn't that Steve turned into some kind of egotistic monster; it was more like he got distracted for a minute in the sudden burst of flashlights . . . But it was long enough for him to lose sight of some of his closest friends.

I must have been a bit of a pain in the arse to be around anyway. I found it hard to be overlooked by the excited fans who would come bustling up to Steve in the street and then give me their cameras and ask me to take a picture of them with their idol. I probably made a few too many caustic jokes about Steve's pin-up status. But we went from talking every day and hanging out several times a week – two young men with an incredibly similar outlook, sharing our experience of the world – to talking only when I could get him on the phone and meeting when he could squeeze me into his schedule. And then I thought, I'm not going to call him until he calls me. And I never heard from him again.

I did run into him at a party a few years later. To his credit, he was sheepish and apologetic. By then he had come out of the other side of celebritydom and had genuine insight into how it had affected him. We exchanged numbers but we never used them. The damage done to our friendship was beyond repair.

In some strange phenomenon of social connectivity, as the chosen few moved into the stratosphere, gathering together in a galaxy of celebrity, with hangers-on and other satellites orbiting endlessly around, the wannabes and might-have-beens and other assorted showbusiness rejects began to congregate in the dark space at the edge of this constellation of stars, telling funny stories about failure to make themselves feel better and bitching behind the backs of their more famous friends. I have to say, my fellow non-achievers were good company. A more extraordinary, talented and delightfully eccentric bunch of people you could not invent. Maybe failure is more character-building than success.

There was Gerry Moore, of course, who had gone back to Ireland, where he made a living as a voiceover artist in radio ads, frequently impersonating singers who could not have held a candle to his own vocal talent. And there was Reid Savage, an erudite raconteur who was also one of the most exciting guitarists I had ever heard. Reid signed to MCA when Ossie was telling us not to and got dropped after one album. I always thought he could have been a great, inventive guitar hero like the Edge but Reid was working his personal magic on the pub circuit, not in stadiums. He was married to Louise Goffin, the only child of classic songwriters Gerry Goffin and Carol King, who had to deal with a very different kind of rejection to the rest of us. Louise put out a lyrically complex, melodically demanding album, *This Is the Place*, in 1987, but every review and interview focussed on the family connection and most found her wanting. 'What's good enough for other people,' she sadly noted, 'isn't good enough for me.' And then there was Frank McGee, a frighteningly fucked-up ball of hyperintensity who had an ugly sex appeal uniquely his own, the charisma of a Hollywood movie star and a wild, poetic streak that should have made him a rock legend, but somehow his band, Jo Jo Namoza, always managed to scare off the A&R community. To be fair, Frank was a scary guy. He once told me that his ideal date was to go back to a woman's home, fuck her up the ass, steal her money and shit in her handbag. But Jo Jo were a strange, taut, funky and utterly unique band and it is the world's loss that they eventually broke up in the face of timidity from the music business, robbing posterity of the chance to enjoy such classics as 'Yes, I Am a Fishhead'. I see Frank pop up on my TV screen every now and then, usually as a policeman or criminal in some low-rent soap opera. He should have been a star. But that's the epitaph of so much talent. Should have been. Could have been. Might have been. If only.

So these were the people Ivan and I found ourselves hanging out with at the tail end of the eighties, as we contemplated what path we were going to take. You know how in American action movies people are always saying things like 'Failure is not an option'? Well, failure was definitely an option. It might not have been the particular option we would have chosen for ourselves but we had, by now, come to the belated realization that such matters were not entirely in our hands.

We were approached by a young Irishman called Paddy Prendergast, who ran an independent record-manufacturing business. Paddy had been an admirer of both Yeah! Yeah! and Shook Up! and was sufficiently enamoured of the quality of 'Invisible Girl' to offer to manufacture the single on credit. I designed a sleeve, using a strange photo in which our faces blurred into the background. Vlad came back and did a radical dance remix for the 12-inch. 'Stop the World' would be the B-side. It was fanciful to imagine that we could achieve chart success without a major record-company machine behind us but, as the single came together, everyone became convinced it would be just the thing to finally win us that elusive deal we had been chasing for so long. Even Barry rejoined the struggle, promising to make it all up to us by paying for a plugger and a press agent. A small distribution company, PRT, became involved, saying they thought it could be an independent hit but that sleeves would have to be reprinted with a barcode and they would need twice as many copies as we had intended to press.

Everyone was getting a bit carried away. Expenses were mounting. But finally, in February 1988, ten years since we first formed a band, Ivan and I released our debut single, 'Invisible Girl' by Shook Up! on our own Planet Pop label. We went down to Brown's nightclub the day it was released. It was a starry hangout, frequented by such pop glitterati as George Michael and Elton John, but we were usually able to blag our way in. We handed a copy of the 12-inch to the DJ, who slipped it into his set, then we sat and watched with big smiles on our faces as London's hippest clubbers grooved around the dancefloor to our music. Maybe everything was going to be OK.

NME slated the single. 'These two sullen pouting young men who bang the drum machine for female victims of incest have honourable intentions, but who benefits? There's a fine line between citing a tragedy and trivializing it. Shook Up! have crossed it.' *Sounds* gave it an ambivalent nod. *Record Mirror* and *Hot Press* were kinder, as might have been expected from magazines that had supported us all along. *Music Week*, however, was a revelation. The industry magazine recommended it to retailers, describing it as a 'dynamic piece of epic dance-orientated pop that is the debut release for the McCormick brothers, helped out by bassist Vlad Naslas of Jack'n'Chill and Brother Beyond's drummer Steve Alexander. A band to watch'. But best of all, Simon Mayo, one of the country's most popular DJs, started playing the record on his top-rated Radio One show. We were being listened to by millions. Our friends were calling up in excitement and saying, 'I heard you on the radio.'

It was up to the general public now. But I thought I'd give it a kick start, so I went into Virgin in Oxford Street, the biggest record shop in London, and flicked through the racks, looking for my own face. I was nowhere to be found. So I went to the counter and asked for a copy of 'Invisible Girl' by Shook Up!. 'We haven't got it, mate,' said the clerk. I asked him to order a copy for me. He disappeared for a moment, to check the store computer.

'How are you spelling that?' he said.

I wrote it out for him. He disappeared again.

'There's no such record,' he said, when he returned.

'I can assure you there is,' I insisted.

'Listen, mate,' he said, 'if it's not in the computer then it hasn't been released – all right?'

'It's on the radio,' I said.

'Maybe it'll be out in a few weeks,' he said, 'but it's not on the schedule.'

I walked out of the shop in a daze. What the fuck was going on? I went into another record store. Same story. And another. Same story. No such record. Never heard of it. Doesn't exist. Are you sure you've got the spelling right? 'Invisible Girl' was an invisible single.

I called Barry and he gave me the bad news. There had been some kind of cock up at PRT. I don't remember what the specific problem was now but the distribution company was in trouble and went out of business later that year. Our singles never made it out of the warehouse. Except in Germany, apparently, where I believe we sold sixty-four copies.

18

So we gave up, right? That's what you're thinking. The penny must have dropped by now. Surely, we had finally woken up to the realization that we just weren't wanted? It was time to accept defeat. Lay down. Roll over. And get a proper job, a suggestion that most working adults we knew were increasingly prone to make.

But we had just sold sixty-four records in Germany! So, ha! There was firm evidence that somebody loved us. And what about Simon Mayo? One of Britain's best-loved DJs had played our song – proof, if ever it was needed, of our commercial potential. And besides, we had a couple of thousand copies of the single, retrieved from PRT, which we needed to flog in order to pay our debts.

It was too late to stop now.

So we began to put another band together with the justification that anyone who took an interest in our single should be able to see us perform. But it was all being done in a rather half-hearted fashion. It was as if we were afraid to go back into the record companies, afraid to make another push for attention lest they turn around and say, 'Oh no, not the McCormick brothers again.' Since we found ourselves unable to even contemplate going through the rigours of auditioning another 150 drummers and other assorted musicians, we conceived a plan with our keyboard player, Richard, to play to programmed synths, sequencers and backing tapes, which was all the rage in the wake of the Pet Shop Boys and other electro pop stars. Essentially we only needed the three of us on stage but we would spice things up with a band of babes, recruiting a sax player called Chrissie Quayle and a coterie of female backing singers, Margo Buchanan, Julie Harrington and Rebecca De Ruvo.

The girls were enlisted by word of mouth through fellow musicians. They were an absurdly talented bunch who between them had worked with Tina Turner, Level 42, Billy Idol, Eurythmics, Paul Young and Stock, Aitken and Waterman. They agreed to lend their talents to our cause because they were all convinced, as so many had been before, that record companies would not be able to ignore us. The fools!

I was feeling a bit marginalized by the new musical set up. Essentially all the work was done by Ivan and Richard. I just had to slot my vocals into spaces left by their pre-programmed arrangements. And Ivan and I weren't getting along very well. I detected a kind of exasperation in his attitude towards me. He described me as a prima donna and accused me of being too precious about my art. Ivan always had a swagger of confident physicality about him and favoured the instinctive over the intellectual. Maybe this was partly a path he had chosen to define and separate himself from me. Our songwriting partnership had to strike a balance between my desire to craft lyrics of substance and his taste for feisty dance music but, as we moved into this more techno-orientated area, he became increasingly insistent that I write to his specifications.

'You tell me what you want and I'll give it to you!' I snapped, exhausted by one too many screaming arguments. 'How many choruses? How many verses?'

'I want the chorus to be longer than the verse,' he said.

'Fine,' I said.

'Start with the chorus,' he said.

'Whatever you want,' I said.

'Make it a double chorus,' he said. 'Chorus, verse, chorus, verse. If you have to have a middle eight, keep it short. In fact, make it a middle two! Or forget about it altogether. And then lots of choruses.'

'No problem,' I said.

'Short lines,' he said.

'If that's what you want.'

'And no rape, no vomit, no child abuse, no words you need to look up in the dictionary.'

'Fine,' I said.

I wrote a lyric in thirty minutes. It was called 'Comme Ci – Comme Ça'. The chorus went like this:

It comes and it goes
You got to learn to live with it
It comes and it goes
You got to learn to live without it
Comme Ci, Comme Ça
Like This, Like That
[repeat twice]

OK, so it had a bit of French in it, but Ivan loved it, and there was peace in the household for a while.

Songs are like a diary to me. I can tell what I was going through when I wrote any given song even if I wasn't aware of it at the time. I think that song was about me and my brother. It was about everything we had been through and the inevitable separation to come. As Ivan had demanded, it wasn't exactly subtle.

We had to move out of the flat. The landlord wanted to sell the building. It felt like the end of an era, the curtain falling on five years of partying. We had one last blow-out which resulted in our long-suffering neighbours finally calling the police. It may have been the fireworks display we staged in the bedroom that upset them. Ivan and I wound up in a two-bed flat in West Hampstead, which, despite its name, bears no relation to the upmarket Hampstead. It's more like East Kilburn. Or, as we used to call it, Wild West Hampstead.

There was an aspect of my brother's behaviour which was really starting to bother me. He was conducting simultaneous relationships with two girls, his long-standing girlfriend Cassandra and the ringleader of our Oriental fans, Ina Hyatt. I was in no position to lecture him about his attitude towards the opposite sex but I disliked being caught up in his deceit and having to lie on his behalf to both his girlfriends. I wrote a song which I thought might get this message across, entitled (without delicacy) 'Somebody's Gonna Get Hurt'.

'Is that song about me?' asked Ivan, when he read the lyrics.

'Yeah,' I admitted.

'I love it,' he said. 'I wanna sing this one!' Which wasn't quite the reaction I had hoped for.

We debuted the new-look Shook Up! at a sold-out gig at the Rock Garden in March 1988. It was a storming success. The sound was sleek and modern. The girls were fresh and feisty and sang like the pros they were, wrapping my vocals in blocks of warm harmonies. Ivan and I had a new look: long hair (I hadn't been to the barber since Rob Dickens declined to sign us on account of my haircut), cut-off jackets and jeans with belts made out of motorcycle chains. The buckle of mine said 'Shook'. The buckle of Ivan's said 'Up'. So as long as he stood to my left nobody would think we were called Up Shook.

The sheer thrill of being back on stage, under the lights, in front of a noisy audience got my enthusiasm up for a while. But the limitations of the synth line-up began to present themselves when Barry got us a college gig in front of a less sympathetic crowd. We were tied to the programmes. With a live band you could move things around, speed up, slow down, jam songs together, improvise. You had room to manoeuvre. In front of a late-night, drunken, student audience, I could feel them slipping away and there was nothing I could do about it. My between-songs patter just grew steadily more desperate. We did not get called back for an encore, which was a first for a Shook Up! concert. I threw a tantrum in the dressing room, fuelled by the generous allocation of alcohol Barry had negotiated for us in our contract rider. 'Maybe you should just sample the fucking vocals as well as everything else and I could stay at home,' I snapped at Ivan.

'Well, at least that way you might stay in tune,' Ivan whipped back.

'Girls! Girls! Break it up,' intervened one of our backing singers. 'It wasn't that bad. They're students. They're drunk. What d'you expect?'

Ah, but that was the problem in a nutshell. By now we expected to be playing to people who actually wanted to hear us. We had worked so hard for so long it was mortifying to find ourselves right back where we started.

We decided to go for one final push. We recorded a new demo, featuring 'Comme Ci – Comme ça', 'Somebody's Gonna Get Hurt' and a song called 'Back in the Machine' that gave a few clues to how we were feeling:

> There's a sound machinery makes as it's grinding to a halt
> The death rattle of pumps and chains as the arteries clog
> And that's the only sound I heard for an eternity
> Nothing seemed to work anymore, and that included
>   me . . .

And that was only the spoken intro.

We needed a review to set things in motion but we were old news by now and it was difficult to get music papers interested. But there was an obvious solution to that little problem. After all, I had been accused in the past of making up my own reviews. So . . .

I had a friend called Gloria.

Or, as Van Morrison might have put it: her name was G! L! O! R! I–aye–aye–aye–aye–aye–aye . . . Or, as U2 would have sung it: Gloria in te domine. Gloria Exulte!

It was Gloria Else, actually.

'You know you've got the same name as a U2 song,' I said to her once.

'You who?' she said. Gloria was not particularly interested in pop music. As a recent divorcee with two very young boys to bring up, she generally had more pressing matters to engage her attention. But I was interested in Gloria. In fact, she was the first woman who had stirred my genuine interest since Joan's departure. Gloria was (it was widely agreed among our friends) something special. She was gorgeous and vivacious, with a lively spirit and infectious laughter. And she had the most beautiful blue eyes. And lips like cushions. You could have made a sofa out of her lips. I wanted to settle down on that sofa, make myself really comfortable. Oh, I had it bad for Gloria. I was always volunteering to help her out, with babysitting and other duties. I was a regular one-man single mother's support unit.

But Gloria had other ideas. She was a former neighbour from Belsize Crescent and had seen a few things. To Gloria, I was a long-haired, feckless, unemployed musician who slept all day, partied all night and, as she once pointed out, seemed to have a different woman with him every time he walked out his door.

'That's only 'cause you won't go out with me,' I countered.

'I don't mind going out with you, Neil,' she said. 'I'm just not staying in with you.'

I'll tell you another thing I liked about Gloria. She was serene. She seemed to be enshrouded by a bubble of calm. My life was a swirl of chaos and emotional turmoil. Her flat became a refuge, a port in my personal storm.

Anyway, as you may have already noticed, I am nothing if not persistent. I was prepared to play a long game with Gloria. Right now, I saw her great charm as an asset to be exploited in the cause of getting Shook Up! a review. I asked Gloria to call *Melody Maker*, claim to be a student and ask how she could break into music journalism. I knew that music papers were desperate to recruit female journalists and I knew exactly what they would tell her: go to a gig and send in a review. I counted on her telephone manner to make sure they would be paying attention when the review arrived.

Shook Up! had a gig lined up supporting Auto Da Fe, a veteran Irish Goth band, in the Mean Fiddler. After the show I wrote a review. I was nice enough about Auto Da Fe. But I was really nice about the support band. I maintained an edge of sarcasm, however, so that *Melody Maker* did not smell a rat.

Shook Up! promised to lead us into a wonderland of temptation: safe sex, guilt-free sin and love's sweet salvation, launching into 'Faithless', a solid pop groove that could be covered by Kylie Minogue in leathers and fishnet stockings. Three girls and three boys coming together in close harmony, Shook Up! never let up for an instant, ripping through six would-be hits as if warming up for a *Top of the Pops* chart countdown.

Melodic, dance-worthy, gorgeously coutured, there had to be something wrong and it reared its head halfway through when the handsome, flaxen-locked lead vocalist stopped grinning for a moment and said, sincerely: 'This is a song about something that goes on all around us, though we never see it, it's a song about child abuse.' Suddenly, you realize that at the heart of this pop dream machine lie more angst-ridden singer-songwriters, yet the resultant 'Invisible Girl' is funky enough to keep feet on the dancefloor and sad enough not to offend. After the show, band members mingled with the audience selling copies of the single version of the track. Anyone that desperate for success deserves a shot (and, in a perfect world, to be shot as soon as their 15 minutes is up).

OK, maybe I was laying it on a bit thick. But it did the trick. Gloria's review was printed in the next issue and all the record companies sat up and took notice. Meanwhile, Gloria was fending off excited calls from *Melody Maker*, who wanted to commission her to do a feature and wondered if she could pop into the office to say hello to the editor and maybe she would like to have lunch? The next time they rang, I told them Gloria had been summoned back to South Africa to attend her grandmother's funeral. She was never heard of by the rock press again.

We had often been told it was a mistake to manage ourselves – if only from the point of view that, to the unimaginative at least (a category which definitely included A&R departments), artists should never appear to be interested in (or even capable of understanding) the brutal, cut-throat world of business. Managers made plans. Artists had visions. And besides, I knew I had upset a few too many people with my outspokenness. So, in the absence of the real thing, we decided to invent pseudo-management. Ivan's friend trainee Doctor Martin and my friend Gloria (who had rather enjoyed the whole *Melody Maker* subterfuge) agreed to pose as a vibrant new management team and do the rounds of the record companies. I would brief Martin and Gloria on who they were about to see and what tack they should take, then sit at the back during the meeting and look as baffled by all this high-powered business talk as any self-respecting artist should be.

We set up a showcase in the Theatre Museum, an unusual and attractive space in the centre of London. Everything was arranged for the convenience of the record companies. Elegant invitations (and subsequent reminders) were sent out with maps and offers of transport. It was early evening and mid-week, so as not to disturb their doubtless hectic social lives. As our representatives, Martin and Gloria assured them that we would be performing only four songs, then they could be about their business. It was an entirely cynical and contrived attempt to bring the mountain to Mohammed, since Mohammed evidently was not prepared to go to the Rock Garden.

The remarkable thing is, it worked like a dream. Virtually every record company turned up, even some we hadn't invited. We dimmed the lights, blasted through four songs, and left them to discuss it among themselves.

Afterwards, Martin and Gloria were mingling with the music business when a senior record executive approached them. 'This is the most impressive showcase I have ever attended,' he informed them. But he wasn't interested in signing Shook Up! He wanted Martin and Gloria to manage one of his acts.

Still, the prognosis was good. Well, it was OK. The head of Chrysalis Publishing wanted to see us the next day. Arista indicated positive interest. Various others nodded in approval. After all that effort, it was disappointing not to get a firm offer. But it was something. And something was better than nothing. Just about.

We went to Browns that night (not for the first time). And slipped into the VIP room (again). And drank champagne (on someone else's tab, naturally) and toasted the future, celebrating as if we had been granted the keys to the kingdom rather than just been allowed another glimmer of light through the crack of a partially opened door. Boy George was there and we chatted about Vlad, who was producing some tracks for George's new album.

'He's a very strange man,' noted Boy George.

'He certainly is,' we confirmed.

'Do you think his girlfriend is really psychic?' wondered George.

'Well, she said we were going to be the most successful group in the world,' said Ivan.

'Funny, she said the same thing to me,' sniggered George. 'I said, "Too late, dear. Been there, done that."'

Elton John was in the VIP room. And so was George Michael. And so were we! This was where we belonged. Only, I made the mistake of going downstairs to the dancefloor and when I tried to return a bouncer blocked my way.

'All my friends are up there,' I said.

'That's too bad,' he said.

I thought I might as well try it on. I mean, if anybody looked like a pop star it was me. So I bristled with outrage and demanded, 'Don't you know who I am?'

'Yeah, I do know who you are,' said the bouncer. 'Now fuck off!'

There was no single moment when I decided it was over. But if giving up this ghost of a career was the result of a series of little epiphanies, then I certainly experienced one there. I stood shaking with embarrassment in front of the bouncer then snapped, 'Fine!' turned round and walked out of the club. The bouncer knew who I was. But did I? I took the night bus home, on my own. I needed time to think.

What was I supposed to do? I could feel it all slipping away now but I was clinging to the cliff face of my career by broken fingernails, hanging on with the grim determination of the truly desperate. I felt that if I let go I would be in freefall, not spinning towards the freedom of an unimagined future but plummeting helplessly to the jagged rocks below. Fame and Fortune were the twin peaks of my desire. But why did I feel it was so imperative to scale these particular mountains? And why would I feel such a failure if I never made it to the summit? These were questions that needed to be answered.

I spoke to Bono. We went for a long walk in the countryside and I poured it all out, my hopes, my fears, my feeling that I had so much to give, all this creativity bubbling up inside me with no outlet, until the pressure was building like a volcano in my head. I feared spontaneous combustion.

'Get a life,' said Bono.

'What?' I said, not sure if I heard right.

'You've got a life,' repeated Bono. 'You don't even see it. You're so occupied by some imaginary future life you barely even notice that you're living now.'

'I'm not living the life I want,' I wheedled.

'You can't always get what you want,' said Bono.

'Don't start quoting Rolling Stones songs at me as if they were Zen aphorisms,' I complained.

'Life is what happens to you when you are busy making other plans,' said Bono.

'John Lennon said that,' I pointed out.

'I am John Lennon,' said Bono. I looked closely at him. His face was in shadow, silhouetted by the radiant sun behind his head. 'I am John and I am Paul and I am Mick and I am Keith and I am Elvis and Jimi and Bob and Johnny and I am all of rock'n'roll. Look on my works, ye mighty, and despair!'

Shit! I woke up with my heart pounding. The Bono dreams were getting worse. Sometimes I would be on stage with U2 in front of a stadium full of roaring fans and suddenly realize I didn't know the words to the songs and Adam, Edge and Larry would all be looking at me with exasperation and then Bono would come out and take the microphone from me. Sometimes we would be playing our guitars and talking about songs and having a rare old time but other people would come into the room and I would find myself getting pushed further and further away until they were all surrounding him, listening to him sing, and I was blocked out completely. Sometimes I would find myself outside the red rope that cordoned off the group from their fans. Sometimes I would find myself inside the red rope, happy and basking in the presence of my starry friends, acknowledged as one of them, which felt even more humiliating when I woke up. How could I be so craven in my need to be part of U2? I didn't want to feel any different about Bono than I had ever felt, yet he was taking on this strange, archetypal role in my subconscious, a rock God presiding over all that I desired.

U2 released a new album in October, *Rattle and Hum*. It's a great album, I think, mixing live music with studio recordings while on tour in America in a rootsy attempt to embrace rock's rich heritage. It has some fantastic songs on it. The Bo Diddleyesque evocation of naked hunger that is 'Desire'. The broodingly atmospheric travelogue 'Hawkmoon 269'. The sweeping, string-laden, epic love song 'All I Want Is You'. But the truth is, it fucking annoyed me back then. I thought, Who are they to declare themselves heirs to the all-time greats of rock'n'roll? Bono barely even knew who Bob Dylan was back when we were teenagers and now he was writing songs with him, with Bono and Dylan co-credited as lyricists on 'Love Rescue Me'. And on the opening track, 'Helter Skelter', the group who had once happily described themselves as the worst covers band in the world dared to take on my idols. 'Charles Manson stole this song from the Beatles; we're stealing it back,' proclaimed Bono, as they launched into a sloppy rendition of the *White Album* rock classic. I was really irritated by that. That song belonged to me as much as it belonged to anyone, more than it could ever belong to blow-ins who never even owned a Beatles record growing up. They did a similarly hastily rehearsed cover of Dylan's 'All Along the Watchtower'. When Jimi Hendrix recorded that song he made it his very own. The best that could be said about U2's version was that they made it to the end.

But the one that really got my goat was 'God Part II', their sequel to John Lennon's myth-shattering 'God', which climaxed his first post-Beatles solo album. Lennon's gentle, melodic epic had been an attack on belief systems, a litany of everything he had lost faith in (from 'I don't believe in Jesus' to 'I don't believe in Beatles'). 'The dream is over,' he poignantly concluded.

Bono took another tack. Over a pummelling, monotone bass and drum track attacked by savage guitar bursts, Bono snapped out short, pithy couplets acknowledging the contradictions between conviction and practise ('I don't believe in excess, success is to give / I don't believe in riches but you should see where I live . . . I don't believe in deathrow, skidrow or the gangs / Don't believe in the Uzi it just went off in my hands'). Each verse concluded with an almost wistful declaration: 'I believe in love'. Bono's faith in the power of love struck me as unconvincing in the harsh and cynical eighties. And it seemed to fly in the face of Lennon's own disillusionment. I thought of Lennon's weary, poignant put-down of his own failed idealism: 'I really thought love was gonna save us all.' That could be the ironic inscription on his gravestone, the famous last words of a peace advocate who went down in a hail of bullets, slain by one of his own followers. Bono's attempt to revive that idealism seemed at odds with the bleak things he had to say ('Don't believe in forced entry, I don't believe in rape / But every time she passes by wild thoughts escape'). The most perplexing contradiction came when Bono sang: 'I don't believe in the sixties, the golden age of pop / You glorify the past when the future dries up'. Yet the song was written in homage to a sixties icon and included on an album that glorified the past in its musical styles and points of reference.

It seems obvious with hindsight that my anger had more to do with my own frustrated desires to establish my place in the rock hierarchy than any inherent flaw in U2's song, but I was incensed enough to compose a song of my own, a very raw blues in E minor that amounted to a kind of atheistic, nihilistic, existentialist declaration of disbelief.

> I don't believe all men are equal, that's a rumour put
>   about
> By them who have it all and don't want to let it out
> I don't believe the meek will inherit the earth
> Till it's been robbed of all its minerals and fucked for
>   all it's worth

It was full of nasty couplets, including one about Bono: 'I don't believe in rock stars preaching from the stage / Instead of acting high and mighty, I wish they'd act their age'. And I let my maker have it too: 'I don't believe in nothing I can't smell, taste, touch or see / I don't believe in God and He don't believe in me'.

I called it 'God Part III'. I sent it in a letter to Bono. I don't know what I expected his response to be. Was he supposed to write back admitting that I was the real rock genius and it was time for him to step aside and let me take over?

A couple of weeks later, I attended the premiere of the *Rattle and Hum* film in Leicester Square. There was Bono, on the big screen, where I had always wanted to be. Larger than life. The mixed emotions U2 inspired in me were impossible to ignore any more. As much as I admired them, their success was costing me something deep inside, knocking chunks out of my already badly battered ego. Surely something you love shouldn't make you feel bad? This was the music that had inspired me to want to be in a band yet, watching them in the cinema, I felt each uplifting chord and high-minded sentiment contrarily dragging me down. I had been upstaged even in the drama of my own life. The scale of U2's fame seemed to mock me, making the minor achievements of my own existence seem pathetic. U2 made me feel small. The very idea that they could affect me in this way made me feel even smaller.

Afterwards there was a party in the Science Museum. Well, if you've got to throw a party somewhere . . .

Ivan and I made our way down. Outside, huge searchlights arced across the night sky and crowds gathered in the cold to try to catch a glimpse of their heroes. We showed our invitations and strolled into the main hall, where the skeleton of a Tyrannosaurus Rex stood tall and savage, making all the partygoers appear insignificant, mere mortals heading inevitably to our own personal extinction. There were a lot of people mingling about, none of whom I knew. I looked around for U2.

And there it was: the red rope, just like in my dreams, cordoning off the stars from the rabble. A horrible shiver ran through me, a sense of hallucinatory *déjà vu*, as if my personal nightmare was being enacted in the real world. Stone-faced bouncers guarded the entrance to the sacred inner sanctum. Special passes were required, which we didn't have. I didn't know whether to approach the red rope and expose myself to the potential humiliation of rejection or just accept that my close connection to U2 had been severed. Our worlds had shifted out of alignment. Maybe I should count myself lucky to be at the party at all, drink the free beer and toast the success of my old friends. At least, one day, I could tell my grandchildren I was there when it all began.

But Ivan was having none of it. He went up to the rope and waved. Edge turned and waved back. And the next thing I knew, we were inside the cordon and our old friends were greeting us like, well, old friends.

'We were wondering if you had made it,' said the Edge. 'What did you think?' And we chatted a bit about the film, its strong points and its weaknesses. For someone who takes the role of guitar hero, the Edge seems curiously lacking in ego. Indeed, lacking in edges. He not only accepts criticism but also seems to be interested in it, turning it over with analytical detachment rather than engaging with it as if it were a personal attack. In school, he could bristle with the competitiveness of any of our contemporaries, sometimes resorting to sarcastic humour in his attempts to fight his corner, but over the years Edge has grown progressively calmer and more centred. Success, of course, breeds confidence, but it was clear that he was also fortified by the strong inner convictions of his faith.

Adam was in ebullient form, grinning widely as he approached to ask if I still possessed that first bass guitar we had both owned.

'I'm sure it's around somewhere,' I said.

'I'd like to buy it back off you,' he said.

'It'll cost you a bit more than sixty quid,' I said. 'You really ripped me off when you sold me that plank.'

'Name your price,' he said. 'I've come into a bit of money since then.'

At some point in the evening, I sat down with Bono.

'That song!' he said, rather pointedly.

'I'm sorry,' I said.

'You've got the sickness,' he said. 'Your songs make Leonard Cohen sound cheerful.'

'I've been feeling a bit jealous,' I admitted. 'You know, I can't believe in anything. I just can't. But I look around at where people are in their lives and I find that the people who have a strong belief system seem to do better than those of us who have nothing but confusion.'

'You're suggesting that belief and confusion are mutually exclusive,' countered Bono. 'I don't think so. I think belief gives you a direction in the confusion. So what's really bothering you?'

'I can't believe you wrote a song with Bob Dylan,' I said, barely able to disguise my envy.

'How jammy is that?' laughed Bono. 'You know the strange thing: I was staying in LA, right, and I had a dream one night about Bob Dylan, and I woke up and just started writing that song. And it's about a man who people keep turning to as a saviour but whose own life is getting messed up and he could use a bit of salvation himself. I wrote a couple of verses and I didn't really know what to do with it, but I thought, I'm a rock star, right? And I've actually got Bob Dylan's number ... somewhere! So why don't I give him a call? So I go over to his house and I told him I've got this song, it's not finished, and he says, "Play it to me," and he just started making up lyrics on the spot. It was incredible, whole verses just came pouring out. And so I actually got to finish the song with the man in my dream!'

'I hate to admit this,' I said, 'but I've been dreaming about you.'

'I'm not sure if I want to know about that,' said Bono.

'I'm not sure if I want to tell you!' I said. 'I don't want you in my dreams! They're private!'

'I'll try to remember that next time I'm wandering about at night looking for somebody's head to get into,' laughed Bono.

'I'd appreciate it,' I said, but I couldn't bring myself to take this matter any further, to tell him how I was really feeling. 'So what was Dylan like to work with?' I asked instead, bringing the conversation back to safe ground.

'You know, he recorded a lead vocal on that song but then he wouldn't let us use it,' said Bono. 'It's incredible. People still say he can't sing but I learned more about phrasing and delivery just listening to him sing that song than I think I've learned in ten years on stage. Every line he sings, it's like the truth, he's got absolute conviction. I wish he'd let us put it on the album but he had some excuse about not wanting to conflict with the Traveling Wilburys' record. I don't know if that was true or if the song was just a little close to the bone. There's a lot of despair and regret in there. I think maybe he got cold feet about portraying himself in that way. I'll tell you a funny thing, though. We're in the studio, right, laying down the vocal, and he says, "Uh, can't use that verse." I'm like, "What's the problem, it's a fantastic verse." It was one of his verses, which he'd just sung off the top of his head. And he says, "Uh-uh, can't use it." And I said, "Why not?" He said, "I've used it before!" And he had!'

I was laughing at Bono's impersonation of Dylan's weirdly undulating voice, shaking my head with incredulity at the whole situation. Bono seemed equally amused, revelling in the absurdity of his farcical encounter with this legendary hero. And for a moment we seemed united, just like when we were schoolboys, looking at this fantastical world of rock dreams from the outside, noses pressed to the glass. I had a nice time with Bono at the *Rattle and Hum* party. It was like old times. We chatted all night, while people buzzed about trying to catch his attention. We revisited all our usual topics, flogging the same hobby horses just to see if there was any life left in them. Then it was time to go.

'God bless,' he said.

'Yeah,' I said. 'Same to you.'

It would be a long time before I saw him again.

19

Dreams don't die easily. They limp towards the horizon, staggering from their wounds, muttering to themselves, trying to convince anyone who will listen that it's the cavalry coming over the horizon, not just a cloud of dust.

Well, that's how it was for Ivan and me, anyway. There was no dignity to be found in the death of ambition. Not even relief that it was all over, bar the post-mortem. We just dragged that carcass as far as we could, then sank to our knees, exhausted, still baffled about how it could have come to this sorry pass, silently wondering if this could really be the end. The slow and bitter end.

Which went something like this.

Shook Up!'s negotiations with Chrysalis Publishing became bogged down in detail. Chrysalis were definitely interested but there was something else going on in the background, another agenda that was hard to get a handle on. They offered to let us record some new demos at their in-house studio. One of the songs they wanted us to record was 'Sleepwalking'. We didn't tell them we had already recorded it twice. What the hell. Maybe it would be third time lucky.

While we were in the studio, the engineer got called out to an unusual assembly of Chrysalis staff. He returned a bit shaken and told us they had been addressed by the MD. The company was being taken over by EMI. There would be major changes ahead.

Ivan and I went upstairs to see the publisher we had been negotiating with. In a sombre mood, he admitted he wasn't in a position to sign anything. Maybe next year. If he managed to retain his job.

It was the same old story. Ivan and I had heard it so many times now it was difficult to even get worked up by each new cruel twist in the tale. It was almost as if we expected it. We were despondent but refused to admit defeat. In public, anyway. Or even to each other. But in the dead of night, well, that was different. There was one thought tossing around my head, one question that only I could answer. Is it over?

Arista, too, were going through a complete overhaul and put us on the long finger. That was a position we were used to occupying by now. Paul Tipping was an experienced manager who had taken up the running after the showcase, helping us negotiate the Chrysalis contract that never was. He felt we would get a deal with Arista or one of the other companies that had expressed an interest if we could push it through before they broke up for Christmas. But it was already November and the clock was ticking. Paul told us frankly that we needed to have a contract signed, sealed and delivered by December or when the record companies we were dealing with came back after their holidays they would have forgotten all about us. But what more could we do to press our case? What could we give them that they hadn't already heard? Nothing. The pot was empty. Hit us and we rattled.

Paul's prediction turned out to be right on the money. But it wasn't only the record companies that forgot about us. So did Paul.

And still we didn't sit down and say, 'That's it.' Wave the white flag. Surrender. We didn't look each other in the eye, shake hands and say: 'We gave it our best shot. It was not to be.' Rather, we skulked around, avoiding each other, seeking refuge in the arms of women.

I was in love. For the first time, I felt I could actually say that without fear, without equivocation or concern about commitment. And it may be that failure released me from the prison of ego and ambition, so that I no longer contemplated the future with the greedy eyes of a child in a candy store. Or it may be that love was a safe haven for my wounded ego, because love makes everybody special. Everyone can be a star in the constellation d'amour. Our loved ones loved our songs. They'd ask us to play for them, even when no one else wanted to listen any more. Maybe I could not believe, like John Lennon and count-less other dreamers, that love would save me. But at least love would lick my wounds.

The object of my ardour was Gloria. And when she finally reciprocated, after a long siege on the stronghold of her heart (itself a damaged but well-fortified citadel that had survived a drawn-out war of attrition with her ex-husband), I was temporar-ily elevated to seventh heaven, king of all I surveyed. In the warmth of her embrace, I could overlook my failures. I could even give thanks for the crooked path my life had taken, telling myself that it had led to this wonderful woman. The fact that she was a single mother with two young children did not daunt me. Her little boys became my new playmates. In retrospect, of course, I can see that motherhood may have been part of her appeal, as I sought refuge from my broken dreams in the bosom of a ready-made family. But Gloria was no pushover. For the first time in a decade, I had a girlfriend capable of resisting my charms and standing up to my wiles. When we were together our love was sweet and crazy, in the first bloom of emotion, but she had other priorities. She did not want her kids to know we were dating, which made me feel as if I was on permanent probation, sneak-ing out of the house at three in the morning so that I would not be there when they got up for breakfast.

Ivan's own romantic life was even more of a mess. In my song, I had predicted that somebody was gonna get hurt. As it turned out, everybody got hurt. When Cassandra discovered that Ivan had been two-timing her she was understandably devastated. But Ina's triumph at becoming the only woman in Ivan's life was short-lived. She became upset by my brother's game-playing and returned to her family in Indonesia. Ivan adopted the pose of wounded lover, although it was clearly he who had done the wounding. When the latest deal fell through and he had no one to turn to make him feel better, he decided to head out East to find Ina and tell her he loved her.

You might be wondering how he could afford to do this, since we were both supposed to be on the dole. Well, we had been caught up in a back-to-work initiative, one of a multitude of schemes specifically designed to get work-shy skivers like us off the unemployment register. This particular scheme was called Enterprise Allowance. We actually got slightly more money (the increase was incremental but when you were as poor as we were every little bit counted) and we did not have to sign on any more (a big plus for such a pair of lazy good-for-nothings). The downside was that it lasted only a year, after which we were on our own. We had to do a couple of day-long courses, which were supposed to tell us all we needed to know about the enterprise culture, and then we were supposed to start our own business. It was entirely ridiculous, of course, but it effectively got people off the dole and made it incredibly hard to get back on, so you were more or less forced to get up off your arse and find a job. The days of free money were coming to an end. Anyway, Ivan buggered off to Indonesia on the pretext that he was importing fancy Oriental chess sets.

I told my Enterprise case worker that I was going to set up as a freelance journalist. Even though I could not admit to myself that the group was finished, I had been carefully considering my employment options for a while. I put in a couple of days on a building site, coming home physically shattered and completely caked in dust and dirt, all for £25 cash-in-hand, which was enough to convince me that I was not cut out for manual labour. I thought about graphics and design work but, while I had been an art director at nineteen, my dexterity with a scalpel and cow gum was somewhat behind the times. Computers had become the principal design tool. Scanning the employment ads, I realized I was no longer qualified. A decade out of work will do that for you. I could probably have found work as a cartoonist but coming up with one joke a fortnight for the strip I was doing for *Hot Press* already felt like hard graft. A gag a day would be worse than working nine to five. So it would have to be journalism.

I loved writing. And I had written some good features over the years, when something had particularly perked my interest or I had just been desperate for money. But I did not want to be a professional journalist. And in particular I did not want to be a rock critic. I had heard so many musicians complain that rock critics were just frustrated rock stars, to fulfil that cliché would have been the ultimate admission of defeat. But I wrote off a few half-hearted letters to magazines, enough to keep my case worker off my back.

Had I actually gone to a job interview, the only people who might conceivably have employed me were some dirty bikers magazines. Or maybe a gazette for the great unwashed. I had always been vain. Mirrors were my friend, a cheap substitute for the TV screens I wanted to see my face in. So I suppose it is rather telling that I had grown a scruffy great beard which covered half my face. What with the long, unkempt hair and the scuffed leather jacket, I was starting to attract nervous glances from strangers. Not that I could blame them. I looked like the kind of person I would cross the road to avoid.

Then disaster struck. Or potential disaster, at least. Ivan and I were summoned to interviews with our Enterprise case worker, to see how our business plans were progressing. The problem being that neither of our plans were progressing at all, besides which, Ivan wasn't even in the country, his lengthy absence being somewhat against the rules of the scheme. But fuck 'em all. The unemployment bureaucracy held no fear for me. The interviews were scheduled a day apart and I decided I would attend as both McCormick brothers. Ivan's came first. I showed up with my hair wild and my beard bushy, wearing loud clothing and behaving like a complete moron. I got some weird satisfaction from the case worker's withering appraisal of Ivan's business scheme.

'You say you are planning to import exotic Indonesian chess sets?'

'That's the idea,' I said.

'So on your business card – if you can call this square of cheap cardboard a business card – why have you stuck a picture of a plain, ordinary, common-or-garden pawn, and not one of your exotic chess pieces?'

'Good point,' I said. 'Why didn't I think of that?' The real answer, of course, was that I had made the card myself and I didn't have any pictures of exotic Indonesian chess pieces in my possession. Indeed, I had no idea what such a thing would look like.

The next day, I returned to the office as myself. The case worker liked me much better than my brother. I shaved off my beard (to Gloria's great relief). My hair was tied up in a pony-tail. I was wearing glasses. I had on a tatty suit. I played Ivan as a loud-mouth but presented myself as quiet and withdrawn.

'I have been writing to magazines with ideas,' I said, showing the case worker my rejection letters. 'It's a very competitive busi-ness but I think I am making some headway.'

'What makes you think that?' asked the case worker.

'Well, the rejection letters are getting more polite,' I pointed out.

My case worker was very helpful, giving me some useful tips on how to proceed. 'You're living with your brother,' he noted as the interview drew to a close.

'Yes,' I said, nervously. Where was this going?

'I met him yesterday,' he said.

'Uh, yes, I know,' I admitted.

'Your presentation is much better than his,' said the case worker. 'Maybe you could give him a bit of help.'

'Oh, he never listens to anything I say,' I said. 'He likes noth-ing better than the sound of his own voice.'

'I rather got that impression myself,' laughed the case worker, sympathetically.

'I hope he wasn't too obnoxious,' I said.

'You're the one who's got to live with him,' pointed out my case worker.

The whole episode put a bit of a spring back in my step. I even thought I really *could* do a bit of journalism. Where was the harm? At least it would keep my case worker happy.

I spoke to a contact at the *Sunday Times Magazine*, sending in some of my *Hot Press* clippings instead of one of my deliberately hopeless letters. They were apparently impressed, commissioning me to interview Sinead O'Connor. They may have been swayed by my ever-so-slightly exaggerated claim to have known Sinead since she was a little girl (well, I had met the young chanteuse once while she was rehearsing with In Tua Nua).

It was a prestigious assignment. The beautiful, shaven-headed, ethereal-voiced Irish singer was already infamous for her outspoken and combative views but I felt sure that, with our shared background, we would get along just fine. My interview technique had improved somewhat since that first, painful encounter with Fay Fife and the Revillos, but I did not want to leave anything to chance so I prepared an extensive list of questions. Sinead, however, did not seem to take it quite so seriously. For one thing, she was distinctly unimpressed by my assertion that we had met before, muttering dismissively, 'Don't remember.' She sat in the offices at Chrysalis, eating a curry, communicating between mouthfuls in sentences of one word. Or less. We got through my questions in ten minutes flat – without producing anything resembling a printable quote.

Floundering for a topic with which to engage her, I decided to broach her exotic spiritual beliefs. Drawing on something she once said about how we choose our own parents before we are born, I asked her why, since she was always complaining about her mum, she didn't choose a better one. She became incensed and announced that our meeting was over. I suggested leaving her to finish her curry in peace and then perhaps starting the interview over. In a remark that contained cutting echoes of Fay Fife's degrading appraisal of my skills, she snapped, 'That wasn't an interview. That was more like a conversation on a bus!'

I knew I had blown it, but what could I do? I decided to leave. Sinead, however, would not let me. Not that she was filled with remorse. She just wanted the tape of our conversation. 'You're going to make a fool of me,' she snarled.

'I think you're doing a fine job of that all by yourself,' I snapped back. She made a lunge for the tape recorder and we briefly tussled over the table. But Sinead was half my size and when I would not release my grip she went running out of the room to get help. I tried to make my escape but was accosted by Sinead and a female press officer on my way downstairs. 'Sinead would like you to hand over the tape,' said the embarrassed press officer, while the pop star stood behind her, urging her on. I pointed out that I did not work for Sinead or Chrysalis. 'Sinead feels you are going to use the tape against her,' said the press officer.

'Well, Sinead should have thought about that when she was being obnoxious and refusing to answer my questions,' I said.

'They were shit questions,' yelled Sinead.

'I takes two to do an interview,' I yelled back. 'I didn't need to come down here and waste my time watching you eat lunch. If you don't want to talk to the press then don't talk to the fucking press but don't ask me to sit there while you don't talk!'

Sinead was absolutely livid, her face red with rage. 'Be like that!' she snapped and stormed off.

The press officer continued to plead with me all the way out of the building.

The *Sunday Times* were not impressed. They wanted a puff piece on a soulful Irish singer, not a blazing row on the stairs. But I didn't really care. I didn't want to work for the *Sunday Times* anyway. I wanted to be a rock star. I wanted it so bad it hurt. I wanted it the way a child wants the toys he has thrown out of his pram. I wanted what I had always believed was rightfully mine and I couldn't understand why the nasty grown-ups wouldn't let me have it.

Ivan returned from Indonesia, accompanied by Ina. I was relieved to have him back. I had written seven songs in his absence, all of which could have benefited from his melodic touch. The titles tell their own story about the state of my mind. 'I Let It All Slip Through My Hands', 'Careless', 'The Love that Harms', 'Poison', 'A Long Time Coming', 'Mad', 'What's It All About?', 'Stick to Me'.

That last song was pure, abject desperation.

Stick to me
Please stick to me
We made it this far
How much farther can it be?

Ivan read the lyric through and gave me a curious, knowing, almost pitying smile. He worked on the songs but it was hard to engage him in conversation about our future, how we might proceed or, indeed, whether we should proceed at all. He ducked out of discussions and I suppose I was afraid to force the issue in case he stated the obvious.

It's over.

They don't want us.

Time to move along.

It was hard to escape the impression that Ivan was a bit, well, pissed off with me. He didn't exactly make much of an attempt to disguise it. He would frequently roll his eyes when I was talking. And sigh. There was lots of sighing. Or I'd be in the middle of expounding my current Theory of Life, the Universe and Whatever and he would loudly interrupt, often to change the subject entirely, and just start talking across me. And there were a lot of petty domestic rows, about whose turn it was to do the dishes or whose sausage in the fridge had been eaten by whoever (it was my sausage, by the way. It was always my sausage. My cheese. My milk. And his excuse, the hardy perennial: 'It was only a sausage!'). He had developed a very short fuse but only, really, when it came to me.

Deep down, I understood what was going on. This was his (perhaps long-overdue) rebellion against the tyranny of Big Brother. He wanted to demonstrate that he was an independent entity, not beholden to me in any way. Because we had really been together too long. All our lives. And for all that time I had the built-in advantage of being the senior party who had established a pre-existing order. He had come along and just been integrated into my world as a kind of appendage: me, myself and I(van). I thoughtlessly relied upon him the way you might rely on your limbs. You wake up in the morning; your legs and arms are where they always were. They work in a predictable fashion. You don't spend much time contemplating what life would be without them, do you? But Ivan was getting ready for an act of amputation.

The insightful reader may be well ahead of me here. Because, in so many ways, from the tiny to the significant, Ivan is the absent party in this tale. He was always around, but he is to be found between the lines, more than in them. I may sketch an acquaintance in a few sharp sentences but what can I really tell you about my brother? I could say he was the most significant person in my life. But just how well did I know him? I respected his musical talent. I enjoyed his fast-firing wit. But I never really had to engage with him as a person any more than you have to engage with yourself. I took him for granted.

I have come to think that Ivan, in many respects, was shaped in reaction to me. He was determinedly anti-intellectual, because I was intellectual. He chose to occupy a space that was physical, emotional and instinctive, leaving the reading, philosophizing and reasoning to me. As a child, I was always admired in our family for my artistic ability and my way with words. When Ivan found music, and applied himself to it, he must have felt he was marking out his own special territory. And then, like some jealous child who prefers his sibling's toys, I invaded that space and made him share it with me.

But still, it would have been OK (as, indeed, it was for many years) if only it had all added up to something. But we had got nowhere, and had nowhere left to go. And somewhere deep within his psyche (because Ivan would never admit any of this, not even to himself) the child was roaring. He took my toys. And he broke them!

I still find it almost impossible to have this conversation with my brother, more than a decade on. He just shrugs and denies any ill will. But it was there in his behaviour, in his cutting comments, impatience, rudeness and general air of disregard and disrespect. Ivan blamed me for our failure to achieve the fame and fortune we both desired. He blamed the complexity of my lyrics. My unwillingness to compromise. My arrogance in deal-ing with the music business. My stage presence (he always thought he had more stage presence than me). My singing (he rather fancied that he sang better than me, too). He probably thought Rob Dickens was right about my haircut, for that matter. He blamed me and maybe he didn't even have to have a specific reason why. He just needed to take it out on somebody.

A large group of us went out for dinner for Gloria's birthday. Ivan stood up and said he had something to say. We presumed this was going to be a toast to the birthday girl but instead he announced that Ina and he were getting married.

This was quite a bombshell. Ivan was the last person whom anyone present would have considered the marrying kind. He was considered a bit of a party animal, renowned among our friends for his wild behaviour and general sense of impropriety. And he was a womanizer who made my own forays into that area of human endeavour appear insignificant. I think it is fair to say that, over the years, he had treated Ina like shit, two-timing her, spurning her, chasing her away when she was around then chasing after her when she wasn't. But here they were, tying the knot. It was hard not to see this as a kind of wounded act, salve for the scars of disappointment and rejection. Ina was spirited and funny and eccentric but they always made for a chalk-and-cheese couple. She liked her material comforts. He liked to bum around. She wanted to settle down. He wanted to travel. And boy, could they argue! Even when they actually got married, later that year, it was one of those occasions when guests were muttering under their breath that it wouldn't last. And, indeed, it did not. They divorced a few years later, leaving Ina with a badly broken heart.

So anyway, there we were, at Gloria's birthday dinner, which quickly turned into an engagement party. Gloria was pissed off because she felt her celebration had been hijacked by Ivan. And I was pissed off because it became clear that Ivan had proposed six months earlier but had chosen not to tell me his plans, even though they had significant impact on my own. Ina confided their intention to travel the world for a year before considering where they might settle down.

I was looking for a chance to catch Ivan alone, to speak to him away from the chatter of happy-ever-after platitudes. But he kept out-manoeuvring me, ensuring there was no possibility of a private word. Until the very end of the evening, when I followed him to the toilet. We stood side by side at the urinal. It was an appropriate setting. It wasn't just piss that was running down the drain.

'So,' I said.

'So,' he replied.

When you had been together for as long as we had, you can say a lot with just one word. My 'so' was laden with hurt and betrayal, full of weary accusation, but shaded with a question, grasping for a last fading glimmer of hope. His 'so' had the firmness of confirmation and dismissal. It was cocky and a little bit cruel. And it was final.

We stood and urinated for a while.

'That's it, then?' I said.

'That's it,' he confirmed.

Then we zipped up and went our separate ways.

And still I could not quite accept that it was done and dusted. I was like a boxer who doesn't know when he's beaten. I had taken one hell of a pounding. There was blood all over the ring. The whole crowd was yelling for me to stay down and take the count. But some primitive instinct was still in operation, compelling me to struggle back to my feet. A voice in my head saying, 'One punch, that's all it comes down to. You can still take this guy.'

Officially, I was considering my position. My guitar playing was improving with practise. I was still writing a lot of songs. Maybe I would be better off on my own.

One more blow had to land.

One more straw to break this stubborn camel's back.

And it fell, cruelly, one night in bed with Gloria. We lay there in the aftermath of passion and I was talking about the future, imagining all kinds of wild scenarios, when she gave it to me straight.

'I love you, Neil,' she said. 'I love being with you. You make me laugh, you're always good to me. But I can't make a life with you.'

'Why not?'

'Look at yourself!' she said, sweetly, sadly. 'You haven't got a job. You never have any money. You don't take responsibility for anyone or anything except yourself and barely even that. You live in your head. All the time. Your whole life is dreams about the future. When are you going to wake up? Life is going on right here, right now. I'm trying to get on with my life. And I can't count on you. 'Cause, let's face it . . .'

'What?' I said, resentfully.

'Nothing,' she said, thinking better of it.

'Let's face what?' I insisted.

'You're a loser.'

I recoiled as if slapped in the face.

I recoiled in the way you recoil from the truth. From a truth you've tried to hide from yourself. From a truth that hurts.

'I'm not a loser,' I said, as much to myself as her.

20

It wasn't as if I just snapped to attention and went to work. But what Gloria said preyed on my mind. And, over the course of 1989 and 1990, I started to get my act together.

I guess I had a head start as a journalist. I knew the craft, having made my mistakes in Ireland and eventually finding my voice under the guidance of Niall Stokes and all my *Hot Press* colleagues. I had some flair for language, a lot of curiosity and a low tolerance for bullshit, all of which served me well, but there was something more besides. I wasn't some bright-eyed kid coming out of college. I had been living a life, loving and losing and learning hard lessons. I wouldn't go so far as to describe myself as mature but I had a deep well of experience to draw upon.

And I had something to prove. I really applied myself to the task in hand. Because if this was going to be my profession, I didn't just want to get published – I wanted to do great things. I wanted to write articles nobody else could write. I wanted them to rip off the page and grab readers by the scruff of the neck. If I was going to be a journalist, then I would take it as a licence to investigate and explore, to gain access to places where ordinary civilians are not always welcome, to find out about people whose stories are rarely told, to go on a voyage of discovery. My co-conspirator in this regard was my friend Leo, who was driven to achieve something extraordinary with his photo-journalism. It wasn't kudos he was looking for. It was penetration. We talked up a storm, the pair of us. We (perhaps arrogantly) decided that too much journalism merely skimmed the surface. We wanted to get right inside our stories, to illuminate the dark corners most journalism never even noticed.

I suppose, to some extent, this was a kind of transfer of

ambition. If I couldn't be a rock star then I would be a press star. But there was something else besides that. A genuine immersion in the task. A commitment to doing something worthwhile. And, with each published article, I slowly rebuilt my shattered dignity and restored my pride in myself.

I wasn't writing about rock'n'roll, either. Anything but music. I was fascinated by the underbelly of life, where losers like me congregated, seeking out ways to get their own back on the world, and so I went in search of it. And one day, I got lucky.

I used to read the Irish newspapers, just to keep up on events back home, and had been following the case of Martin Cahill, widely alleged to be the General, the notorious kingpin of Dublin's crime scene. The focus of the most concentrated operation in Garda history, he was openly accused in the media, denounced in parliament and (perhaps most damagingly of all) discussed in the pub. Anonymity is usually considered an essential element of a successful life in the underworld, yet Cahill had achieved a status usually reserved for pop stars and actors: he was a household name. Maybe that's what drew me to him. Here was someone who had fame thrust upon him, unwanted. What made the story easy to sell to the editors of GQ magazine, however, was that fame was a burden borne with considerable humour by Cahill.

Kept under constant police surveillance, he told reporters outside court that he was moving into the security business, quipping: 'Since the Gardai go everywhere we go we can offer an armed Gardai escort for the movements of large amounts of cash.' Cahill was a serial joker, a godfather in Mickey Mouse boxer shorts who would drop his trousers to mock his persecutors. Yet despite all the publicity, he maintained a curious kind of obscurity. While he was appearing in court for a breach of the peace, a succession of Gardai witnesses failed to point Cahill out, though one detective was prepared to have a go, declaring: 'He is wearing a wig, a false moustache and glasses and if he took down his hands from his face I could identify him.' Everywhere Cahill appeared in public, he kept his features hidden behind balaclavas and ski masks. He was a villain who somehow reflected the country that spawned him. America had Al Capone, the personification of suave, swaggering, organized violent crime. England had the Krays, brutal and trendy. And Ireland had the General, a gang leader with a sense of humour.

GQ wanted to know if I could get an interview. And I confidently said, 'Why not?' Well, actually, I could think of a good few reasons why not. Law-enforcement officers who had crossed Cahill in the past had been kidnapped, car-bombed and knee-capped. And then there were the oft-repeated rumours of him peeling the skin off an informer's legs, and nailing a suspected betrayer to the floor. But I was not really sure about the protocols of crime journalism and thought it only reasonable that, if I was writing about the General, I should give him the opportunity to put forward his side of the story.

It was easy to find out where he lived. Even my parents knew. They were enthusiastic about my occupation, which hinted at a previously unsuspected streak of respectability in their errant son. 'I never thought you were cut out for the rock scene,' my dad declared one day, blissfully writing off his own part in my history. 'I always thought you'd be better off as a writer!' He drove me over to the lair of Ireland's most notorious criminal and hung about outside, fearful lest his son's new career come to a brutal end before it even got started.

It was hard to miss the General's redbrick house in Cowper Downs, an affluent suburb of south Dublin. There was a police surveillance team parked outside. I don't know what they made of me — I doubt I looked like one of the General's usual visitors. My hair was still worn in long, rock'n'roll locks, I was dressed in denim jacket and jeans and I had a notebook and pen tightly clutched in my hands. I was shaking with nerves as I opened the garden gate. I was not encouraged by the sight of a solemnly threatening sign, 'Beware the Guard Dog', featuring an ominous silhouette of a vicious Rottweiler.

The barking started immediately, loud and agitated. I advanced across the messy garden, silently praying that the dog was safely locked up. I had just about reached the front door when I caught sight of it, hurtling towards me, teeth bared. It couldn't have stood more than six inches tall, a tiny black puppy that all but rolled over and wet itself at my feet. I took a deep breath and rang the doorbell.

After what seemed like forever, the door was opened by a spotty, teenage boy. 'Is Mr Cahill in?' I inquired, my mind reeling as I tried to come to terms with the unexpected domesticity of the situation. Where were the henchmen, the thugs that might be expected to be protecting their boss? 'Da!' yelled the kid, before disappearing back inside. Whatever next?

The figure who appeared at the half-open doorway did not conform to any popular image of a major-league criminal. He was short and portly, dressed in well-worn trousers and a stained T-shirt, a few long strands of hair clinging hopelessly to his bald pate. The air of physical disrepair was not helped by his bent, yellowing teeth. He watched me closely as I introduced myself, running through a prepared speech, my voice trembling, the notebook in my hand bobbing up and down. When Cahill smiled his whole faced seemed to light up. 'Are you nervous?' he asked, softly spoken, his thick Dublin accent shading his words with lilting reassurance. He reached out to tap my arm. 'You don't believe everything you read now, do you?'

And that's what I was after. That's what I wanted to hear. Because everything I knew about the twilight zone we call the underworld I had read in books and newspapers or gleaned from films and TV. I wanted truth. Hard, unvarnished truth. That was what brought me to Cahill's door.

I met with Cahill twice, and interviewed him at length. 'You don't want to talk to me about crime, do you?' he asked me, with a gently mocking air. But of course I did. He proved a loquacious conversationalist, although predictably guarded on certain subjects. He developed a curious way of talking about things in the third person, like an expert giving his opinion, but always the answers came wreathed in knowing smiles. 'I hate liars,' he'd say, 'but sometimes I have to lie. D'y'understand?' A more genial gangster you could not hope to have met. Yet there was no doubt Cahill held the propensity for extreme violence, and that this reputation helped him in his trade. 'You want to know if there's something nasty underneath this smile?' he asked me, when I pressed him on the issue. 'Crime is a way of life,' he said. 'Sometimes something bad will happen when you do the crime.'

For me, the essential banality of Cahill's world was a kind of revelation. Here was the most notorious figure in Ireland, sitting in a messy living room, offering me cups of tea while he discussed acts of criminality as casually as my dad might have chatted about his working day. There were scribbled drawings of the Teenage Mutant Ninja Turtles pinned to the wallpaper. Children ran in and out of the rooms, and he greeted them affectionately. Yet he once nailed a man to the floor, an act he would blithely consider part of his job.

The article caused a minor sensation when it was published and I began to discover what it was to be a wanted man. After years of having doors shut in my face, suddenly they were swinging wide open and I was beckoned through with open arms. *Esquire* magazine wanted to commission me. When I informed *GQ*'s editor, Michael VerMeulen, of this development, he just snapped, 'You can't write for *Esquire*!'

'Why not?' I asked.

'Because we're going to make you an editor!' I'm sure he just decided that on the spot. Michael was an inspirational American, under whose editorship British *GQ* became the biggest-selling men's magazine in the country. He rather took me under his wing, making me first a contributing editor and then editor-at-large, an overblown title for a fantastically attractive position which involved going into the office only two days a week (to participate in editorial discussions and commissioning), leaving me free the rest of the time to pursue my writing.

I began to write more crime features. I met armed robbers, muggers, burglars, gangsters, fences, drug dealers, conmen and even killers. I had dinner in their homes, drank with them in their pubs and clubs and occasionally, when things hadn't turned out according to plan, visited them in prison. My encounter with Cahill had made me realize something all too obvious. All these people, regularly demonized in the media, but with no access to it, had stories to tell, and were mostly eager for the chance to have them chronicled. I never offered my approval, and it was never asked for. All they wanted to know was that I would honestly report what they had to say. I was flattered once to find an article I had written on pimps blown up and pinned to a wall in Charing Cross police station. A Vice Squad detective told me that they were amazed that I'd managed to get pimps, normally the most secretive of criminals, to talk about their business so frankly. I went to Bradford and investigated the murder of a prostitute. I interviewed a psychopath who had been boasting that he was Britain's most prolific killer. I hung out with armed robbers and armed policemen on a quest to find out just how easy it was to buy an illegal gun in the UK (it took me three months but I eventually got my hands on an Uzi). I spent a month on the job with a crack dealer, worrying about whether I too was liable to get arrested if the police actually caught him in the act. I put time into these stories, often considerably more time and effort than the financial remuneration justified. But I wanted to get things right.

And I was having adventures. I was reckless, taking stupid risks. I went all the way to Russia to attend a rave, dropping acid with members of the Mafia who were so unhappy with what I wrote they threatened to have me killed (mind you, I already had a psycho writing threatening letters from prison, so they would just have to wait in line). I went to South Africa to explore a country riven by Apartheid and somehow got stuck halfway up a cliff, alone in the middle of nowhere (I really thought I was going to die that time, but somehow sheer embarrassment at the notion of expiring so uselessly and pathetically gave me the will to pull through). I went to America and travelled the country getting drunk in bars with complete strangers until I got robbed by a stripper in Nashville and had to talk my way back to London with only $25 to my name. I had a good time in the States. I got roaring drunk with Billy Joel in a bar, where we persuaded the manager to let us have a lock-in and boozed away till daylight. A couple of Billy's old New York cronies showed up, and a very dubious bunch they turned out to be. I particularly remember a guy called Rocco. 'Would you fuck the waitress?' he kept asking me. She was kind of an ugly waitress but then Rocco was no oil painting himself. 'I'd fuck the waitress,' he admitted. 'But right now, I'd fuck a can of worms.' Billy got on the piano and we ran through some rock'n'roll standards. As I recall, my rendition of 'Twist and Shout' (with Billy on backing vocals) was particularly well received.

OK, so I did some rock journalism. But only the big guys. I drew the line at talking to up-and-coming stars – that would have been too painful. When I saw bands on stage – any band, any stage – I was sick with envy. I wanted to jump up and grab a guitar and show the audience what I could do. This is not a good critical position. But I met some of my heroes. I spent some hours being charmed by Leonard Cohen, one of the most gracious and eloquent gentlemen I have ever encountered. And I rode around LA in a limousine with Keith Richards, drinking vodka and listening to old Motown records on the radio (we were only supposed to drive from a video shoot to Keith's hotel, but he was having such a good time telling me about the musicians who played on each track that he instructed his driver to keep going, waving his vodka glass and slurring, 'Just drive. Drive all night!'). Maybe I never made it as a pop star. But I could console myself that, in the less starry firmament of journalism, I was beginning to shine.

In May 1992 I was in the GQ office when a call came in from U2's office in Dublin. They wanted to make sure I had tickets and passes for the band's forthcoming gig at Earl's Court. It was U2's first British show since Wembley Stadium five years before. I was surprised and flattered to have been tracked down. Although I had spoken to Bono a couple of times on the phone, I hadn't actually seen anyone from the U2 camp in years. I never even caught up with Adam to sell him the old bass guitar – though I had been in search of it, when I was back in Ireland, thinking of all the money I could make. It was last seen in the possession of Yeah! Yeah!'s old bassist, Deco. But when I went round to his house Deco handed me what I can only describe as the neck of a bass guitar with a tiny square bit of wood attached.

'What's that?' I said.

'It's the old Ibanez,' he said.

'What have you done to it?' I shrieked.

'I sawed the body off,' he said, cheerfully. 'I wanted it to look like one of those Devo basses. Don't worry. It still works.'

My dreams of screwing a small fortune out of Adam evaporated. 'It's worthless now,' I said, despondently contemplating the wreckage.

'Oh, come on, Neil,' said Declan. 'It was always worthless. It's just a cheap piece of crap. But now at least it looks really cool!'

Anyway, I went along to the Earl's Court show with Gloria. I wanted to introduce her to Bono. When I wasn't travelling on assignment, Gloria and I were living together in her flat in Belsize Crescent, the very same street where Ivan and I had partied a decade away while dreaming of stardom. But things were very different now. I had embraced the concept of fidelity and responsibility and my relationship with Gloria had blossomed from there. Once I had shown that I was serious about getting my act together, Gloria supported me during my struggle to establish myself as a journalist and I was doing my best to repay her faith. We were becoming a family. The kids were easy to love, as kids generally are. You just open up your heart and they'll move in. I wasn't their dad but I was becoming something else, maybe even something better: a guy they liked to be with, somewhere between parent and friend. Life was taking a whole new shape for me. But I made a very peculiar discovery when I first mentioned the U2 gig to Gloria.

'Are you really friends with Bono?' she said (the band were so famous now, even Gloria was aware of them).

'Of course!' I said. 'I've told you before.'

'Yeah, well, you tell me lots of things,' she shrugged. 'I'm never sure when you're pulling my leg.'

'You mean, you don't believe me?' I said, incredulously.

'Well,' she said, quite reasonably, 'I know most of your friends. How come I've never met him?'

I couldn't really explain that. If I wanted to get hold of Bono, I had to call U2's office and speak to an assistant who would pass a message along, usually telling me something discouraging about where he was on the planet doing great work in the name of social justice and what a backlog of calls was building up for him.

Sometimes it would be weeks before he would actually call back and then it was pure chance if he caught me. There would be a voice on my answer-phone saying, 'I will hound you down!' So I'd have to call his office and start the process all over again. It was, really, too much to go through for something as trivial as touching base. It was not just that access was restricted by the channels of success, but also that everyone wanted a piece of Bono now. On one of the few occasions when I got hold of him (or he of me) he was interrupted by an assistant and came back to say, 'I've got to go; I've got the President on the other line!' 'Which president?' I asked. 'Good question! Which president?' he asked his assistant (it was the president of Ireland, by the way). With world leaders, film stars and supermodels to compete with, I was somewhere near the back of the queue and I just couldn't bring myself to make the effort required to push to the front.

And the thing is, maybe I even preferred to maintain my distance. I still woke up in a cold sweat sometimes from a Bono nightmare and I didn't like that at all. U2 were so popular they had become inescapable. They flashed like a beacon on my personal horizon, a constant reminder of everything I had failed to achieve.

Still, I was looking forward to seeing them again. As a live band, they were my touchstone: the first group I had ever seen perform, and the finest. And as friends, well, it would be interesting to find out where I stood.

The Earl's Court show was part of U2's extraordinary Zoo TV tour, which started out in arenas before moving on to stadiums. *Achtung Baby* had been released in 1991, a superb album of big, complex, emotional songs delivered with a contemporary cut and thrust that saw U2 shift away from their dalliance with roots music to reconnect with modernity and art rock. They sharpened up their image: there was a lot of flash and humour. Critics claimed they had embraced irony but there was really no irony in the songs, which were as substantial, soulful and committed as ever. The irony was in the packaging. U2 embraced the contradictions of their place on the world's stage: passionate Irishmen being feted as superstars in the trivial, gossip-hungry universe of celebrity. And they embraced the contradictions of their own personalities: true believers with a sense of humour. They decided to have fun.

And the Zoo TV shows were a lot of fun. And a lot more besides. It was a hi-tech multimedia art-installation extravaganza with heart and soul, a breathtaking spectacle of flashing slogans, pre-recorded images, live footage and random television channels bombarding the senses from walls of interactive video screens. Bono remained the lightning rod for the audience, the conduit for communal experience, but he was conducting this symphony of collective emotion with a weird new vitality, channelling everything through the character of the Fly, a representation of his own darker self, dressed in black leather and black shades, a barstool pundit from hell, a creature every bit as provocative as Gavin Friday in his Virgin Prunes heyday.

The Zoo TV concert was constructed on an incredible scale, but with U2 at its centre it seemed a living, breathing thing. It was truly the most amazing live event I had ever witnessed. Could rock'n'roll really really have come this far? And could it have been brought all this way by the same bunch of kids who had rocked the school gym with Bay City Rollers covers?

You could say I was impressed. And I was genuinely looking forward to telling the band so. All my reservations receded as Gloria and I made our way backstage. I had some very impressive plastic-laminated passes which eased our passage through a massive throng of well-wishers. As much effort seemed to have gone into the backstage set-up as had into the show itself. Guests with ordinary VIP stickers were restricted to a common-parts bar but our laminates admitted us to a white-tented tunnel, past a bar set aside for less well-connected associates, leading to a large hospitality marquee, with Zoo TV screens displaying random footage and waitresses dishing out sushi and champagne. There was a smattering of celebrities. Elvis Costello was there. And Chrissie Hynde. And Sinead O'Connor. I had met them all in my travels, and said hello, introducing them to Gloria (well, all except Sinead, of course, in case she wanted to search me for a tape recorder). There was no sign of the band, however. I thought perhaps they would come out to meet and greet once they had freshened up. But time passed. And then I noticed Elvis, Chrissie and Sinead being led away by a girl with a clipboard and escorted down another tunnel. Into a further chamber.

I approached the security guard at the entrance of the tunnel, with a sinking feeling in my heart.

'Sorry,' he said, politely. 'That pass doesn't let you through here.'

I turned back to Gloria. 'Let's just go,' I said. I felt heavy with disappointment but I didn't want to countenance such a feeling, that sense of debasement so familiar to me from my dreams.

'I thought you wanted to say hello,' said Gloria.

I could taste the bitterness welling up, a childishly petulant reaction to seeing celebrities being accorded the privilege of a personal audience while I was left outside. But I didn't want Gloria to suspect that such pettiness might reside within me. I wanted to be bigger and better than that. I had to accept that whatever personal connection I had to U2 had been eroded by time and changing circumstances. They had moved far beyond me. That part of my life's journey was over.

'I just want to go home,' I said.

21

Sometime in late 1995, I was sitting in front of my computer in my office above the bookie's in Piccadilly, deep into a feature on the murder of my old friend the General and his supplanting in the pecking order of the Irish underworld by an equally bizarre character known as the Monk, when I received a call from Sarah Sands, the new deputy editor of the *Daily Telegraph*. I had not spoken to her before. My contacts in the world of journalism were curiously limited. Despite my relative success, I could never really work up the enthusiasm to engage in the practice of networking by which most of my fellow freelance journalists seemed to survive. I was on a retainer from GQ and I was confident that when I was done with one story I would always pick up another commission. But I knew the *Telegraph*, of course. It was one of Britain's most venerable and popular newspapers. Its politics were some way to the right of my own, with strong affiliations to the Conservative party and the old British establishment, but I often perused its pages. The *Telegraph* always had well-written and well-researched national news coverage, which often provided me with inspiration and leads for the kind of hard, criminal features I favoured. Anyway, Sarah made me an unexpected offer.

'As I am sure you are aware,' she said, 'Tony Parsons is leaving.'

'Yes,' I said, even though I was aware of no such thing. I didn't know Tony Parsons had ever been at the *Telegraph*, let alone that he was leaving it. But I suspected that such an admission might be a mistake. Anyway, I knew who Parsons was: an ex-*NME* punk who had gained a reputation as one of Britain's most pugnacious and opinionated arts journalists.

'We were wondering if you would be interested in taking over his column,' said Sarah.

'Certainly I'd be interested,' I said, trying to sound as calm as possible. A column is the dream of most journalists, a forum of your very own from which to spout your theories and opinions (and I had a lot of theories and opinions festering away in the dark catacombs of my mind). And a column in Britain's best-selling broadsheet newspaper . . . Well, it might not mean the same thing to me as getting a number-one single but in my business this was definitely *Top of the Pops* material. Still, it would help if I knew what this column was supposed to be about.

'Can you meet with me to talk it over?' inquired Sarah.

'Any time,' I said.

'How about now?' she said.

'No problem,' I said. 'Can you give me an hour or so?'

Actually, I had a big problem. Quite apart from not knowing exactly what we were supposed to be talking over, I had been engaged in a major writing stint for several days, during which I had not paid much attention to my appearance. I had a few days' growth of stubble on my face. And I was compensating for the lack of heating in my office by wearing a pair of woolly trousers and a big, shaggy jumper. I did not feel like prime *Telegraph*-employment material. But I had an idea. I ran up Regent's Street to the *GQ* offices and threw myself at the mercy of the girls in the fashion department. They fitted me out in an ultra-sharp suit, shirt and slightly extravagant tie (which were intended for an up-coming fashion shoot), gave me a shave, sprayed me with some cologne and dispatched me looking every inch the *GQ* man. Sarah must have been impressed, at any rate. She offered me the job on the spot. But what job? I was on full alert for clues.

'I think you would be ideal material for the *Telegraph*,' said Sarah. 'You're young . . .'

(These days it wasn't often I was called young but journalism is very different to the music business, and in a newspaper whose most famous correspondent, Bill Deedes, was pushing eighty, I suppose a thirty-four-year-old could be considered a spring chicken.)

'. . . dynamic . . .'

(I could tell she liked the cut of my suit.)

'. . . you're a really terrific writer . . .'

(What can I say? I just felt flattered that somebody had noticed all the good work I had been doing.)

'. . . and you can bring a wealth of your own experience to the job . . .'

(What experience was she getting at, exactly?)

'. . . Because, unlike most people in this profession, you've seen it from both sides . . .'

(I wasn't sure I liked where this was going.)

'. . . You've actually been there and done it.'

'I certainly have,' I said. Hoping she wasn't going to ask me to elaborate on where I had been and what I had done.

'I think you would be an outstanding rock critic for the *Daily Telegraph*.'

I nodded thoughtfully. My past had caught up with me. Well, it was bound to, sooner or later. But there was one thing we had to get straight.

'I've never liked the term "rock critic",' I said.

'Whyever not?'

'It's not all rock music, is it?' I pointed out. 'What if I wanted to write about a rapper? Or a reggae singer? Or a disco queen?'

'I take your point,' said Sarah. 'What term do you prefer?'

'Pop,' I said.

And so I started writing a weekly column for the *Telegraph*. I had a picture byline: 'Neil McCormick on Pop'. And if that sounded like I was high on lemonade, it was a small price to pay for not having to admit I had finally accepted the destiny fate had clearly marked out for me, staggering down the byways of fame and fortune, from putative rock star to embittered rock critic.

Actually, not that embittered. To no one's great surprise but my own, I found that I enjoyed my new role. I had my soapbox from which I could rant and rave about the evils of the music business but also champion the music that I loved, be a voice for the artist rather than the corporations, celebrate talent (in its hugely diverse array) while keeping tabs on the cynical machinations and manipulations of the industry. Music had never stopped being part of my life, even if I had become a regular consumer rather than an active participant. It still infected my imagination. I couldn't pass a record store without wanting to scour the racks, looking for gems. Gloria sometimes complained that there was never a moment's respite from music in our household. So if I was going to play it, listen to it, read about it, think about it, talk about it, then I might as well write about it too. And, once the cork had been removed from that particular bottle, there was no stopping me. I was frothing over. I kept ringing up my editor on the arts pages and asking for more space. 'I can't possibly explain the rebirth of ambient music as part of club culture in 800 words,' I'd complain.

'Well, what kind of length do you think you need?' the long-suffering Sarah Crompton would sigh.

'I need a book,' I'd say.

'I can squeeze in 1200 words,' Sarah would generously reply.

'But there's so much to say!' I'd wail.

And as the musical representative of Britain's biggest-selling broadsheet, I got to meet, well, pretty much everybody I ever wanted to meet (and a few others besides), from Aaliyah to Warren Zevon (and all points on the alphabet in between).

I never met Kurt Cobain or Tupac Shakur (both dead by the time I was getting started) and I haven't yet met Madonna, Michael Jackson, Prince, Bruce Springsteen, Eminem or even, for that matter, Robbie Williams (I must be the only person in the British music business who hasn't met Robbie, but it's not as if I am holding my breath). On the other hand, I got drunk in a bar with Debbie Harry (still my beating heart). And we got along famously, once we had got over my impertinent comments about her appearance. 'Fuck you, you fucker!' were, as I recall, Debbie's words to me when I suggested that she might have put on a little weight since the years when her portrait used to adorn my wall. 'There are chubby-chasers in the world too, you know!' she added, laughing richly. And I had dinner with Elton John, David Beckham, Posh Spice and Lulu on the same night. Actually, that was at an album launch, where I staggered in from my drunken encounter with Debbie and sat at the wrong table by mistake. But they were very gracious about it. Elton didn't know who I was but chatted away happily and, I am told, later inquired who was the handsome fellow in the shaggy jumper (an item of punk-rock clothing I had worn in Debbie's honour).

And I went shopping with Michael Stipe in LA. We were sitting in the sun, sipping cappuccinos, when Daryl Hannah stopped and said hello, engaging the rock superstar in friendly, frothy chat. 'That was such an LA moment,' said Michael, after-wards. 'I've never met her before in my life.'

And Mick Jagger bought me champagne in Cannes. And I was served by a butler in Sting's garden. And a Sugababe sat on my knee at a P-Diddy party in Barcelona. And I bumped into Boy George in a crowded square in Shanghai, where he hugged me and said I wrote the nicest things anyone had ever written about him, then spent the next twelve hours trying to seduce me (admonishing me for my habit of saying 'Fuck me!' to express surprise, he declared, 'If you say that once more, I'm going to have to take you up on it'). And Bob Geldof invited me to his fiftieth birthday. It was fancy dress. 'You can come as a cunt,' he told me. 'Then you won't need a costume.' And a Beatle once rang me at home.

'Paul called,' said Gloria when I got home one evening.

'Paul who?' I said.

'I don't know; he just said his name was Paul,' said Gloria. I ran through all the Pauls I knew but she insisted it was none of them. 'I'm sure you know him, though,' she said. 'His voice was very familiar.'

The mystery was solved when he called back. 'Can I speak to Neil McCormick?' said a warm, lightly Liverpool-accented voice.

'You're speaking to him,' I said.

'Well, you're speaking to Paul McCartney,' said my caller.

'Gosh! Hello, Paul!' I declared.

'You believe me, then?' said Paul.

'Yeah, why not?' I said.

'Usually I have to spend the first half-hour convincing whoever I've called that it's me,' he explained. He had obtained my number from his press officer. He wanted to thank me personally for an article I had written about the Beatles' songwriting partnership. I had argued that it was silly to talk (as so many critics did) about Lennon *or* McCartney. It's Lennon *and* McCartney. 'I could never say those things, but what you wrote expressed exactly how I feel,' he told me. So while I had him on the phone I bombarded him with Beatles questions, which he gracefully answered. And it couldn't have been too painful, because actually he rang me several times. It got to the stage where the kids were putting their hands over the receiver and yelling, 'It's that Paul McCartney on the phone again!'

I think I have been a kind critic. Which is not to say I haven't occasionally mocked and denigrated people's creative efforts (I prefer to write about music I appreciate but when a major star releases a new recording it is part of my remit to say what I honestly think about it); and I have certainly attacked those aspects of the business I find most abhorrent, such as the overcommitting of resources to cynically contrived, lowest-common-denominator manufactured pap. But I hope I brought to my music journalism a sense that music is created by people, and that whether it is to my taste or not, I believe most people try to do the best they can. Even musicians.

And I discovered David Gray. Well, I was the first national UK journalist to champion his cause, anyway, when *White Ladder* was still on his own kitchen-sink label, before he signed it over to East West and went on to sell some five million albums world-wide, perhaps the greatest word-of-mouth success in the history of the music business. David had been making music for over a decade to little avail, having been dropped by three different labels. I was so impressed with his home-made album, I got a number for his record label, called up, identified myself and asked if it would be possible to set up an interview with David Gray.

'This is David Gray!' said the excited voice on the other line.

David's long struggle for recognition has made him the patron saint of Lost Causes. His name has become synonymous with the triumph of talent over hype, personifying the battles of the little guy against the big, brutal industry machine. He has been lauded as an example of how Talent and Perseverance (those twin watchwords I once spouted as a mantra before my perseverance finally ran its course) can sometimes result in triumph. But David said something that really struck home for me, words I have passed along to many a struggling artist: 'I've been chewed up, spat out and through it all have come to some sort of wisdom,' he claimed. 'I don't blame the music industry. Although there's gross incompetence on all levels, and I'm sure that talent by the bucketload gets crushed and thrown by the wayside, I've come to realize that the buck stops with you as the artist. Unless you've got huge amounts of money and the force to manufacture success, what you've actually created has to convince people of its own accord.'

And so mostly, despite my initial reservations, I enjoyed my time as a music journalist. Mostly. I have to admit that there were occasions when a sense of envy or resentment would well up.

Like when some pop star who had a co-writing credit by dint of sitting in a studio chipping in the odd idea while teams of established professionals assembled their record would start talking to me (me!) about the craft of songwriting. 'Listen up,' I wanted to say to Natalie and Samantha and Mel, 'I know more about the pain and beauty and goddam art (not craft!) of songwriting than you could possibly imagine.' But I had to keep my peace. Because they had hits. And I had a bunch of old demos rejected by the same record companies who turned them into stars.

Or when some joker whose looks and luck had carried them way beyond where their talent truly warranted started complaining about how hard it was to be famous. 'Come on,' I wanted to scream at Gavin and Dolores and Simon, 'you got more than you ever deserved, so fucking make the most of it.' But I couldn't say anything. Because they had it. And I hadn't. And that is all that counted.

Or when the dread subject of Destiny reared its ugly head. And some star who had everything they ever wanted started talking about how it was *meant to be*. Did they really believe that shit? I mean, was it really and truly fatalistically inevitable that Kylie Minogue and Jason Donovan would some day top the charts? And that I would be sitting in other people's hotel suites, listening to the inane drivel of lucky dopes with half my talent?

Not that I was bitter. Oh no. But whenever anyone, no matter how genuinely, supremely, indisputably talented they might be, started talking as if their fame was preordained, I wanted to turn off the tape recorder and say, 'Listen, buddy, let me share with you an open secret, spoken freely in the streets but never even whispered in the corridors of power: it's a big world out there and sometimes, despite all of your best efforts, events get out of your control.'

I once met Rob Dickens at an awards ceremony. He was no longer head of WEA, yet remained one of the most significant individuals in the British music business. But in my private realm of demonology Dickens was the number-one monster. His dismissal of my band had been so cruelly arbitrary. I had never forgotten that Bill Drummond told me his boss had refused to even listen to our music before tearing up our contract. A mutual acquaintance introduced us. And then promptly froze as she realized what she had done.

'You dropped my band from your label,' I said to him, as we shook hands.

'You'll have to remind me,' he said, smirking. 'I've dropped a lot of bands.'

'Shook Up!' I said.

'Ah, yes,' he said. 'Bill Drummond's lot. Well you never made it, did you? So I was right.'

The *fucker*! I wanted to headbutt him right there, break his nose and leave him bleeding on the floor, maybe kick him while he was down, so he could see how it felt. But I thought it would probably be conduct unbecoming of a representative of the *Daily Telegraph*. So I just smiled and let go of his hand.

We could have made it. I still believe that. I just think it would have required a bit more imagination than by-the-numbers industry guys like Rob Dickens have ever displayed.

So anyway, after all these years writing a newspaper column and consorting with the great and the good of the music business, I'm often asked who is the most famous person I've ever met. It always feels like a trick question. I could say Dylan but I just stood next to him once. And Paul McCartney is pretty famous, but we've only talked on the telephone. The truth is, the most famous person I have ever met is a guy I first got to know in school in Dublin when I was fourteen years old.

I ran into Bono again in May 1996, at a funeral. Bill Graham had died of a heart attack, aged just forty-four, his years of heavy drinking having taken a lethal toll. I went back to Howth to pay my last respects to a man who had been a mentor to so many of us, the best rock journalist ever to have come out of Ireland by a country mile, the man who discovered U2 when really there was not much to discover, and befriended them, believed in them, guided them, challenged and inspired them. But he inspired a lot of other people besides, myself included. The small band of brothers and sisters that put *Hot Press* together back in those early days are bound together for ever by a shared history of long nights of music, laughter and fucking hard work keeping Ireland safe for rock'n'roll. I had spoken to Bill during a visit to Dublin shortly after landing the *Telegraph* job. He had been full of encouragement (after he got over asking me to return a record he loaned me over fifteen years before – when it came to music, Bill never forgot anything). I remember thinking it was good to know that I could draw on his incredible musical resources. If I was ever stuck for an idea, I could call Bill and just listen to his rambling discources. Bill was a gushing river of ideas and insights; you could spin entire articles out of the tributaries of his conversation.

But it was not to be. We would never again have the pleasure of his rich, wild, kind and frequently rather inebriated company. Bill was gone.

He received an incredible sending off in a funeral as eccentric as the man himself. The entire Irish music business seemed to have come to pay tribute and it was standing-room only in Howth church, an enormous, Victorian-era greybrick monstrosity overlooked by gargoyles in the centre of the village. A weave of fiddles and guitars from folk band Altan welcomed us in. Maire Ni Bhraoinain of Clannad filled the rafters with her soft, ethereal voice as she sang a mournful Gaelic lament before the Gospel reading. But it was not an unduly sombre occasion. I still chuckle whenever I think of the parish priest receiving an offertory gift from Liam Mackey, the priest standing there in all his fine robes in front of the altar solemnly holding a copy of Miles Davis's *Bitches Brew* above his head (the psychedelic cover of which features a naked black woman with prominent breasts). During Communion, Bono sang Leonard Cohen's elegaic 'Tower of Song' from the balcony, with backing from the Edge and members of Altan. Gavin Friday sang Dylan's 'Death Is Not the End'. And then Simon Carmody of Irish trash-rock band the Golden Horde gave a plaintive, shaky, solo rendition of New York Doll Johnny Thunder's 'You Can't Put Your Arms Around a Memory' while Bono, Edge, Gavin Friday, Niall Stokes, Liam Mackey and another old friend, John Stephenson, carried the coffin into the bright sunlight. That was the hardest moment. I suppose we all thought of ourselves as young and were still getting used to the very notion of mortality among our contemporaries. A few of us made the trip out to Fingal Cemetery, where Bill's coffin was laid into the ground to the lonely strains of a jazz trumpet.

Afterwards, as tradition dictated, there was a wake in the Royal Hotel in Howth. I was trying to comfort a highly emotional Liam Mackey, when Bono and Ali sat down at our table. It had been a long time since I had seen them, but no words were spoken about that. Edge joined us. And Gavin. And we toasted Bill. 'He was not an ordinary man,' said Bono. 'He made so many connections he could introduce you to yourself. I'm so glad I knew him. I'm really going to miss hearing that tuba of a voice, like a whole brass section in your ear at four o'clock in the morning.'

The afternoon dragged on with stories and drink, as these occasions must, and a small ragged band of us found ourselves still toasting him late into the night, in Dublin club Lillie's Bordello. I don't remember at what stage Bono made his farewells but I do remember talking to him about my little sister, Louise, who was the latest member of the McCormick family to have become involved with U2. She had been employed as an assistant engineer on sessions recording B-sides for the *Achtung Baby* album and got along with Bono so well he started using her to record his personal demos. Louise had been a fan of U2 since the earliest recordings. At the age of thirteen she played my copy of *Boy* over and over, until even I was in danger of getting sick of it. But she had a great equanimity about her, and took employment by her teen idol in her stride. Louise had been very quiet around the studio, apparently, and it was a while before she even mentioned that she was related to Ivan, Stella and me. 'Where would U2 be without the McCormicks?' Bono joked.

'I often wonder where I would be without U2,' I replied. 'Probably a fuck sight better off.'

'Ah, don't be like that, Neil,' said Bono.

'You know, I've got my own column in Britain's biggest-selling broadsheet newspaper, with a nice little picture of me on top,' I pointed out. 'I've got more than a million readers, so they tell me. The BBC send camera crews around to my office whenever there's a breaking music story. My granny got all excited 'cause she saw me on the six o'clock news. I'm a regular guest on half a dozen radio shows and, if you get up early enough in the morning, you might see me on the couch on breakfast TV. And still I feel like a failure. It's ridiculous. I never got the kind of fame I always wanted but under almost any other circumstances I would probably be the most famous person to have come out of my class at school, at least. But I had to go to school with you!'

'You're not the only one of my friends who complains about how hard it is knowing me,' said Bono, smiling.

'Everybody's got their dragons to slay,' I grumbled.

'Yeah, but you've got to kill Bono!' chuckled Bono. This notion seemed to amuse him greatly. 'That's it! You've got to kill me,' he laughed. 'It's for your own good! And mine!'

'I don't begrudge you a thing,' I said. 'I think you got everything you deserved. What I worry about is: does that mean I got what I deserved too?'

We started to establish a new relationship after that, a mixture of the personal and professional. My music column provided an excuse to stay in touch. I could ring Bono for quotes and comments without feeling like I was hanging on his coat tails. The rise of the mobile phone also meant there was a number where I could leave a message for him personally, anywhere in the world, without having to go through a retinue of assistants. And he started calling me a little more often, whenever something brought me to mind.

Like when U2 decided to call their next album *Pop*.

'I don't believe it,' I scoffed. 'How many times have you told me you don't make pop music?'

'I've grown to like the word "pop",' he laughed. 'That pop thing you've always been into, I used to think it was a term of abuse. I didn't realize how cool it was. It's the grown-ups who called it pop music. And now we've all grown up. Some more than others!'

We were talking about the meaning of pop, when he went off to fetch a dictionary from his shelves. 'I've got a great definition of pop,' he insisted. 'Let me see. *Pox. Practise. Pram. Prant. Prang.* God, all my words! *Pratfall. Preach. Prayer rug.* Hold on, I'm past it. Here we go. P-o . . . POP. *Pop, poppy, pop. To make or cause to make a light, sharp explosive sound.* Isn't that great? Or how about: *an informal word for father.* I like that, I like that a lot.' He idly continued his amble through the dictionary. '*Popcorn.* And then *pope.* That's my favourite. Pop is the Pope after he's dropped an E. I'm gonna get a T-shirt made up: "Pop John Paul II".'

'How about "Pop John Paul George and Ringo"?' I suggested.

Bono referred to these chats as 'our ongoing dialogue'. We had lunch one day and talked, just for a change, about God. 'Religion is responsible for a lot of bad things that have happened in the world,' Bono admitted after one of my more stinging critiques. 'But I have to say, it's probably done a lot of good things too. It's sort of politically incorrect but if you look around you, at practical things missionaries have achieved in some of the toughest areas of the world, hospitals and schools in Nicaragua and Calcutta, well, I don't want to be the defender of religion, but if I had to be, I probably could. Apart from the odd Spanish inquisition.'

Afterwards, we rambled around a labyrinth-like bookshop. When we were leaving, he handed me a copy of Leo Tolstoy's *The Kingdom of God is Within You.*

I laughed, but I was flattered. 'Do you still think there's hope for me?'

'There's always hope,' said Bono.

I was flown out to San Francisco to see the PopMart tour, watching from the mixing desk in the company of Liam and Noel Gallagher of Oasis. The biggest band in Britain had just played a support slot to the biggest band in the world. 'Fuckin' mad, man. Mad!' Liam kept saying, in tones of wonder, at the unfolding of what was undoubtedly the most impressive multimedia extravaganza since, well, the last U2 tour. Never regarded as the most articulate of people, Liam nonetheless has a distinctive way of expressing himself. 'This is the first time I've seen U2,' he declared. 'Now I understand! It's . . . phwoarghghghgh!'

I knew exactly how he felt. PopMart was insanely spectacular, appealing on every conceivable level: artistic, intellectual, emotional, visual and musical. U2 played beneath an arch of glittering neon, before an enormous video wall alive with inventive pop-art imagery. A guitar solo was delivered to a mind-bending psychedelic display, spread across 700 square metres of screen. The group arrived for encores inside their own glitterball UFO. The show had constant momentum and was delivered on a scale that made the full moon, suspended in a cloudless sky over the open-air baseball stadium, look like just another part of the lighting rig. Yet there remained room for personality, improvisation and intimacy. Bono displayed that gift he has for transcending the problem of physical distance with the generosity and humanity of his performance.

After the show, Liam (who appeared to have made an early assault on the backstage supplies of alcohol) hijacked the sound system in U2's dressing rooms. 'You gotta listen to this,' he insisted. 'This is fuckin' great!' It was the new Oasis album, fresh from the studio. As music boomed from the speakers, Liam clutched Bono by the shoulders, singing the lyrics of every song directly into his face. Quickly catching hold of the choruses, Bono sang along. The Edge nodded his head approvingly.

'People say Oasis songs are obvious, but the way the melodies relate to the chords is quite unusual,' he observed in his typically analytical manner. 'You get the feeling you have heard the songs before, but they still surprise you.' Moving with the animal grace of some magnificent simian creature, Liam spread his arms wide and bellowed, 'Stand by me, wherever you a-a-a-are . . .' An intimate gathering of backstage revellers (including film star Winona Ryder and her beau from US punks Green Day, models and singers Lisa M and Lisa B, maverick Scottish DJ Howie B and producers Nelle Hooper and Hal Wilner) watched in open admiration, applauding this astonishing private performance. Noel sat on a sofa taking it all in, a perpetual, secret smile playing on his lips.

Somehow I wound up in a corner with Bono, in a drunken conversation about the symbolic meaning of the giant olive perched on top of a giant stick which towered over the stage while U2 played songs of faith and doubt, passion and reflection, love and war. I mean, what was all that about, I wanted to know. Three chords, the truth . . . and an olive on top?

'There's an entire philosophy that comes with the word "pop",' Bono was telling me. 'You were always banging on about it and I can see that now. You were right. Did I ever tell you you were right?'

'You've told me about ten times tonight already,' I said, 'but you can keep telling me if you want. It's music to my ears.'

'We're in a commercial world and pop artists like Warhol wanted to be part of the real world; they didn't want to be on a gallery wall, they wanted to make prints and make it accessible. Warhol was one of those people who, rather than trying to dodge the contradictions of his situation as an artist working in the commercial world, actually enjoyed it and drew from it. He embraced the contradictions. There's freedom in that. Freedom for us to get away with our songs, which are spiky and bitter and there's a brokenness to them. You just wouldn't get away with them unless you surrounded yourself with neon and cosmic glitter. This is the nineties! It's a decade that's like this great party and its hangover. And I think there's something in facing that, in facing the other side of the party. Because no one can live that life without it turning in on you and getting shallow.'

'So let me see if I've got this right,' I said. 'The olive represents freedom. And it also symbolizes a decade of excess. The night before the millennium after.' Well, blame it on the late hour, blame it on the champagne, beer and wine flowing backstage, but all that seemed to make sense. Sort of. 'But what about the forty-foot lemon beneath the giant olive?'

'You've got to have a lemon,' said Bono. 'A vodka and tonic without the lemon is just not the same thing.'

Bono announced a visit to a bar called Tosca's, which was being kept open for the band. It was a favourite watering hole of his, a bohemian writers' enclave, once a haunt of Charles Bukowski, Sam Shepherd and Tom Waits (Bono's brother named his Dublin restaurant in honour of Tosca's and their father's life-long love for opera). The last few diehards piled into a minibus. Edge and Liam were on the back seat, Noel squeezed in between Bono and me, clutching the singer's knee as he babbled with excitement about the concert and enthused about U2 songs he admired. And then, with startling synchronicity, the minibus radio, tuned to a late-night station, began to play U2's hit 'One'.

'This is the greatest song ever written!' yelled Noel. And he and Liam started to sing it at the top of their voices. Swept away by the brothers' exuberance, Bono and Edge joined in. And as we rolled down some San Francisco highway, long after midnight, four of the world's greatest rock stars raised their voices in an impassioned, impromptu rendition of a song of unity and brotherly love. 'We are one,' they sang, 'but we're not the same / We've got to carry each other, carry each other . . .'

And I sang, too. Because if this was anybody's song it was my song. The song of Bono's doppelgänger.

We are one. But we're not the same.

I recall, at some point in the ensuing drunken revelry, Bono clambering on to the bar at Tosca's to deliver an operatic aria. And Nellie Hooper dragging his girlfriend Lisa B out by her hair, apparently enraged that she was talking to me. And the newly married Liam sneaking off into the night with Lisa M, with whom he conceived a child. And many, many hours later, Bono rounding up the stragglers (Edge, me and a couple of girls) to go watch the sun rise over the Golden Gate Bridge.

And by the time I woke up, in the early afternoon, with a sore head and a smile on my face, whatever lingering envy and resentment I might have felt towards my old friends had faded in the California sunlight. And I thought about what a privilege it was knowing them. And getting to see their remarkable story unfold, up close and personal. And to be invited, from time to time, to join in, to sing along, to share the adventure.

Like the time we went to Rome to visit the Pope.

It was 1999 and Bono and Bob Geldof were campaigning for Jubilee 2000, a charitable organization that wanted to persuade world leaders to drop the debt crippling the Third World. They had been promised an audience with Pope John Paul II at his summer palace in the Alban hills. 'He does command a very large constituency,' as Geldof (an avowed atheist) pointed out in typically pragmatic fashion. They wanted a journalist to accompany them, so I was invited along for the ride.

Bono and Geldof made for an extremely odd couple: the former an upbeat, optimistic idealist motivated by his long-lasting commitment to Christianity; the latter a belligerent, pessimistic, atheist cynic who seems compelled to do good work almost despite himself. Together, however, they represented a genuinely dynamic duo: two Irish rock stars on a mission to save the world. The night before, conversation had dwelled on Irish showbands of the seventies rather than global economics, but as soon as cameras or microphones were trained on them Bono and Geldof turned into impressive advocates for their cause. They had clearly done their homework, confidently backing up punchy, emotive soundbites with an impressive grasp of salient facts and figures. 'You know the funny thing,' Bono confided, 'in school, you couldn't have paid me to learn this stuff. You couldn't have beaten it into me. But guess what? It turns out I have a facility for it. I read briefing notes and find I can memorize them, no problem at all.'

Maybe it was because this was something that really mattered to him. Still, I knew Bono actually had grave doubts about being a figurehead for the campaign. 'It is absurd if not obscene that celebrity is a door that such serious issues need to pass through before politicians take note,' he complained. 'But there it is. Jubilee can't get into some of these offices and I can. But the idea has a kind of force of its own. I'm just making it louder. And, you know, making noise is a job description really for a rock star.'

Bono's fame had reached quite outlandish proportions. In Italy, where he is a superstar among superstars, his every appearance would cause visible ripples to run through the surrounding area. Traffic would grind to a halt amid the celebratory beeping of horns. Mobs of pedestrians swirled around. Paparazzi jostled for position. Jubilee 2000 had provided a phalanx of bodyguards, all of whom were conspicuously better-dressed than the man they were assigned to protect. Their sharp, grey Italian suits, sleek haircuts and designer sunglasses made Bono (in tatty black jacket and jeans, huge purple shades and brothel creepers) look like a bum who had been rooting around in thrift shops. But, in an era when fame is portrayed more as a burden than a privilege, Bono cut a refreshingly fearless figure, unwilling to allow himself to be cut off from the world by overprotection. Whenever he ventured beyond the guarded confines of the hotel building, he was immediately mobbed by media and public alike. Not the tallest of men, he would at times disappear from view, leaving his bodyguards looking extremely tense as they hovered helplessly on the edges of the scrum. To their palpable relief, Bono would eventually emerge with limbs still attached, smiling as he signed a last autograph or dispensed another soundbite for the TV cameras.

Outside the papal residence, a crowd of onlookers were all yelling for Bono, as a police escort led our minibus through an enormous archway into a vast, walled courtyard, home to the man considered by the Roman Catholic Church to be God's representative on earth. The biblical expression 'in my father's house there are many mansions' would be a fair description of the Pope's residence. The house I grew up in would have fitted comfortably in a single room. Our small entourage was led from one vast chamber to another until we arrived at the aging Pontiff's quarters. I was really looking forward to meeting the Pope. After all, this was the guy who had broken up the Modulators. I wanted to see what God's envoy looked like in the flesh. And I had solemnly promised Bono I would not use this opportunity to trot out my theories about the Godless universe or ask embarrassing questions about the meaning of specific biblical passages. But when we approached the door, true to form, a glorified bouncer (albeit one dressed in the medieval costume of the Vatican Swiss Guard) insisted I wait outside.

I might have fucking known. This was the story of my life with Bono. I never had quite the right pass or sufficient kudos to gain access to the final sanctum. 'Just don't tell them I'm not a Catholic,' Bono whispered to me as he was led inside by the Swiss Guard.

I was left sitting on a stone bench awaiting his return. But I didn't spit and fume and curse my luck. I sat and chuckled to myself about the absurdity of the whole situation. I thought about my friend, and what an amazing person he had turned out to be, a complex, gregarious, immensely compassionate individual who put himself on the line, again and again, for the things he believes in.

Over the years, Bono and his bandmates had campaigned for Amnesty International, Artists United Against Apartheid, Live Aid, Self Aid (a charity set up to help the unemployed of Ireland), CND, Greenpeace and Warchild. U2 had protested against the construction of a nuclear-waste processing plant at Sellafield, a power station in England that was notorious in Ireland for dumping waste into the Irish sea. The band did an enormous amount to highlight the plight of war victims in Bosnia and, throughout years of conflict, supported the besieged citizens of Sarajevo. They pledged time and significant funds (including all the profits from their single 'One') to raise AIDS awareness. And they played a small but significant part in the Northern Ireland peace process, when Bono brought the leader of the Democratic party, John Hume, and Unionist leader David Trimble out on stage to shake hands during a U2 concert in support of the Good Friday Peace Agreement in 1998. 'We're going to have to start finding other ways to get our message across,' Bono once joked to me. 'I'm terrified that if U2 make another big statement about peace, war might break out just to knock me off my high horse.'

Watching him in Rome, working the media, banging the drum for the starving of the world, pushing himself to the limit of exhaustion and beyond for a cause that had the potential to change the world, I was moved almost to tears. I saw what he put into it and what it was taking out of him. The Jubilee campaign had engaged so much of Bono's time and energy it had knocked U2 for a loop, setting back the recording of their latest album by a year. 'It is such a big idea, the biggest idea I have ever heard,' said Bono, 'I just couldn't walk away from it. This is not just throwing pennies at the poor; it is looking at the whole structure of poverty. But it's getting to be a sore subject with the others. It really is. They've been very patient with me but it's not easy for them waiting around in the studio while I go to visit the Pope!'

Bono could give an interview masterclass. At the centre of a veritable media riot, he remained impressively focussed on his cause, stating and restating the case for debt relief with a potent combination of charm, sincerity, wit and conviction. While Geldof discussed strategy with the Jubilee 2000 delegates before departing for business meetings in Rome, Bono answered the same questions over and over again, gamefully attempting to inject something fresh into each interview. Although visibly tiring as the day wore on, his voice growing hoarse from ceaseless talk, the subject matter always seemed capable of engaging him. 'It's a moral question more than an intellectual one,' he insisted during a telephone interview with *Newsweek*. 'You can argue all you want with the idea – and I've had some extraordinary arguments with some extraordinary minds – but in the end it's a moral issue and if we can't make this happen it says much about moral torpor.'

'Just how unhip is this?' Bono laughed as he put down the phone. 'I might as well get myself a bowler hat and briefcase.'

A day that had begun with an early-morning phone interview with Radio Four's *Today* programme finally ground to a halt close to midnight in a chaotic little office in Rome, where an old rug had been taped to a wall to provide a colourful backdrop for a live satellite link-up with CNN's American news team. Bono was clearly beginning to lose it, stumbling over his sentences and improvising a reggae song about the funky pontiff when the link went down for the fourth time. 'You better get me out of here before I start saying things like "the poor should give the rich what they want",' he jokingly warned an assistant.

We dined al fresco at a swish restaurant beneath a full moon in Rome, toasting the health of the frail, eighty-two-year-old pontiff who had released a strong statement in support of their cause. Geldof, true to form, provided a lone dissenting voice, casting doubts on whether they were really any closer to their goal, but with wine flowing freely even his pessimism was considered grounds for another toast. A few hours earlier Geldof had cheekily asked the Pope for a set of rosaries for his dad but now launched into a not untypical rant about the sheer ridiculousness of religious belief. I pointed out that he and Bono made quite a pair. 'Bono is a Jesuit priest,' declared Geldof to much laughter. 'With a mullet hairdo! Have you ever noticed how he walks with his hands clasped in front of him?' Geldof was talking loud enough to be sure Bono was paying attention. 'And I walk with my fists clenched by my side! You don't have to believe in order to have a sense that things ain't right, and they can be put right. God is such a psychedelic notion anyway, this superbeing who fixes everything. Is the whole world on drugs? It's just so improbable!'

'When you come out with all that stuff it makes me laugh,' declared Bono, throwing an arm around Geldof's shoulder. 'You are so close to God. Closer than most people I know.'

It was the only time I have seen Geldof lost for words.

By two in the morning, only a few stragglers were left. Even Geldof had made his excuses, declaring that he owned a flat in Rome he had never seen (ah, the trials of the multimillionaire life). Bono, however, was resisting all attempts to persuade him to call it a night. Although due to catch a six a.m. flight to Washington with Harvard economist Jeffrey Sachs to meet American senators, he was apparently determined to re-establish his rock'n'roll credentials. 'Sleep is for economists,' he joked. Late-night traffic was still streaming by as Bono slipped away from his minders, beckoning me to follow. I wasn't sure what he was up to but tagged along as he strode out into the middle of the road, holding up a hand to dramatically halt an oncoming car.

Had I been on my own, I'd have undoubtedly been run over by an irate motorist and left for dead in a Roman thoroughfare. But Bono brought the traffic to a complete standstill. The driver of the car in front of us was practically squealing with delight as a rock star leaned in his window, cheerfully inquiring if he knew anywhere round here we could get a drink. It was then that I noticed the car was full of transsexuals. Before Bono's minders had worked out what was going on, we were squeezing into the back seat to perch on the knees of some hairy Italian ladyboys. Which is how come at four in the morning we were seated at a small table in a packed nightclub between beautiful people of indeterminate gender, drinking complimentary champagne while a scantily clad babe tried to attract Bono's attention by dancing on the table. 'Remind me, what's this rock–star thing all about?' Bono mused, puffing on a giant cigar. 'Ah yes. Screaming girls. Fashionable clothes. People playing guitars. Got it!'

And I thought, rock stardom couldn't have happened to a nicer and, frankly, more deserving guy. He's certainly put it to a lot better use than I ever would have.

22

Bono's father, Bob Hewson, passed away at four a.m. on Tuesday 21 August 2001, aged seventy-five, after a long battle with cancer. Bono was at his father's bedside when he died. But that very same day, he flew to London to perform with U2 at Earl's Court on their All That You Can't Leave Behind tour. Kneeling down on stage in front of 17,000 strangers, Bono made the sign of the cross. 'This one is for my old man,' he told the crowd, his voice heavy with emotion.

I've seen a lot of U2 shows over the years, all of them special in their own way, but that show was something else, a whole other level of rock'n'roll, life and death riding on power chords and a howling voice. Songs already imbued with intense qualities of spiritual yearning gained whole new dimensions of meaning, overflowing with terrible poignancies and heartbreaking ironies. 'I will be with you again,' sang Bono at the end of 'New Year's Day', evoking the aching rawness of his bereavement. 'I'm a man, I'm not a child,' he wailed on 'Kite'. 'I know that this is not goodbye . . .'

The atmosphere in the arena was crackling with unseen forces. Primal energies were being unleashed, feelings too great to be contained within any one person were somehow transmitted and shared between thousands. Bono leaned out to the crowd with grief, love, loss, hope, anger, unfailing optimism. And they reached back to him, a sea of hands, reaching up to let him know they cared.

Afterwards, I went backstage with Gloria, where I was greeted by the Edge. 'We were wondering if you had made it to the show,' he said, a comment that made me feel valued, especially in front of Gloria, who had never quite got over her suspicions that my relationship with U2 was largely in my mind. The Edge looked exhausted and shell-shocked, sweat glistening on his brow. 'That was a tough one,' he admitted. 'I don't know how he got through that.'

There was no need to resort to clichés about how the show must go on to understand what Bono was doing on stage that night. Those who knew him understood that he wanted to be there, perhaps even needed to be there, working out his innermost feelings in the place he feels most at home. 'Great performers are supposed to play to the back of the hall,' he once told me. 'But really driven performers, I think you'll find, are playing to one person. It might be a lover. But it might be your father.'

Bono had never talked to me much about his dad. It was the death of his mother that seemed to loom large in his psyche, the unseen force that was always driving him on, but the peculiar thing was that he once admitted to me he could barely remember his mother. 'I even forget what she looks like,' he confessed, almost as if ashamed. The key parental relationship was with his father but it was a deeply frustrating one. 'Trying to talk to my old man is like trying to talk to a brick wall,' he would complain. Discussing the effects of his mother's sudden death, he said it was as if 'the house had been pulled down. After the death of my mother that house was no longer a home. It was just a house.' And it was a house of suffering men, who could not communicate. But towards the end of his father's life Bono seemed to have reached a kind of emotional rapprochement with the distant figure with whom he had such a complex, yearning relationship. After he was gone, Bono would love to tell stories about his father, laughing at the recollections with genuine affection, despite the harsh emotional kernels that often lurked at their core.

'I had an amazing moment with my old man the first time he came to America,' he told me, chuckling at the memory. 'I picked him up in a limousine. Now, I don't like limousines but I knew it would have the reaction it did. He wouldn't get in it! So we had to take a taxi! It was in Texas and at sound-check I organized with the lighting people to put a spotlight on him during the encore. I said "I wanna introduce you to somebody, it's their first time in the United States." Holler! "It's their first time in Texas!" Bigger holler! "This is the man who gave me my voice; this is Bob Hewson!" The light came on, 20,000 Texans hooting at him, and he stood up and he just waved a fist – at me! After the show, usually I'm left on my own for a minute just to calm down, but I heard these footsteps behind me and I looked around and it was my dad and his eyes were watering and I thought, "This is it! This is the moment! Finally, he's going to tell me something! This could be very interesting. This is a moment I've waited all my life for." My father was going to tell me he loved me. And he walked up, he put his hand out, a little shaky, a little unsteady, he'd had a few drinks, looked me in the eye and he said, "Son . . . you're very professional!"'

It's the kind of tale where you don't know whether to laugh or cry. Right there, almost tangible, was the emotional gulf that separated Bono from me, the star from the wannabe. 'If you are trying to fill that kind of hole, music and being a performer is an obvious route,' he admitted. 'Ultimately it won't be satisfying, but insecurity is at the root of most interesting endeavours, I find. If you're totally secure in yourself and you were told all your life that you were the bee's knees, well, you're probably gonna wind up with a respectable job in the City or something! And that's what I want my kids to feel, by the way! I don't like being the Boy Named Sue!'

Bono and Ali have four children. Two young teenage girls, Jordan and Eve, and two infant sons, Eli and John. 'I'm so glad I was able to give Bono sons,' Ali once told me. 'He's great with the girls but the relationship between father and son is very special and I don't think he really had that in his life.'

We were out at dinner in Dublin one night, just me, Bono, Ali, Jordan, Eve, a large posse of the girls' teenage friends, Gavin Friday, Guggi, Edge and, well, whoever else might turn up. Bono led his entourage into the restaurant at the Clarence hotel. We had no reservations and the restaurant was looking rather crowded, but the waiters were impressively accommodating, providing two secluded balcony tables for an unspecified number of people, and graciously responding to Bono's rather airy instruction to 'bring food!' with a choice selection from the menu. But then, U2 do own the hotel. We settled into a discreet alcove where we could observe the activity below without ourselves being under scrutiny. 'Do you like this?' inquired Bono. 'I designed it myself!' As we ate, friends kept appearing, Bono bidding them to sit at the tables and join us, until there were at least twenty people gathered around, eating and drinking. There were familiar faces from the old days and a smattering of Dublin's rock glitterati. Shane McGowan, alcoholic songsmith, lurched in to find that Bono, anticipating his arrival, had already ordered his favourite whiskey. Sinead O'Connor settled down at one point and looked at me curiously. 'Have we met?' she asked. I denied everything.

Ali was looking stunning. With her lustrous black hair, knowing eyes and smooth skin, the years had been extremely kind to her, perhaps aided by the kind of luxurious lifestyle that massive wealth can provide. Not that Ali lived a particularly pampered existence. Besides being mother to four and wife to a force of nature, Ali had studied politics at university, attaining a social-sciences degree, and had become a noted activist in environmental causes. Talking politics with Ali, though, was a slightly surreal affair, since she and Bono were acquainted with so many world statesmen. When she said, 'I really like Tony Blair,' you were never entirely sure if this was a policy or personal endorsement. Discussing the American presidency, she said, as if it were the most unremarkable aside, 'We flew to Africa with the Clintons last week to see Nelson Mandela.' As you do. 'Chelsea's the one to watch,' advised Ali. 'Bill and Hillary are incredibly smart but Chelsea's got both their brains.'

Her own daughters seem to have been blessed with their mother's looks while exhibiting something of their father's social fearlessness, happily talking to anyone who spoke to them and holding their own in the midst of an increasingly unruly assembly. 'A woman asked me for my autograph today,' revealed Eve, with a mixture of pride and incredulity. 'I said, "What do you want my autograph for? I'm only twelve! Ask my dad!"' They both sat pressed up against Bono, excitedly relating their day's incidents to their father, who seemed somehow able to pay attention to everyone – his daughters, their friends, his own friends. Sitting at the head of the table, Bono struck me as a king among his courtiers, yet he appeared oblivious to this effect, almost wilfully unaware of the central part he played in so many lives.

'You know, Neil, your life and my life are not so different,' he said to me, as we chatted about events in London, where I had bought a terraced Victorian house to accommodate the impending arrival of my first baby. I may have snorted at his comment. I felt in debt up to my eyeballs, in the midst of rapidly mounting domestic chaos, and couldn't help thinking that the bill for the evening's soiree, which Bono would generously pay without a glance, would probably amount to more than a week's earnings for me, a sum that could quickly sort out a few of my more pressing creditors. But that wasn't what Bono had on his mind. 'You might think I live in some kind of rarefied atmosphere, but I've got all the same concerns as you. When you spend time in the Third World, the gap between an ordinary life there and a life in the West is enormous, almost unimaginable. But the gap between where you are and where I am is microscopic. It's just degrees of luxury.'

He told me about a recent family holiday to a chateau in France that he shared with the Edge. 'It is gorgeous. Beautiful gardens. Fantastic views. It is everything you could imagine. And I was standing in the garden, watching the sunset, and it suddenly struck me, "I own this! This is my house! This is my life!" In all these years, that thought had never occurred to me before. Really. Because I've always been in the middle of it. And the house, the money, that's not what's important. It's never been important. It's the family and the work. It's the same things you care about. It's the same things everyone cares about.'

We clinked glasses. 'I've been thinking about this a lot, lately,' he said. Bono was in cheerful, gregarious form. Still, it was hard to escape the impression that his father hovered like a ghost behind our conversation. He was orphaned now, as we all someday will be, and perhaps forced to address the psycho-logical engines that made him tick. 'I've been thinking about what really matters. What can I do that will make my kids proud. What can I do to make a *difference*.'

'I think you've made a difference,' I said. 'Most of us are lucky if we've touched a few lives. You've touched millions. Aren't you the man who saved the world?'

'Oh, fuck off!' roared Bono amiably, perhaps suspecting that I was poking fun at him. Was it that obvious?

'I don't know how you find time to actually fit in your family and U2 around all the charitable causes,' I said.

'You're starting to sound like the Edge,' said Bono. 'Debt relief is not a charity. Seven thousand Africans dying every day of a preventable, treatable disease is not a cause. It's an emergency!'

'See. There you go again!' I laughed. 'You can't help yourself!'

I know that Bono sometimes despairs of his image as some kind of latterday saint. 'I am not in any way at peace,' he told me on another occasion. 'I think the world is a really unfair and often wicked place and beauty is a consolation prize. And it's not enough for me. It just isn't. There's always been a kind of rage in me and it does still bubble up.'

We were propping up the bar of the Clarence, being liberally supplied with drinks we didn't have to pay for. 'I have some influ-ence here,' Bono told me, waving the barman over again. It was late in the evening, we were waiting for Ali to arrive before head-ing off to a party, and we were quite drunk. Talking about God, fame, politics, pop: all the usual subjects. Solving all the world's problems over a pint. Or five. And there may have been some whiskey chasers involved. And a couple of cigars. And this was after Bono had told me he had given up drinking and smoking because it was playing havoc with his voice. But that was another conversation. Right now, Bono was talking about the burden of fame. Not the usual stuff about autograph-hunters and stalkers and paparazzi and oh it's lonely at the top. But about the moral burden that he just could not shy away from.

Jubilee 2000 was supposed to have been a year-long campaign

leading up to the new millennium but it was so tantalizingly close to achieving its incredible goals that the deadline kept being stretched. It had turned into an ongoing Drop the Debt campaign, to which Bono's personal commitment threatened to dwarf all his previous charitable efforts. Its demands on him were huge. He was so much more than a figurehead. He and Geldof could get things done. They could mobilize popular consensus. They could get world leaders like Tony Blair, Bill Clinton, George Bush, Jaques Chirac and Vladimir Putin to engage with the issues and make substantial commitments. And, behind the scenes, they could get into the offices and homes of all the less noted senators and governors and ministers and financiers whose co-operation was essential to turn the platitudes and promises of politicians into a functioning reality. Because, as Bono put it, 'between the agreement we've managed to secure to cancel a hundred billion dollars in debt and actually getting the money to build hospitals and schools, immunize children against malaria, educate people about the HIV virus, is a lot of red tape and bureaucracy and it's of Kafka-like proportions, everyone passing the buck and people hiding in the smallprint. And we're going after each one of them! But it's very frustrating. And I keep thinking there must be people more qualified to do this than me!'

'Maybe there aren't,' I replied. 'This is where you find yourself at this place in time. I used to think how are they going to solve the Northern Ireland problem? They needed an individual to rise above the mire. They needed a Nelson Mandela. And they got . . .'

'John Hume,' said Bono.

'So the debt idea came into focus and they needed a figurehead. You put a politician up there and nobody is going to pay any attention. You put a concerned movie star like Richard Gere up there and it falls apart. He can't carry the world with him. People would be suspicious. They'd mock him. But you're one of the most famous people on the planet and look at what got you to where you are. You've got the passion, the intelligence, the faith, the conviction and twenty years of history that says this guy really believes in what he does. You are the right man, in the right place, at the right time.'

Bono laughed. 'You could talk a blind man into crossing a motorway.'

'And never forget you've got God on your side,' I said.

'You mean the life-long argument I have with my maker?' he smiled, ruminatively. 'I'm not sure if we're on speaking terms at the moment.'

'Welcome to the club,' I said.

'The belief that there is love and logic at the heart of the universe is a big subject. If there is no God, it's serious. If there is a God, it's even more serious!' He laughed. 'Sometimes I think it takes a lot more courage not to believe. I don't know what gets you through the night.'

'I haven't quite given up on finding God,' I said. 'I'm keeping my options open for a deathbed conversion.'

'You have always been such a crank!' laughed Bono. 'Even in school. What I always kind of looked up to in you was that you were just a nagging question! Just rooting and scratching for whys and wheres and whos and hows. You were more curious than I was, back then. I think maybe I've caught up with you.'

It took me a while to digest this. 'You looked up to me?' I finally blurted out. The possibility had never occurred to me that I might ever have been, in some small way, my hero's hero.

'Have I ever told you, if I hadn't become a rock star I always thought I'd like to be a journalist?' said Bono.

'Any time you feel like giving it a shot,' I said, 'we can swap places.'

Epilogue

There may yet be a twist in this tale. Whether it is just another twist of the knife buried between my shoulderblades remains to be seen.

I never stopped writing songs. Never stopped playing my guitar and singing. I just stopped trying to foist my efforts on the rest of the world. I stopped looking so far outside myself for validation. My songs were my poetic diary, an emotional record of my life with Gloria, our ups and downs, my struggles with stepfatherhood, my state of perpetual existential crisis in my ongoing search for meaning and purpose. They were probably the best songs I had ever written but they were only ever played to myself, my family and my closest friends. To my own surprise, I found that was audience enough. Just about.

And maybe that was further evidence that I never really had that God-shaped hole Bono talked about, that dark engine of stardom, that motherless black hole of naked desire sucking in all the attention it can get. 'If you were of sound mind you wouldn't need 70,000 people a night telling you they loved you to feel normal,' he admitted to me once, before adding, reflectively, 'It's sad, really.'

But still I had the music. It may even be true to say that music meant more to me than ever. Because once you have dived into the stream of music that flows like a torrent through the history of mankind, once you have truly surrendered to its power, immersing yourself in its nurturing force, only a fool would crawl to the bank and shake himself dry. Playing a musical instrument is not just a conduit to the latent joy within you, it is a vehicle of release from all the constricted emotions and petty frustrations and little disappointments of everyday life. Music is a channel to the spirit. It is a gateway to yourself. I don't know how I would get by without my guitar.

And then, for my fortieth birthday, Gloria bought me an electric Custom Telecaster and amplifier. Big mistake.

To celebrate the occasion, I assembled a motley crew of musical contemporaries to perform in a local pub under the name Groovy Dad (because we are dads, and we are groovy). One of my fellow rock rejects, Reid Savage, now a graphic designer, was lead guitarist and musical director. We had a set-builder on drums. An astrophysicist on bass. Ivan came along and joined in on backing vocals. We opened a short but lively set with a version of Led Zeppelin's 'Rock and Roll'. Which seemed appropriate. It really had been a long time since I rock and rolled.

Too long. I may have given up on dreams of rock stardom (or, fairer to say, they had given up on me) but our nostalgic excursion pungently reminded me of the pleasures of performing music for its own sake. Our little band was made up of regular civilians, none of whose job description included the word 'musician', but they were all talented players who had once been in bands and never lost the love of their chosen instrument.

'You know what?' I said to Bono, when he rang to wish me a happy birthday. 'Music is for life, not just for Christmas!'

Bono laughed. But he pronounced himself much enamoured of this concept, pointing out that the very notion of making a living out of music is a relatively recent phenomenon. As young men growing up in Ireland, it was possible to witness astonishingly resonant folk sessions in pubs where the players were local fishermen or farmers. 'There's a strange idea that music is a way to get rich quick,' said Bono. 'But it never even used to be a paying job. It was a part of the community, something people did on the side.'

And it became something I did on the side. I started an occasional, informal gathering of musical friends under the name Songwriters Anonymous. I billed it as a 'twelve-step programme for singers and songwriters who cannot resist the urge to perform'. Except that I could only come up with six steps:

1. Turn up
2. Tune up
3. Sing up
4. Hit the bar
5. . . . er . . .
6. That's it

I was a bit concerned about the *Daily Telegraph*'s pop critic stray-ing from the realm of gamekeeper into the terrain of the poacher, so, to preserve my anonymity, I performed as The Ghost Who Walks, a name from an old comic book. It seemed appropriate. Because, as far as music was concerned, I felt like a ghost slowly coming back to life.

Those evenings were a lot of fun. The quality of the music played was fantastic. Old bandmates like my brother and Margo Buchanan turned up and did their bit; new friends came along too, successful working musicians such as Robyn Hitchcock, Steve Balsamo and Jamie Catto; but the real revelation was how many civilians who had never pursued a musical career got up to perform songs they had written themselves, wonderful songs full of heart, soul, wit, insight and passion. It occurred to me that whatever problems the music business has in developing new stars, it is not for want of talent.

A friend had started a small label, Map Music, and frequently prevailed upon me for advice and guidance. In return, I got the use of his cramped but well-equipped studio. I started to record some of my songs, drafting in Reid as co-producer. Our philos-ophy was simple. Get the best musicians we could find and let them do their stuff. Bang it down fast. Worry about it later. The idea was to have some fun. We weren't concerned with what anyone else might make of it because it wasn't for anybody else. For the first time in my life, I was making music solely to satisfy myself. And the result (to no one's surprise more than my own) was the richest, most fully realized music I had ever made. Other musicians would come in and rave about what we were doing.

'You could get a deal with this,' my friends kept telling me. But I wasn't sure about that at all. I had been bitten too many times by the music business. I thought we could stick it out quietly and anonymously on Map as a no-budget, Internet-only release, so that it would exist, at least. Maybe I could have a bit of fun with The Ghost Who Walks in my column. Get my fellow rock critics to review it without actually telling them who it was.

One morning, I woke up from a vivid musical dream. All night in my sleep I had been singing a song. I was singing to God, even though I did not believe He could hear me. I was singing about the idea of God in all its heavenly glory and earthly cruelty, addressing a living universe with the questions that had tormented me all my life. And as I sang my song to God, the music I could hear in my sleepy head was suitably divine (there is no music like the music of your dreams), a huge gospel choir of voices, raised in praise and torment. And then, the strangest thing happened. God sang back to me. The really peculiar thing is He sounded quite like Bono.

I pulled myself awake, jumped out of bed and started scribbling down everything I could remember. It just came pouring out, in short, sharp couplets with an A-A, B-B rhyming scheme. It took me about fifteen minutes to write it all down. And there it was. Complete on the page, like a gift from heaven or my subconscious: my whole life-long struggle with divinity captured in a song. I picked up my guitar and started strumming. And the first chords I played fitted perfectly. It was the fastest song I had ever written. And maybe the best.

And another strange thing happened. A weird moment of synchronicity. Bono phoned. It was not like he called every day. We seemed to be speaking more often than ever before but still, months could pass between calls. But there he was, on the end of the line while I was still bursting with enthusiasm and excitement for my new creation.

'I've written a song,' I told him. 'It's called "I Found God".'

'That'll be the day,' he laughed.

'Well, at least I'm still looking,' I said. 'Do you want to hear it?'

'Do I have a choice?' he joked.

I had him on the speaker-phone. So I picked up my guitar, and sang him my new song.

I found God in the first place that I looked
I found God in the crannies and the nooks
I found God underneath a stone
I found God, didn't even have to leave my home
I found God

I found the Buddha sitting cross-legged by the door
I found Jesus nailed and bleeding on the floor
I found the Prophet up to his neck in sand
I found God wherever I found man
I found God in a hundred different places
With a thousand different voices and a million different
    faces
I found God

And I found God down the smoking barrel of a gun
I found God in bones bleached white beneath the sun
I found God amongst the killers and the rapists
I found God between the proddies and the papists
I found God in temples turned to rubble
I found God on the pulpit stirring up more trouble
I found God on both sides of the war
With the bigots and the fascists, kicking down my door
I found God

And I said, 'My God, my God, what have You done?
Why is this life so hard for everyone?'

And God said . . .
'I found you before it all began
I found you when the universe went bang
I found you in the cooling of the stars

I watched worlds collide, I wondered how we got this
   far?
I found you crawling from the sea
I found you hanging with the monkeys in the trees
I found you before you found me
I found you and I set you free
Free to stand on your own feet, free to watch the sunrise
Free to be what you can be, free to be what you despise
Free to glory in the truth, free to swallow your own lies
'Cause I'm coursing through your bloodstream, I'm
   staring through your eyes
I found you.'

And I said, 'My God, my God, what have we done?
Why is this life so hard for everyone?'

At the end of my impromptu performance there was a moment
of silence. And then Bono declared, 'I wrote that song!'

'You wish!' I said.

'I have been trying to write that song my whole life,' he said.

I played 'I Found God' at the next gathering of Songwriters
Anonymous. And all these great singers in the room started
joining in with the coda, until I could hear the gospel choir
of my dreams. And afterwards people kept coming up to talk
to me about the lyrics. Everybody seemed to hear different
things in it, finding a reflection of their own beliefs. Some
heard a religious devotional. Some heard a philosophical
discourse. Some heard an atheist anthem. That song had a power
all of its own.

I recorded it at Map studio, with eight of the best singers I
knew backing me. The album (because I now realized that that's
what it was) was coming together and I started seriously wondering what I was going to do with it. Still, I was busy writing my
column. I could record only when the studio was free and I
wasn't too busy and I had a bit of money spare to pay for musicians and engineers, so the whole process was dragging on, which

suited me fine. It meant I could delay deciding where this was all going.

One day, I was working in my office when my phone rang. My caller had a bold opening gambit. 'I believe you have described me as the biggest arsehole you've ever met!' boomed a patrician voice.

'Who is this?' I inquired cautiously.

'Nick Stewart,' my caller replied.

I had to think for a minute, but finally the penny dropped. It was the Island A&R man who had signed U2 but rejected Shook Up! 'Mr Stewart,' I said. 'I did not call you the biggest arsehole I ever met. I called you *one* of the biggest arseholes I've ever met! There were plenty of other A&R men in my black book.'

Laughter rolled down the telephone line. It turned out that Nick was a big fan of my newspaper column. He was head of international A&R at BMG now, where he also ran his own label, Gravity. Nick invited me to dinner. We got along famously, the disappointments of the past long forgotten. At the end of the evening I gave him a four-track CD of The Ghost Who Walks without telling him what it was. I just asked him to give it a listen and let me know what he thought.

Now Nick also had a late-night weekend show on Virgin radio, for which he was known as Captain America, in which he would play a mix of alternative country, Americana and classic singer-songwriters. And, unbeknown to me, on his next show he played one of my tracks.

You'll never guess what song he played (and no, it wasn't 'I Found God') . . .

It was a new version of 'Sleepwalking'. It was the only old song of Ivan's and mine that I had recorded. It's just such a gorgeous song, I couldn't resist laying it down again with the great musicians I was working with. And the radio phone lines lit up while it was on. Callers wanted to know where they could get their hands on this record.

'I don't think its actually available,' admitted Captain America.

He invited me out to dinner again. 'Tell me about The Ghost Who Walks,' he said.

'Well,' I said, uncomfortably. 'He's a singer-songwriter. He's been around. He's not that young.'

'Hmm,' said Nick, thoughtfully. 'Can I meet him?'

'Uh, I don't know,' I said. 'He doesn't like publicity.'

'This is you, isn't it?' he laughed.

'My secret is out,' I confessed.

'Can I put this out on Gravity?' he politely inquired.

I was genuinely taken aback. I didn't know if I wanted to put it out on a major label with everything that would entail: promotion, touring, driving in a van up the M1 to play some godawful toilet in the middle of nowhere to a bunch of drunken students. I had responsibilities these days. A mortgage. Children. A life. A nice, easy life, supported by a good job that I really enjoyed.

I suggested he let me finish the album and then we would talk again.

I discovered something very strange then. When you say no to a record company, they become even more eager. Nick kept calling up to see how things were progressing.

And I kept putting him off. It was ironic. After all those years chasing a deal, I had a record company chasing me and I wasn't even sure if I still wanted a deal. I didn't want to get excited. I didn't want to start dreaming of stardom. I didn't want to get caught up in the mania of my youth. And maybe I didn't want to risk disappointment. My heart had been broken by the music business too many times before.

But the time came when I had to admit I was finished. I had twelve tracks that I really liked, enough for an album. Musically, it was wildly varied stuff. I wanted it to sound like all the music I had ever loved jumbled together, as if the listener was lost in their favourite record store. Lyrically, there was a darkness to it, perhaps because the inspiration to write usually came to me when I was suffering. There were songs about death, addiction, loss, apocalypse and man's inhumanity to man, the same kind of stuff I used to write for Shook Up!, really, but without the pop froth. I sent copies to a few close friends. The response was very encouraging. But the card from Bono meant most of all to me.

Neil,
Heard your CD: it's extraordinary. A row of 10s. A couple of 7s on the production. 'I Found God' is a classic. 'My Black Heart' . . . these songs are as good as it gets. The palsy has made your sickness even deeper!! You're disturbed . . . you will never be released from Songwriters Anon.
    Your fan,
        Bono

As it happened, Nick had spoken to Bono too. 'He talks very highly of you,' Nick reported. He asked me to come and see him in his office at BMG.

'This is a work of Godlike genius,' said Nick, perhaps exaggerating somewhat but I wasn't complaining. 'It deserves to be heard.' And he offered me a deal. It was a small deal, a long way removed from the kind of figures Ossie Kilkenny used to bandy about, but it was tailored to my unusual circumstances. Which was that I made it clear there was no way I was going to give up everything to hit the road and promote this with the desperate energy of a young wannabe. 'In publishing terms,' I explained, 'I don't need to be a best-selling author. I'd be quite happy being a minor poet.'

'I believe we can shift 10,000,' he said, which would make it economically viable. 'It deserves to sell 100,000. But most of all it deserves to be out there. I'd be proud to have this on my label.'

And so we shook hands on a deal. He said he would get contracts drawn up. I said I'd get a solicitor.

I left the office in a daze. I could hardly believe what had just taken place. Better twenty-five years late than never, I thought.

I called my brother. He had remarried and lived down the country these days. He had a covers band called 29 Fingers who played weddings and he composed music for low-budget TV programmes. He was proud to make his living as a working musician even if it was a long way from the fantasies of fame and fortune we had once mutually entertained. 'You're never going to believe this,' I said. 'I've been offered a record deal.'

'Congratulations,' he said grumpily. I knew enough about envy to understand how he was feeling.

'It's just a small deal,' I said, to try to make him feel better. But a dangerous thought was cannoning off the walls of my mind. Nick said it deserves to sell 100,000. What if I was to get out there and really work it?

When I got home, I popped some champagne with Gloria. 'I was thinking I might take a couple of months off when the record comes out,' I told her. 'Give it a real go. You never know. I'm too old to be a pop star now but there's a lot of people my age out there looking for quality music and if I can just get this in front of them, Nick reckons we could shift 100,000. And that's only the beginning. I'm already thinking about the next album. I know I can make a better record than this. I want to make a masterpiece. I want to make a record that moves the world. This could be the start of something big, babe. It could change our lives.'

A week later, Nick Stewart was made redundant.

Addendum and Acknowledgements

It's hard to know where to end a life story, since life rolls remorselessly on. But let me fill you in on a few delicious ironies that have unfolded since I completed the manuscript.

I gave up on The Ghost for a while there. I had wasted enough time flogging dead horses. Gloria and I moved house and had a gorgeous baby boy, who we have saddled with the name Finn Gabriel Cosmo Else McCormick (I figure if he ever decides he wants to be a rock star, he should have a range of names to choose from). So, one day, I was sitting in my temporary office in my basement, surrounded by packing crates, when the telephone rang. It was Mel Gibson's office calling from Los Angeles and they wanted to know if they could use my song 'Harm's Way' on an album of music inspired by his film *The Passion of the Christ*. Naturally, I tried to act as if this kind of thing happened to me every day. I certainly didn't want to blow my cool by asking how on earth they had even heard my music. The truth emerged the next time I spoke to Bono. 'It was Ali,' he told me. 'She listens to your album a lot. It was on around the house and she just kind of took control of it. Then Mel's office called to talk about music that might suit *The Passion* and she said, "You've got to hear this song", and played it down the phone to them! But here's the really funny thing: she didn't even know who it was! She asked me and you should have seen her face when I told her it was you. It was very funny. And the crushing irony is that the first song released by you on a major label is from *The Passion of the Christ*! Come on! And you say you don't believe in God!'

'Obviously He works in very mysterious ways,' I said.

'It just proves that God has a great sense of humour,' said Bono.

Meanwhile, my album, 'Mortal Coil', passed through various hands, leaving a predictable trail of havoc in its wake. I

can hardly bear to tell you about how the head of a top independent music publishing company offered me a fantastic deal
. . . only to have his parent company go out of business (the
knock-on effect of an independent distributor going bust
owing millions). He lost his job. He couldn't hold me in any
way responsible but I think we both harboured lingering suspicions that the curse of McCormick had struck again. Anyway,
with the help of Nick Stewart, a music man to his core, and
The Divine Comedy's manager Natalie DePace, my album
received a limited UK release through Vital distribution in
September 2004. It got some kind reviews and has sold
moderately well through Amazon UK. You can find out
more on theghostwhowalks.com. Anyone interested in hearing the music of Yeah! Yeah! and Shook Up! can find links
on realshookup.com and neilmccormick.co.uk.

I have lots of people to thank but let me start with one who
invades every corner of this book. Bono has been immensely
encouraging to me ever since I called him to tell him I was
thinking of putting my sorry saga in print. I told him my opening line and then listened to him guffaw with laughter for about
two minutes. 'It's not that funny,' I grumbled. 'I could have been
famous!' I would just like to say, one more time, for the record,
how much I admire the man. I was particularly impressed that,
after he read the manuscript, he wanted to make only one change.
And that was to add the phrase 'tongue-in-cheek' to my revelation that they played a version of the Bay City Rollers' 'Bye
Bye Baby' at their first gig. 'It's been an ongoing debate between
us,' said Bono, 'but you have to believe me: when we did the Bay
City Rollers it was because they were a fucking teen band and
we thought it was funny! The track listing was unhip enough
but, even so, cast your mind back to being a fifteen-year-old boy
– if you were into rock music, you hated the Bay City Rollers.
It wasn't that we thought they were cool. No one thought they
were cool! But as it happens the things we thought were cool
were just as uncool! By the way, for the record, in those early
gigs everyone in the band got a choice of material and Adam's,

I think, was the Eagles, Edge's was Rory Gallagher but my uncool choice was the worst of all. It was responsible for "Nights in White Satin".'

I'm glad we cleared that up.

I'd like to thank Ali, too, who is always fiercely protective of Bono. I suspect she viewed this enterprise with a healthy degree of scepticism but she has never been less than gracious to me. Well, almost never. I do remember driving (erratically) with Bono in Dublin one evening when Ali called on the car speaker-phone. 'Here's a voice from your past,' said Bono, announcing my presence. After exchanging pleasantries, Ali said, rather pointedly, 'Just remember to take everything he says with a pinch of salt.'

'I always do,' I said.

'I was talking to Bono!' she objected.

After Bono hung up, he laughed. 'I thought she meant me as well,' he admitted.

People have asked how I remembered things with such clarity. Well, there were diaries, letters, tapes, photographs and lots of old friends to jog my memory, but it is worth making the point that this is my version of my life and not everyone remembers things exactly the same way. And so, in particular, I would like to express gratitude for the forbearance of my brother, Ivan, whose life story this also is. He did not agree with everything in the manuscript but asked for only one tiny change.

I am acutely aware that people have full lives that intersect with mine only at various points, and so I apologize if any of my friends and relatives feel caricatured or reduced by my manuscript in any respect. I know my older sister, Stella, sometimes worries that the only way she will be known to the world at large will be through her imbalanced relationship with me. So, for the record, she's a bright, vibrant woman, devoted to her son, Nicholas, with a very full social life. And she insists she did not scratch my copy of 'Seasons in the Sun' in front of me with a nail file. Apparently she smashed it behind my back. At any rate, it's all Terry Jacks deserved for making my adolescence such a misery.

I love my family. There are many more dimensions to them than can be contained within the pages of this story . . . but if they want to set the record straight, frankly, they are going to have to write books of their own. My parents remained stubbornly proud of their children, even if we never quite achieved the things that once seemed possible. When Ivan and I gave up on our musical dreams, my dad started saying that Louise was always the real musical talent in the family (she's certainly a better singer than I could ever be). But Louise eventually gave up on music too, moving to Cork to raise her beautiful daughters Juliet and Ophelia. When my book and album came out, I couldn't help but notice that dad started to swing back around to the idea that I was the real talent in the family. He was probably just waiting for me to repay all that money he invested in me. Sadly, he passed away, suddenly and unexpectedly in November 2004 but at least he got to vicariously enjoy some of my small success. He was particularly impressed when an editor at the *Daily Telegraph* described him as the real hero of the book, an appraisal dad shared with anyone who would listen. Rest in Peace, dad.

I want to express my gratitude to all the other people who have become characters in my book. In particular, my ex-girlfriend Joan Cody. I am sorry that I broke your heart once. I hope reading about it has not been too painful. All I can say in my defence is that I was young and had a lot to learn about love. Joan is back in Ireland now; she has two fantastic children but currently no man in her life. She has, however, an abundance of admirers. When I go back to Howth, I am most renowned among the younger men of the village for having once squired the divine Ms Cody!

I've lost touch with Barbara McCarney. She married my old bassist John McGlue and they moved to Australia. I gather that they are now happily divorced.

This is in danger of turning into an Oscars acceptance speech, but I'd like to thank all the musicians who put up with the battling McCormick brothers over the years. Great bonds are formed in bands, and Frank, Deco, Vlad, Damien and Steve will always be in my heart. But in particular Leo Regan remains my very close friend, a man of immense integrity who helps keep me on the straight and narrow. Leo has gone on to become a Bafta-winning director, no small achievement.

In the U2 camp, I'd like to thank Edge, Adam and Larry, who have always treated me with friendship and respect, even though I still don't know which one of those bastards vetoed Shook Up!'s single behind my back. Paul McGuinness has always been extremely friendly towards me, perhaps because he still harbours the delusion that I was once a member of U2. Sheila Roche, former number two at Principal Management, has been kind and helpful over the years and did everything in her power to facilitate this book. Anton Corbijn was extremely kind to let me use one of his classic photos for the British cover, especially given that he was initially very reluctant to let anyone tamper with his picture. But he read the book and got the joke. I only knew Candida Bottaci at Principle via email but she became a great ally to my cause. I would also like to thank Louise Butterly and, in particular, Regine Moylett at RMP, publicists to U2. Regine was a contemporary of mine on the punk scene in Dublin, where she played in bands and ran a clothing shop, No Romance (and can therefore be held directly responsible for some of my worst fashion excesses). Bono (who is very good at deciding what other people should do for a living) persuaded her to get into PR, where she has been a fantastic success. Regine has a quality of kindness, thoughtfulness and consideration rare in this business, and she has always been available to help me out even though this project really runs right outside her remit. Thanks also to Regine's husband, Kevin Davies, who supplied the fantastic US cover shot. And a special mention to my great friend Darren Filkins, the photographer who dropped into Anton's picture. Darren could have written his own saga of life as a might-have-been, having quit the embryonic Blur to devote himself to photography, but, in his case, the choice never weighed heavily upon him. He is a superb guitarist (who guests on The Ghost Who Walks album) but a better photographer.

This book owes a great deal to the encouragement, perspective and advice of my hugely experienced agent, Araminta Whitley, her fantastic assistant, Celia Hayley, and my enthusiastic and thoughtful UK publisher, Rowland White. And I am immensely grateful for the kind words and ongoing support of my American publisher, Lauren McKenna, and US agent, Sarah Lazin.

I would never have got this far without the support of my dearly beloved Gloria, whose giggling as she read selected high-lights was immensely encouraging. Mind you, she still hasn't seen the passages dealing with sexual and narcotic excesses. I'm a different man since I met you, babe. And this book is especially for her sons, the lights of my life, Abner and Kamma. I hope you're not too shocked by what I got up to when I was your age! Remember, just say no to drugs, kids. And for my beautiful Finn – one day you'll read this and find out more about your dad than you really want to know. Just remember, we all had to start somewhere!

This has now run on longer than the credits on a hip-hop album. But, as I said at the start, books have to end somewhere. So this is it.

Postscript to second edition, 2011

As I may have already pointed out, life goes on. And on.

And so it was that, in February 2010, I found myself sitting in a ramshackle social club somewhere in the hills outside Belfast with my brother Ivan, brooding over a black, black pint of Guinness, while a primped-up band pranced about on a dingy stage beneath cheap red and blue spotlights. Cigarette smoke hung in the air, a naked girl was shaking her tasselled tits in my face, and I was battling an almost vertiginous sense of unreality, a whirling vortex of conflicting emotions, breathless nostalgia, stabbing shame, overwhelming pity, empathy, pride, anger, embarrassment.

On stage, a handsome singer in a red shirt and black tie postured and hiccupped, his every move and vocal inflection reeking of youthful ego, ambition and pretension, while his deluded band murdered a half-decent song.

My song.

Which he had every right to trash within an inch of its life, because the naïve, precocious, prancing idiot on stage was me, thirty years younger.

So what did that make the grey-haired cynic twitching nervously in the shadows?

A different me, with decades of lines and weight and experience weighing him down. I felt like a chasm in the space–time continuum had ripped open and was about to swallow me up when, mercifully, a voice called 'cut', the music suddenly stopped, the band froze, and a different thrum of chatter and activity filled the room, as if everyone present had been mysteriously released from a spell. As my narrow point of focus pulled back to once again take in the cameras, lights, clipboards, microphones and cables of the film set, a creamy English voice broke through the shadowy buzz of action, bringing me back to Earth with a bump.

'So what did you think of that, darling?' enquired Nick Hamm, the director. 'You look like you've seen a ghost!'

'That was great!' announced my brother, who has never really suffered from the curse of self-consciousness.

I could still feel my younger self's eyes on me. The actor, Ben Barnes, was probably only looking for some approbation from the character he was playing, but to me it felt like so much more. I wanted to go up to myself, shake me by the shoulders, and say, 'What the fuck do you think you're doing?'

Imagine that. Imagine having the opportunity to address your younger self, explain some of the facts of life, avert mistakes that haven't yet been made, put yourself on the right track. Who hasn't had the thought, 'if only I knew then what I know now'? I could spell out some home truths and maybe spare myself a world of pain to come. I might even have been able to ease my younger mind, persuade myself not to treat everything as a matter of life and death, enjoy the moment and the music and the people and accept wherever it was taking me, and maybe get through that thick skull that success and failure are not diametric opposites but merely illusory staging posts on a much bigger journey.

Fat chance, of course. I know how my twenty-year-old self would have reacted to some middle-aged music critic quoting Kipling's advice to 'meet with Triumph and Disaster and treat those two imposters just the same'. I'd have thought, 'Out of the way you balding, bitter old Buddha, can't you see I'm going to be a star?' And then maybe tried to cadge a drink and explain my latest theories about the future of pop. But if none of my older self's words of philosophical wisdom were getting through, I could have at least passed on some practical tips and helpful phone numbers. That's something I know my younger self would have appreciated.

Of course, I didn't say any of that. It was just a film, after all. And just an actor. 'Ben,' I said, 'it's uncanny. Watching you is just like looking in a mirror.' Well, maybe one of those mirrors they have in designer clothing shop dressing rooms, with very flattering lighting, subtly curved to make you look thinner.

Most people who have films made about them have done something worthwhile, or at least of historical significance. There are warriors and world leaders (from Alexander the Great to Joan of Arc, Ghandi to Che Guevara), sportsmen and rock stars (Ali, Babe Ruth, Elvis, Buddy Holly), movie icons and artists (Chaplin, Van Gogh, Picasso) and sometimes notorious outlaws (Jesse James, Bonnie and Clyde, John Dillinger). Not me, though. All I did was fail, repeatedly, abjectly and quite unheroically. Then they made a film about it. I have been immortalized in celluloid as a total loser.

Nick Hamm contacted me quite soon after my book was first published in 2003, to say that he wanted to option the film rights. Now that was a call I had secretly been waiting for my whole life. Still, I thought he was mad. It's such a sprawling, anecdotal story, spread over a lifetime, in which redemption, if it occurs, is almost all internal, a slow, psychological and philosophical acceptance of fate. Nick saw it as an everyman story, because most people have much more experience of failure than success. The world may have become obsessed with fame and fortune but the pyramid geometry of showbusiness requires far more of us to be propping up the bottom than standing in glory at the peak. Nick had made a few films in his time, with varying degrees of success and, perhaps more importantly, failure. Something about my story spoke to him, and he impressed on me how determined he was to get it made.

It took six years from that first meeting to the cameras rolling in Belfast.

The movie business is a bastard. I may have had a horrible time trying to make it as a rock star but I still count myself lucky I didn't pursue my earlier ambition to become an actor.

You need so much money to make a film, and so many people are involved, and so many things can go wrong that, watching from the sidelines as the production rose and fell, scripts were written and revised, money was offered and retracted, shooting dates came and went, I began to think it is a miracle any film ever gets made at all. After a while, my initially rather delightful interactions with Nick became limited to annual phone calls to renew the rights, in which he tried to negotiate me down with pleas of impending poverty and nervous exhaustion. 'You have ruined my life, darling,' he told me during one late-night phone call. 'You have ruined my life.'

At least, in best theatrical tradition, he was still calling me darling.

Things began to heat up in 2009, with a new producer on board – Ian Flooks, who used to be U2's booking agent. But as the production started to come together, and the script went through its fourteenth revision, new issues emerged. 'The problem with your life, darling,' Nick told me, 'is that there's no third act.'

'That is because it's a life, Nick,' I pointed out.

'Don't worry, though,' he smirked. 'We're going to give you one.'

I wasn't sure I liked the sound of that.

Meanwhile, my real life had got even more entwined with U2's. Bono liked my book so much, he asked me to write his. And so I became U2's ghostwriter on their autobiography, *U2 by U2*. It was the best-selling music book in the world in 2006, although I'm not kidding myself it was because I had my name attached.

It was an interesting journey; I got to see how U2 operate from the inside and saw for myself how they earn their luck with talent, honour, commitment and sheer bloody mindedness. We wrote that book, took it apart and put it back together. It was supposed to take a year but it took two, sucking up my life in pursuit of something idealized and intangible, because U2 didn't just want a hagiography to take up space on the shelves, they wanted a book that got to the very heart of what it meant to be in the band. We took it right to the wire, making last-minute adjustments even as the printing presses ran. And, at the end, after all the work I had done, the hundreds of hours of interviews, the painstaking weaving of a poetic narrative from so many different voices, the endless discussions and debates with designers and publishers, the band went off to take all the plaudits. I didn't even bother going to the book launch. Who wants to speak to a ghost? As Bono said, toasting me at an after-hours bar, 'You have joined a very exclusive club of people this band has driven mad. Now you know how U2's producers feel.'

Oh, but we had some more adventures. I was around for the final recording sessions of *How To Dismantle An Atomic Bomb*. I walked into the studio during a take of 'Vertigo', and as Bono sang, 'Your love is teaching me how to kneel,' he dropped to his knees and said, 'Hey, Neil!' I hung out on Vertigo tour dates, spent a week on the road in America, and I was in on the start of Live8, as Bono and Geldof's expanding campaign to persuade rich nations to drop African debt came to a head with a massive concert in London, and a lobbying campaign at the G8 summit of world leaders at Gleneagles, in Scotland. I took my little boy on his first protest march. Well, I marched. He rolled along in his buggy.

And I was there for the opening night of the 360° tour in Barcelona, when their space-age adventure with a circular stage beneath a giant alien claw almost never got off the launch pad. At the end of a remarkable show filled with technical breakdowns, the controls of Bono's LED suit had somehow fused with the sweat and heat of his body, so that he couldn't turn his laser-firing jacket off. I watched him being bundled into a people carrier for a quick exit, disappearing down a Spanish highway, firing random red lasers through tinted windows into the dark sky. I imagined ground control trying to bring him back to earth: 'Hewson, we have a problem.' It seemed a curiously fitting exit, as the hi tech and the human fused in unpredictable fashion. The future never quite works the way you want it to.

But I caught up with the travelling sci-fi circus in the UK and US as it evolved and mutated into the greatest show on earth. Well, the latest model, anyway. There was a particularly extraordinary night in the Stadio Olimpico in Rome, when I was standing on the base of the claw, at the foot of the stage, so close to the band we could have all been back in McGonagles in Dublin. But their eyes were focused on another space altogether, over my head. So I turned to see what they saw, and watched the mass of people, 89,000 Italian U2 fans, spreading out across the stadium floor and rising vertiginously up the sides, just a dense, pulsating throb of humanity, absorbing all that music and emotion and powering it back at the band, hands aloft, mouths open in song. There was a mad energy to the moment, an intense feedback of feeling, looping and crackling between rock band and rock fans, with Bono as the lightning rod. And I was struck again by the sheer improbability of all this – that my schoolmate from Dublin had become this fantastic, iconic, ridiculous and amazing 21st-century superstar.

Later, we had a high-speed police escort out of the stadium. 'Do you ever wonder how this happened?' I asked him. By phone. Because he was in one car, and I was in another.

'All the time,' he laughed.

Life is strange . . . and getting stranger every day. At a gig in my local bar, I met a Northern-Irish musician called Joe Echo. When I introduced myself, he said, 'You're Neil McCormick? I'm writing the songs for your film!'

Which is how I found out the producers were not going to be using our original music. I was gobsmacked, even though Ian Flooks patiently explained he wanted a soundtrack with a rock-ier, contemporary edge. After some debate, they agreed to use two of our original songs, 'Sleepwalking' and 'Some Kind Of Loving', in radically rewritten forms. Nick Hamm, for his part, said he just wanted music that worked with each scene, which meant being able to ask his composer for a bad punk song, or telling him to rewrite 'Sleepwalking' as an embarrassing example of jerky Eighties synth pop. For some reason, he thought I might prove resistant to such demands.

'But "Sleepwalking" is a beautiful song, why would you want to ruin it?' I protested.

'Exactly!' he said.

I sort of got the point. It still felt like the ultimate insult. They make a film about your life as a failed musician and decide your own music isn't good enough.

I was consulted on casting. The first time I saw a screen test of an actor playing me I wanted to crawl out of the room with embarrassment. The great Scottish poet Rabbie Burns has a famous couplet: 'O would some power the giftie gie us, to see ourselves as others see us.' But I am not convinced this is a gift at all. Writing my story, I have had a chance to acknowledge my worst characteristics with the ironic awareness of an older and wiser self. Maybe I was the butt of the joke but at least my narration allows me the grace of acknowledging that I am in on the joke. But confronted with this unmediated vision of my youthful gaucheness, my pretentiousness, my tendency to over-excitement and propensity for motor-mouthed bullshit, I wondered how I had ever once convinced myself (let alone anyone around me) that I was destined for great things.

At least the actor eventually cast as me was extremely good looking. Maybe even too good looking, if there is such a thing. Ben Barnes is amongst the most handsome, charismatic young leading men in Britain. He played Prince Caspian in the Narnia Chronicles, for goodness sake. This may have been pretty much how I always saw myself, but I am not sure everyone agreed with this assessment. I said to Nick, 'With his looks and my talent we could have gone far.'

Nick said, 'It's OK, he's playing you as a kind of supergeek. That should be enough to put people off.'

On the set, to distinguish between us, the crew started calling me Real Neil. I wonder how long that will last? I fear I am in the process of becoming my own doppelgänger. I am waiting for the day when I introduce myself as Neil McCormick, and the response is 'Rubbish. You look nothing like him.'

Or maybe just a disappointed 'You were much better looking in the film.'

I suggested we get Brendan Gleeson or Colm Meany to play Bono. You know, a good Irish character actor, preferably old, overweight and balding. That would have been the ultimate revenge.

In the event, they cast young Irish actor Marty McCann. He

was spooky. I was on set for a scene at the launch party of *The Joshua Tree* when Marty walked in, in character, and I just caught him out of the corner of my eye and turned, thinking, for a split second, 'It's Bono. What's he doing here?' Marty had a way of jutting his chin and pumping up his chest, the walk of a boxer getting ready for the big fight, that spun me back twenty years through time. Then he would drop the whole thing, and chatter away in a merry Northern-Ireland accent.

While they were shooting, I called Bono and told him the actor playing him was more like him than he was himself.

'Just as long as he's tall,' said Bono. And then added, after a moment's thought, 'And modest.'

Tall and modest. Well, perhaps not the characteristics most people would associate with Bono.

So, in an effort to bring this enterprise to some conclusion (this being not so much a third act as a fifth), the book you have just read has become a film. If you've seen it, you will know it doesn't stick too closely to the original. Film has its own language, and the screenwriters went to some lengths to create visual metaphors for what was, essentially, an internal, psychological journey. And they gave me that third act, which is a lot more dramatic than anything I managed to come up with for myself. I think of it as a kind of riff on the themes of my book, my life in a parallel universe, where I still don't get to be a rock star, but I do get the best lines.

Ivan, on the other hand, tells everyone that is exactly the way it was. He was the real star in the family. And I ruined his life.

People tell me the film is very funny and I am prepared to believe them. I can only watch it through my fingers, squirming with humiliation.

As a child, of course, I firmly believed that one day someone would make a film of my life. It just never occurred to me it would be a comedy.

Still, like I said at the start of this book, what seems a whole lifetime ago . . .

. . . I always knew I would be famous.

He just wanted a decent book to read ...

Not too much to ask, is it? It was in 1935 when Allen Lane, Managing Director of Bodley Head Publishers, stood on a platform at Exeter railway station looking for something good to read on his journey back to London. His choice was limited to popular magazines and poor-quality paperbacks – the same choice faced every day by the vast majority of readers, few of whom could afford hardbacks. Lane's disappointment and subsequent anger at the range of books generally available led him to found a company – and change the world.

'We believed in the existence in this country of a vast reading public for intelligent books at a low price, and staked everything on it'
Sir Allen Lane, 1902–1970, founder of Penguin Books

The quality paperback had arrived – and not just in bookshops. Lane was adamant that his Penguins should appear in chain stores and tobacconists, and should cost no more than a packet of cigarettes.

Reading habits (and cigarette prices) have changed since 1935, but Penguin still believes in publishing the best books for everybody to enjoy. We still believe that good design costs no more than bad design, and we still believe that quality books published passionately and responsibly make the world a better place.

So wherever you see the little bird – whether it's on a piece of prize-winning literary fiction or a celebrity autobiography, political tour de force or historical masterpiece, a serial-killer thriller, reference book, world classic or a piece of pure escapism – you can bet that it represents the very best that the genre has to offer.

Whatever you like to read – trust Penguin.